SATAN'S
FALSE
PROPHETS
EXPOSED

Michael D. Fortner

Trumpet Press, Lawton, OK

Abbreviations & Volumes Used:

CEV — Contemporary English Version
ESV — English Standard Version
GNB — Good News Bible
GW — God's Word translation
KJV — King James Version
LIT — Green's Literal Translation
MEV — Modern English Version
MKJV — Modern King James Version
NCV — New Century Version
NKJV — New King James Version
NIV — New International Version
TLV — Tree of Life Version
CWD — Complete Word Study Dictionary: New Testament, by Spiros Zodhiates

Author: Fortner, Michael D.
Title: Satan's False Prophets Exposed
1. Charismatic Movement 2. Christian doctrine 3. Signs and wonders 4. False prophets 5. Word of Faith

ISBN-978-0998217277

Learn about other books by the author and watch videos at- www.usbibleprophecy.com

Trumpet Press is a member of the *Christian Small Publishers Association* (CSPA).

Table of Contents

About the Author

Michael D. Fortner is a journalist (B.A.) and historian with a God-given ability to figure things out and to think outside the box. At age 20 God called Michael to preach, but he refused, so God sent him into the wilderness for 40 years where he endured very intense trials and tribulations, molding and shaping, and training.

He is also the author of:

Discoveries in Bible Prophecy
The Beast and False Prophet Revealed
The Fall of Babylon the Great America
The Approaching Apocalypse and Three Days of Darkness
and other books.

A Note From the Author

You will notice that in this book there are no "end notes" at the end of the chapter or the end of the book. The reason there are no end notes is because it is very troublesome for a reader to look up a note which may have some important information that will go unread or may only be "Ibid." It is especially difficult to have end notes with an eBook; therefore, the print and eBook editions of this book have been formatted exactly the same, with notes within the text.

Also, all underlining in this book is my own, and is never found in the original quotes. But the all-caps in quotes are in the original.

I use several different translations in this book. One reason is I prefer the reading given of a particular verse in that translation. It does not mean I endorse the entire translation.

Introduction

The cross of Christ is no longer dripping with the blood of our Savior, but is covered with gold dust, and dripping money. There is oil seeping from a prosperity preacher who bottles it and sells it. There are false spirits that cause barking like a dog, levitation, weird laughter, and out of body experiences. Such is the state of many Pentecostal and Charismatic churches today.

While researching this book, I discovered that the problem of false prophets is far worse than I had previously believed. There is significant reason to believe that some Word of Faith (WOF) churches that have signs and wonders, such as gold dust and other wonders, are pastored by the preachers that Jesus warned us about several times, such as when he said there will come many false Messiahs and false prophets who perform such signs and wonders, that even the elect are almost deceived. It is happening now.

There is much disturbing information about the Word of Faith (WOF) movement, Toronto Blessing-inspired revivals, and Prophetic Movement, their doctrines, and their preachers. I discuss the false prophets and how they operate. The Bible gives us a description of these almost true, yet false prophets, and even tells us that they can sometimes perform genuine miracles. I will explain how that is possible, and how their services are a mixture of the Holy Spirit and evil spirits.

I once believed the WOF preachers on TV were either deceived or just stupid, but new evidence has convinced me that many of them are knowingly telling lies because they are trying to milk all of the money they can out of people. But even worse, some are <u>knowingly following Satan</u>. It is a known fact that people have made deals with the devil to become rich and famous movie stars and rock stars. But what most people do not realize is that there are <u>rich and famous preachers on TV</u> that have made the same deal with the devil. They are literally Satan's ministers; the evidence will shock you, and names are given. One TV preacher can be heard on video saying, *"I'm with Satan,"* while another one, after taking an offering, says, *"Tie my money, Satan."*

And some ministers, both true and false, are faking miracles. The Bible tells us that those who engage in fakery and claim that fake miracles are true miracles from God are in danger of being struck down by God like Nadab and Abihu, who faked a miracle. Are ministers falling dead today? Yes, many have died, but many have not, yet.

I present first-hand testimonies from many people who report getting demon spirits after attending one of the Toronto Blessing inspired revivals, or just watching their DVDs.

The majority of the other books previously written against the WOF movement were written by people who oppose all Pentecostals and Charismatics. Those attack books would have been written even if the WOF did not exist. For that reason, the Pentecostals and Charismatics have ignored those books with deadly results. Many Pentecostal churches, perhaps whole denominations, have been infiltrated by the WOF doctrines, even if it is only the prosperity gospel.

I do not oppose original Pentecostalism, because I grew up attending an old-fashioned Pentecostal church that warned us about the false doctrines of the WOF Charismatics. Even though I was warned against the WOF doctrines, in my 20s I came to believe in the prosperity gospel and the basic WOF doctrines, but God eventually opened my eyes to the truth. But now 40 years later that church is teaching WOF doctrines; probably not all of the WOF doctrines, but enough to consider it infiltrated.

Why did this happen? Because most of the famous spreaders

of WOF doctrines were originally Pentecostals. Kenneth Hagin was an Assembly of God evangelist who adopted the prosperity gospel and WOF doctrines and spread them within the denomination. Then he crossed over into the Charismatic Movement and started his own Bible college (1974). I do not believe he taught all of those messed up doctrines early in his ministry or he would have been kicked out of the Assemblies of God.

TBN was founded (1973) by Paul and Jan Crouch who also claimed Assembly of God roots. It is highly probable that he was not WOF when he began TBN, but because of the teaching of Kenneth Hagin and others, he also became WOF. After all, Hagin claimed to be a Spirit-filled Christian who spoke in tongues and prophesied, so Pentecostals listened to his teaching. But as all the other previous books have proven beyond doubt, WOF doctrine is so messed up it is more like Mormonism or Gnosticism than historical Christianity.

So Hagin and Crouch are examples of ministers who started out on the right track but became deceived. The first step along the wrong path was likely the prosperity gospel, followed by the many other doctrines that were originally developed by E. W. Kenyon. Hagin read Kenyon's books, but Hagin was not smart, as will be seen in the examination of Hagin's teaching, so he believed the falsehood of Kenyon.

Many people today wrongly give credit to the WOF for bringing us knowledge of faith and healing, but that is not true. Yes, the WOF has taught on faith and healing, but they did not originate it, Pentecostals and Charismatics were around long before the Word of Faith became widespread. The WOF group merely twisted the teaching on faith and healing, making it unbiblical.

There are many well-known Word of Faith preachers, and all have greatly distorted many doctrines, yet, because they believe in healing and the gifts of the Holy Spirit, they are accepted by Pentecostals and Charismatics. They should be tested as Jesus mentioned in Revelation, *"And you have tested those who say they are apostles, but are not, and have found them to be liars"* (2:2) (MEV). So now there are many churches that have aligned themselves with these false ministers. This means it is becoming more and more problematic to be a Pentecostal or Charismatic.

Because of WOF infiltration, I no longer consider myself Pentecostal or Charismatic, but rather, Full Gospel. The WOF false doctrines are spreading and threatening to take over the entire Pentecostal and Charismatic movement. The Pentecostal / Charismatic Movement needs a reformation, but it will not happen. What will happen is a split in the movement; Rick Joyner calls it a civil war.

I will be attacked for revealing the truth about the false prophets and their false doctrines, but the Apostle Paul said to expose the works of darkness:

> And do not have fellowship with the unfruitful works of darkness; instead, expose them. (Eph 5:11) (MEV)

And so this book will expose those works of darkness in the Pentecostal / Charismatic segment of the church today.

Some people will want to bring out the "authority" gun to question by what authority I speak against the WOF preachers and doctrines, and the false signs and wonders, saying that God has no self-appointed prophets or lone-wolf ministers. This is an argument that has no merit and is used by people who want to silence those they disagree with. The authority teaching is an example of doctrine being taught as truth when it is actually the opposite of the truth.

The apostles discovered a man who was casting out devils in Jesus' name, but he was not one of the official disciples. They asked Jesus if they should make him stop, and Jesus said, "Whoever isn't against us is for us" (Mark 9:40) (GW). So Jesus personally condoned lone wolf preachers! As he should, because he was a lone wolf preacher himself, as was John the Baptist, and Martin Luther. We know what they all accomplished for God.

John Wesley was not allowed to preach in Anglican churches, so he went into the public squares and eventually founded the Methodist Church. When William Booth started the Salvation Army without anyone's permission, he was attacked and reviled by Christians who tried to stop his good work. But when he died, 40,000 people attended his funeral including the queen, and another 150,000 people walked past the casket.

There are many lesser known lone wolf ministers, such as Gladys Aylward (1902-1970) who saved up her salary and bought a one-way train ticket to China, because the *China Inland Mission* agency would not send her. Her life story was made into a movie in 1958 that starred Ingrid Bergman, *The Inn of the Sixth Happiness*. Also, Bruce Olsen (1941-), who went to Columbia with his own money and ended up reaching an entire jungle tribe, and later spoke at the United Nations. He wrote a best-selling autobiography in 1986, *Bruchko*, that is still in print.

They were lone wolf ministers only in the sense that they were not under any human organization. <u>God is the one who calls people into the ministry</u>, not any human organization. Therefore, if God has called someone into the ministry, then he or she is not really a lone wolf and has every right to be in the ministry and to speak what God has called him or her to speak.

With the gospel of success and prosperity spreading like a plague of locusts, and now the false signs and wonders, and false spirits of the "river" outpouring, the Pentecostal / Charismatic Movement is in serious trouble. I can see why Jesus said, *"when the Son of Man comes, will he find faith on earth?"* (Luke 18:8). In other words, will he find true and accurate faith? Perhaps, because the truth is not something most people want to hear. They eat up those "bless me" doctrines.

Chapter 1
Last Days Deception

(1) Truth Matters

All of Christendom needs genuine revival, but especially the Charismatic Movement needs a revival of truth, a Reformation. We delude ourselves if we think that all we need is the presence and power of God, or the anointing; without truth we will end up with spiritualism, divination, and witchcraft. This is actually happening in some churches. A spiritual experience is not enough by itself. If you want a spiritual experience but reject sound doctrine, you will be led into error faster than those who reject anything spiritual and accept only human reason, but that also can bring error.

Paul said there was a time when God overlooked ignorance of the truth (Acts 17:30), but he now requires people to turn from sin and accept the truth. This applies even more so in these last days. Jesus said *"the true worshippers will worship the Father in spirit and truth."* (John 4:23) (MEV).

Some people only seek after a spiritual experience and don't want to dwell on doctrines because they say it causes divisions. *"Just wait until we get to heaven and we will sort it all out then."* But Jesus spoke of the importance of truth, and the writers of the New Testament considered truth important and attempted to correct false beliefs. Your doctrines can keep you out of heaven, so right doctrines are important.

Jesus said *"I am the way, the truth, and the life"* (John 14:6) (MEV) and *"You shall know the truth, and the truth shall set you* _free"_ (John 8:32) (MEV). You cannot be free if you do not know the truth. Anointing is not enough. To follow _The Way of Christ_ you must know the truth. It is not a spiritual experience that will get you to heaven, but the TRUTH.

While some people believe that _"line upon line"_ of human analysis will arrive at correct doctrine, that also is not accurate. Jesus said, _"you have made the commandment of God of no effect by your tradition"_ (Mat. 15:6) (MEV). Church doctrine itself has obscured much truth. You must be able to follow the guidance of the Holy Spirit in your study or you will never understand Scripture. The Holy Spirit can give us understanding that is beyond the ability of mere human reason, but sadly, WOF doctrine is nothing but human reason, and really bad human reasoning at that.

The truth is in the Bible, but because it does not say what people want to believe, preachers twist the Scriptures and make them say what they do not say. Without the Spirit they cannot see what it actually says. You must also have a desire for truth.

> I love those who love me, and those who <u>seek me diligently</u> find me. (Prov. 8:17) (ESV) (See also Matt. 7:7-8; and Jer. 29:13)

Unfortunately most Christians do not seek the truth, but merely seek to back up what they want to believe. Derek Prince wrote a great book called _Protection from Deception_ in which he said:

> Deception – not sickness, poverty, or persecution—is the greatest single danger in the end of the age. Anyone who denies this vulnerability to deception is already deceived, for Jesus has foretold it and He does not err. (2008 edition, page 6)

The truth of the Christian faith is not hard to understand, it is just hard to accept by American Christians who have been raised to pursue the American Dream. They have become blinded by materialism, which is why the prosperity gospel is spreading like a wildfire, but it is not the truth. And because of the popularity of some of the prosperity preachers on TV, the false gospel is spreading outside the Charismatic and Pentecostal segment of the Church:

> Given its departure from the historical, orthodox message of the church, one would think that most Bible-believing Christians would reject the prosperity gospel. However, this is not the case. The prosperity gospel is spreading beyond the confines of the charismatic movement, where it has been traditionally strong, and is taking root in the larger evangelical church. A recent survey found that in the United States, 46 percent of self-proclaimed Christians agree with the idea that God will grant material riches to all believers who have enough faith. Why is this so? The prosperity gospel has an appealing but fatal message: accept God and He will bless you-- because you deserve it. (*Health, Wealth and Happiness: Has the Prosperity Gospel Overshadowed the Gospel of Christ?* by David W. Jones and Russell S. Woodbridge, Kregel Publications, 2011, page 15)

I guess the Christians in Africa and Asia are not real Christians, because they are very poor. Or perhaps the Bible's idea of prosperity is different from the view of Christians in America.

(2) Warnings From God

Paul said that the Holy Spirit spoke, perhaps through a prophecy or perhaps an unknown tongue with interpretation, that in the last days before the return of Christ, many people will fall away from the faith by following <u>doctrines taught by false prophets who are influenced by demons</u>:

> Now the Spirit says clearly that <u>in the last times</u> some people will abandon the faith by following deceitful spirits, the <u>teachings of demons</u>, and the hypocrisy of <u>liars</u>, whose consciences have been burned by a hot iron. (1 Tim. 4:1-2) (ISV)

This is likely a prophecy about the WOF movement today, and the Toronto outpouring. Of course, they are not the only ones that teach false doctrine and lead people into deception. There is no lack of churches teaching half-truths, but the Bible specifically speaks out against the desire for wealth, calling it idolatry.

The Bible tells us not to accept every preacher or every teaching, but to test them to see whether they are genuine or not, but many Charismatics will swallow anything and follow anyone who comes with signs and wonders. They are just asking to be deceived, and <u>are being deceived</u>. Even though the Bible tells us to test the spirits to see if they are from God, the <u>churches today</u> <u>are literally saying that we should not question</u>, but just accept what is happening as genuine. Here are two important verses:

> Dear friends, stop believing every spirit. Instead, <u>test the spirits</u> <u>to see whether they are from God</u>, because many <u>false prophets</u> have gone out into the world. (1 John 4:1) (ISV)

> For you gladly tolerate anyone who comes to you and preaches a different Jesus, not the one we preached; and <u>you accept a</u> <u>spirit and a gospel</u> completely different from the Spirit and the gospel you received from us! (2Cor. 11:4) (GNB)

The Bible warns us in many places to watch out for false prophets, especially in these last days. Jesus said:

> "For false christs and false prophets will appear and display great signs and wonders to deceive, if possible, even the elect." (Matthew 24:24) (ISV)

> "Beware of false prophets who come to you in sheeps' clothing but inwardly are savage wolves." (Matthew 7:15) (ISV)

We now change from verses warning of deception and false prophets to verses about actual deception already in the Church in the first century:

> I have written to you about those who <u>are trying to deceive you</u>. (1 John 2:26) (ISV)

> But I have this against you: You tolerate that woman Jezebel, who calls herself a prophet and who teaches and leads my servants to practice immorality and to eat food sacrificed to idols. (Rev. 2:20) (ISV)

If false teachers were already in the Church, less than 70 years from the death of Christ, you know there are many false teachers today. The wolves in sheep's clothing will be cast into the fire on the Day of Judgment, if not before. Jesus spoke about these false prophets in Matt. 7:

> "Not everyone who says to Me, 'Lord, Lord,' shall enter the kingdom of heaven, but he who does the will of My Father who is in heaven. 22 Many will say to Me on that day, 'Lord, Lord, have we not <u>prophesied in Your name</u>, <u>cast out demons</u> in Your name, and done many <u>wonderful works</u> in Your name?' 23 But

then I will declare to them, 'I never knew you. <u>Depart from Me,</u>
<u>you who practice evil</u>.'" (Matt. 7:21-23) (MEV)

A large percentage of the false teachers are WOF. Based on
what we have learned in this section, it is no mystery that we find
Charismatic preachers who have many signs and wonders happening, but who also preach the wealth gospel and WOF doctrines of demons.

There are two additional prophecies in other writings that say
in the later days there will be many famous false prophets spreading a twisted form of Christianity. The *Epistle of the Apostles* says:

> And he said unto us: There shall come forth another doctrine,
> and <u>a confusion</u>, and because they shall strive <u>after their own</u>
> <u>advancement</u>, they shall bring forth an unprofitable doctrine. And
> therein shall be a deadly corruption (of uncleanness), and they
> shall teach it, and <u>shall turn away them that believe on me from</u>
> <u>my commandments and cut them off from eternal life</u>. But woe
> unto them that falsify this my word and commandment, and draw
> away them that hearken to them from the life of the doctrine and
> separate themselves from the commandment of life: for <u>together</u>
> <u>with them they shall come into everlasting judgement</u>. (M. R.
> James, *The Apocryphal New Testament* (Oxford: Clarendon
> Press 1924), p. 503.)

Notice that this teaching is about striving *"after their own ad-*
vancement," which is the gospel we have today: you can be successful, you can be happy, God has a wonderful plan for your
life, you can be rich, and you will never go to hell. I believe the
"confusion" refers to the fact that the false prophets teach a different interpretation of the Scriptures, one that is convoluted, or
twisted beyond good sense, which is the WOF doctrines, as we
shall see in other chapters.

Another prophecy from the Jewish and Christian *Sibylline Or-*
acles also puts the time period during our day, which are the decades before the coming of the final Antichrist:

> . . . and there will be no consent in doctrines when some deceiv-
> ers arise in the world <u>with great fame, as prophets</u>, and then
> shall Belial come, and do many wonders among men. (*The Si-*
> *bylline Oracles; Revised and Updated*, Floyer, p. 47.)

The Charismatic false prophets are the most famous false prophets the world has ever known, because their TV programs are broadcast around the world. This prophecy does not call them prophets, but that they have fame "*as prophets.*"

Derek Prince said:

> Never underestimate Satan's ability to produce power, signs, and wonders. Most charismatics attribute anything supernatural to God, which is why I have identified the charismatic movement as a likely place for the Antichrist to emerge. (*Protection From Deception*, 2008, p. 148)

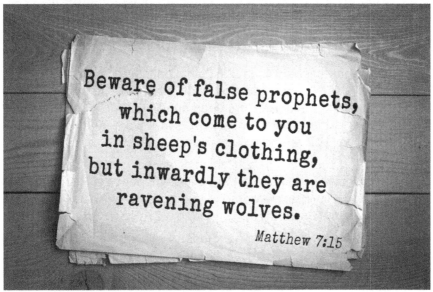

Beware of false prophets, which come to you in sheep's clothing, but inwardly they are ravening wolves.
Matthew 7:15

(3) An Avalanche of Deception

In 2012 evangelist Steve Hill had a vision of a ski slope that was covered with thick snow that was about to cause an avalanche of deception that was threatening to hit the Church. The snow represented false doctrine. He only named a few false doctrines in the book, but it is clear that the WOF is part of the avalanche of deception that is already hitting the Church, as are the false signs and wonders. Here are a few quotes from his book:

> Instead of the true gospel, people are fed a lukewarm, pitiful, watered-down message of the cross of Christ, adding more lay-

ers of accumulating snow up on the mountain. More layers added as more liars are given platforms. (Hill, *Spiritual Avalanche*, p. 26)

This swirling, steady downfall of white powder [false doctrine] can disorient the believer, blinding him as to which direction to go. . . . a spiritual whiteout of unhealthy, unbalanced, and, in some cases, downright unbiblical teaching has blinded the body of Christ in America, and it is quickly spreading around the world. (Ibid, p. 76)

This is another way to test the message: Does it always tell me what my itching ears want to hear, or does it rebuke my flesh? Does it give me a way to avoid the cross, or does it call me to pick up my cross daily? Does it allow me to cater to my sinful desires, or does it call me to die to sinful desires? (Ibid, p. 79)

Many preachers of today, as they continue on in their charlatan ways, deserve to be looked upon as con artists. Where is the brokenness? Where is the deep humility? Where are the tears? Where is the passion for souls? Can anyone find Jesus in this parade of self-promoted piety? (Ibid, p. 89)

And because we preach an imbalanced gospel—emphasizing God's love and ignoring His wrath, emphasizing His mercy and ignoring His justice—we no longer have room for hell and future punishment in our theology. (Ibid, p. 92)

"Brother Steve, we live hundreds of miles from any other large city. I have a good church of fifteen hundred faithful members. They fight to live out their faith. Persecution is an everyday threat. Please, Brother Steve, tell the American preachers that they are destroying us. Their teaching doesn't fit here. If they came here and lived here, they would see. Do whatever you can to stop the constant false teaching that is pouring in. It is confusing and destroying our people." (Ibid, p. 120).

The deceiver and enemy of our souls has slithered into the pulpits of America as he did in the garden and is tempting those with itching ears with fresh snow. (Ibid, p. 143)

Messages on God's blessings, prosperity, and reward abound. They sell books and fill sanctuaries. But what about God's discipline, judgment, penalties, and punishments? (Ibid, p. 167)

The WOF doctrines, the prosperity gospel, the false signs and wonders, and the false spirits of the "river" outpouring are all an avalanche of deception from the pit of hell, but they are not the only heresies spreading in the American Church. Universalism, and other heresies, such as a book and movie called *The Shack* which are full of heresy. The book and movie were promoted by TBN, and the movie by KLOVE radio. Here are twelve heresies in *The Shack*:

1. God the Father was crucified with Jesus.
2. God is limited by his love and therefore cannot practice justice.
3. God forgave all of humanity, whether they repent or not.
4. All hierarchical structures are evil.
5. God will never judge people for their sins.
6. God submits to human wishes and choices.
7. Justice will never take place because of love.
8. There is no such thing as eternal judgment or torment in hell.
9. It doesn't matter which way you get to God.
10. Jesus is constantly being transformed along with us.
11. The Bible is not true because it reduces God to paper.
12. Everyone will make it to heaven.

It is ironic that several ministers were contacted and gave their endorsement of Steve Hill's book, even though they are named here in this book. Hill did not go into much detail about all the false teachings today, or name the false ministers, but not so in this book. I do not just cry out against false doctrine, I examine those doctrines and name many false ministers who teach them. Of course, I cannot include all of them, because there are so many.

Chapter 2:
The Golden Calf

In 2 Kings we read about the king who ruled Israel after Ahab. Jehu killed all the relatives of Ahab; afterwards he gave a festival for Baal and invited all those who wanted to worship Baal. Then his soldiers were instructed to close the doors and kill everyone inside. The reason he killed all the worshipers of Baal is because he had great *"zeal for the Lord"* (10:16). Yet, he did something that seems very strange:

> Thus Jehu destroyed Baal from Israel. 29 However Jehu did not turn away from the sins of Jeroboam the son of Nebat, who had made Israel sin, that is, from the golden calves that were at Bethel and Dan. (2 Kings 10:28-29) (NKJV)

Now, why is it that a king who had so much zeal for Yahweh that he would kill probably over a thousand people that worshiped Baal, yet he did not remove the golden calves from Israel.

The Bible does not give us any clues to this but I greatly suspect that when the people were worshiping the golden calf that they thought they were worshiping Yahweh. So the golden calves became idols of God, even though the Law of Moses speaks against such a thing. This could have been one of the reasons that God sent the Assyrian army to destroy Israel. He had to wipe out those people who had corrupted his true worship, and his holy name.

What does this have to do with the prosperity gospel and Word of Faith, you ask? Paul said that the desire for wealth is idolatry, which was a major violation against the Law of Moses. So it was a serious crime against God. Today, prosperity preachers believe that they are worshiping the true God, but because of their desire for wealth, they are guilty of idolatry; in other words, they are worshiping the golden calf. Like the golden calf, the prosperity gospel has become associated with Yahweh, even though it is idolatry.

Another reason greed is associated with idolatry, is because in paganism the adherent gives offerings and says prayers designed to get specific things from the god. Do a rain dance and you will get rain; so you are trying to manipulate or force a god to give you what you want. So also the prosperity gospel; just give money and you will get more money back. But God does what he has determined is best for us, according to his sovereign will. Also, you become greedy because your desire for material goods grows when you believe that God will grant your desires.

In Ephesians, Paul spoke against the prosperity teachers of his day:

> 5 . . . no sexually immoral or impure person, <u>or one who is greedy, who is an idolater</u>, has any inheritance in the kingdom of Christ and of God. . . . 6 <u>Let no one deceive you with empty words,</u> for because of these things the wrath of God is coming upon the sons of disobedience. (Ephesians 5:5-6) (MEV)

Since greed is idolatry, it means the desire for wealth is the same as worshiping a pagan idol. Whether it is desire for wealth, or desire to keep for yourself the wealth you already have, both are major sins.

Paul said those who teach the prosperity gospel use many "*empty words.*" Today, we would say they are full of nothing but hot air; in other words, their teaching is useless.

Paul goes on to say in the next verse, "*Therefore do not become partners with them*" (5:7) (ESV). The Greek word *summetochos* (4830) means "*partaking with . . . a joint partaker*" (CWD). So Paul even tells us <u>not to become ministry partners</u> with them! I guess there really is nothing new under the sun. When you send money to these false prophets you become "partakers" with them, so you become guilty of their sin of teaching false doctrine. In another place Paul once again likened greed to idolatry:

> Therefore put to death the parts of your earthly nature: sexual immorality, uncleanness, inordinate affection, evil desire, and covetousness, which is idolatry. (Col. 3:5) (MEV)

If you doubt just how greedy the prosperity preachers are, then you probably do not realize how they spend their money. In 1999 Leroy Thompson said he recently bought a dog for $15,000 and a ring for $32,000. He said,

> "I live in a 8,000 square foot house. I am going to build a bigger one now. One that King Solomon would be proud of. . . . I want you [to] know that when the people in my town come past my mansion and they see my Rolls Royce sitting in the driveway, they know there is a God in heaven." (*The Reproach of the Solemn Assembly*, sermon by David Wilkerson)

According to articles in the *Saint Lewis Dispatch*, prosperity preacher Joyce Myers and her husband in Missouri earn over $1.5 million a year and live in a 10,000 sq. foot home. They have an 8-car garage with heat and air conditioning, and a yacht worth over $100,000. Her ministry headquarters is built like a king's palace at a cost of $20 million. It has a pair of Dresden vases worth $19,000, *"six French crystal vases bought for $18,500, an $8,000 Dresden porcelain depicting the Nativity, two $5,800 curio cabinets, a $5,700 porcelain of the Crucifixion..."* The list goes on for some length and includes: a $30,000 malachite round table, a $23,000 marble-topped antique commode (chest of drawers), and a conference table and 18 chairs worth $49,000. The icing on the cake is a $10,000,000 ministry jet.

Another, Juanita Bynum, owns a $5,000 ink pen she uses to sign her multi-million-dollar deals. She spent over one million dollars on her wedding. I suspected that, her being a preacher, she had put her marriage under a curse by spending that much money for her wedding, and sure enough, it only lasted a few years.

Some of you may say that I am not being fair, because most of those prosperity preachers give 10% of their income to orphanages or the homeless, but I believe their claims of giving 10% more likely refers to their ministry income. Either way, look what they do with the rest of the money. The tax collector Jesus ate with was likely not a millionaire, yet he gave 50% of his net worth to the poor (Luke 19:8-9). These millionaire preachers could give 90% and still live well. But then they would not be able to buy a *Bentley* or a diamond studded *Rolex* watch.

If Jesus came today, do you think he would live like the ministers listed above? No! He would set an example by not living in opulence. How many people have gone hungry because these ministers spent money on luxury? You would never see Elijah living in a palace. He did not run away to his summer home, he slept under a tree. Are these prosperity preachers greater than Elijah? Isaiah said:

> They are dogs with mighty appetites; they never have enough. They are shepherds who lack understanding; they all turn to their own way, they seek their own gain. (Isaiah 56:11) (NIV)

You will never see a true apostle driving a *Jaguar* or a *Bentley* unless it was given to him as a gift. But he would probably turn it down or sell it because it is hard to be humble when you live in extravagant wealth, and it does not set a good example. No, true apostles care too much about the poor, and they understand what the Bible teaches on this subject. In other countries true apostles are usually poor.

In 2005 *Forbes Magazine* reported that Paul and Jan Crouch earned over $770,000, a year. They lived in a 9,500 sq. foot home by the ocean in Newport Beach, CA. worth 12.5 million dollars. The home had nine bathrooms, an elevator, a six-car garage, a tennis court, a swimming pool, and a fountain. They have since both died; he died in 2013 at age 79, she died in 2016 at 78. They were the founders of TBN.

Kenneth Copeland has a lakeside home in Texas with 18,000 square feet that cost 4.1 million dollars, according to the Trinity Foundation (see photo below), and he does not pay any tax on it because it is considered a parsonage. This means his ministry owns it, so it was likely paid for by donations, not his personal money. He owns about 2 dozen vehicles, several boats including a racing boat, and several airplanes including a 20 million-dollar ministry jet that cost $5,000 per hour to fly, when fuel prices are low. And he even has a private airport nearby.

I think the TV preachers are trying to see who can build the biggest home.

This is NOT TBN headquarters, the above palace is the <u>personal home</u> of Jesse Duplantis, owned by his ministry so he doesn't have to pay any taxes on it. It is almost as deep as it is wide. According to Justin Peters, the house has 35,000 square feet. He is just too blessed to be bothered by the extreme needs of his poor brothers and sisters.

Chapter 3:
The Way of Balaam

(1) Balaam

Paul spoke out against false teachers when he said, "*do not have fellowship with the unfruitful works of darkness; instead, expose them*" (Eph. 5:11) (MEV). Jesus spoke out against false teachers when he called the Pharisees white-washed tombs; and later Jesus condemned the false teachers in the church at Pergamum:

> But I have a few things against you: You have there those who hold the teaching of Balaam, who taught Balak to cast a stumbling block before the children of Israel, to eat things sacrificed to idols and to commit sexual immorality. (Rev. 2:14) (MEV)

Balaam was a false prophet, not because he gave out false predictions, but because he taught Balak how to lead the Israelites into worshiping the idols of the Moabites. In other words, Balaam was responsible for leading the people into idolatry. Therefore, Balaam was a deceiver. He did this because Balak offered him money. Likewise, there are preachers today who are leading Christians into idolatry for money, which is the prosperity gospel.

Peter specifically connected prosperity preachers with following after Balaam. Read the following verses carefully:

> 3 In their greed these teachers will exploit you with stories they have made up. ...10 This is especially true of those who follow the corrupt desire of the sinful nature ... 14 ... they are experts in greed -- an accursed brood! 15 They have left the straight way and wandered off to follow the way of Balaam son of Beor, who loved the wages of wickedness. ...18 For they mouth empty,

boastful words and, by appealing to the lustful desires of the sinful human nature, they entice people who are just escaping from
those who live in error. (2 Peter 2:3, 10, 14-15, 18) (NIV)

Notice the words, *"exploit you."* In other words, make money
from you! Peter said these false teachers are *"experts in greed,"*
which means they were very good at picking out verses from the
Scriptures and using those verses to convince people to give them
money; this is what prosperity preachers do. They were also experts at taking large offerings. Peter said these preachers have
"wandered" away from true Christianity and were deceiving people for the purpose of financial gain, and specifically identifies
them with Balaam. He said they use *"empty, boastful words,"* in
other words their teaching is useless, while claiming to know
more than other preachers.

Peter said the false teachers entice people who are newly converted, so they do not have the spiritual maturity to see the falsehood of the materialistic gospel. Those who had been Christians
a long time were not falling into this trap because they knew
what the apostles taught. Many people can testify that they once
believed the get-rich gospel, but as they matured in their Christian walk, they saw the truth and rejected the prosperity message,
the very same as I did. Even though I was warned against the
WOF teachings, as an adult I watched Oral Roberts on TV and
read his books, and those of other prosperity preachers. But God
eventually opened my eyes to the truth.

The *Good News Bible* says, *"In their greed these false teachers will
make a profit out of telling you made-up stories"* (2 Peter 2:3). What
kind of stories did they tell? *"This lady gave me an offering, and
within two days she received $500 in the mail. If you want to prosper,
give me an offering. If you want a miracle, give me an offering."* They
will provide you with numerous examples of people who gave
money and got a check in the mail. Well, what about all the people who do *not* give and yet get checks in the mail, or get jobs? Or
what about all the people who gave money yet not only did *not*
get a check, but went more into debt or lost a job? But even
worse, most of those claims are just lies because God does not

honor an offering given to false teachers, and he does not honor an offering given for the purpose of getting even more back.

What they will not tell you about are the large numbers of Christians who are so greedy that they don't even give to their local church, yet they are rich. In his book, *The Way I See It*, Don Basham, one of the founders of the Charismatic movement, said there was a prosperous businessman who was a member of a church he once pastored, *"who boasted he had no need to tithe, because 'I'm a Christian and everything I have already belongs to God'"* (p. 76). This man did not give much money and yet he was wealthy, which goes against the teaching of the false prophets of prosperity.

But let's back up a minute and look at the two previous verses before the passage quoted above in 2 Peter that are on this same topic:

> But there were also false prophets among the people, just as <u>there will be false teachers among you</u>. They will secretly introduce <u>destructive heresies</u>, even denying the sovereign Lord who bought them—bringing swift destruction on themselves. 2 Many will follow their depraved conduct and <u>will bring the way of truth into disrepute</u>. 3 In their greed these teachers will exploit . . . (2 Pet. 2:1-2) (NIV)

This is a <u>prophecy:</u> "*there will be false teachers . . . will bring the way of truth into disrepute. . . . will exploit . . .*" <u>So I fully believe that this is a prophecy about what is happening today</u>. These verses tell us that false teachers will come and bring "*destructive heresies*" that will bring the cause of Christ into "disrepute." WOF teaching and the prosperity gospel has certainly caused the Christian faith to be mocked and denigrated. This happens because even wicked people know that greed is a sin, so why are so many Christians falling for this lie? Only lack of spiritual maturity and good sense and their own desire for money. Then it goes on to specifically tell us that these false teachers will focus on prosperity.

Even in Paul's day, there were many ministers who traveled around preaching only because it was an easy way to make a good living. They were just doing it for money. The *King James*

Version of 2 Cor. 2:17 does not adequately translate the meaning of the original Greek, *"For we are not as many, which corrupt the word of God: but as of sincerity, but as of God, in the sight of God speak we in Christ."* Here is a better translation:

> At least we are not commercializing God's word like so many others. Instead, in Christ we speak with sincerity, like people who are sent from God and are accountable to God. (ISV)

The Geneva translation says many people *"make merchandise of the word of God."* Barnes Notes says the original Greek denotes one who waters down wine and resells it to make as much money as possible, like a peddler. The ESV says, *"For we are not, like so many, peddlers of God's word."* The NIV says, *"Unlike so many, we do not peddle the word of God for profit."*

The plague of the prosperity message spread within the Early Church the same as it has today. The apostles had to face this problem, and we can again read Apostle Paul's denunciation of the prosperity message and those teaching it in the following verses; pay special attention to the underlined words:

> 3 If anyone teaches false doctrines and does not agree to the sound instruction of our Lord Jesus Christ, 4 he is conceited and understands nothing. ... who have been robbed of the truth and who think that godliness is a means to financial gain. 6 But godliness with contentment is great gain. 7 For we brought nothing into the world, and we can take nothing out of it. ...
>
> 9 People who want to get rich fall into temptation and a trap and into many foolish and harmful desires that plunge men into ruin and destruction. 10 For the love of money is a root of all kinds of evil. Some people, eager for money, have wandered from the faith and pierced themselves with many griefs. (1 Timothy 6:3-10) (NIV)

How could it be said any clearer? Paul obviously was talking about ministers who were teaching Christians a way to get rich from the Scriptures, which Paul called *"false doctrines."* Paul said that anyone who desires to get rich in this way has departed from the faith, and that we should be content with what we have. Does this sound like a man who believes in the prosperity gospel?

Not a chance! The NKJV says: *"supposing that gain is godliness."* The literal translation says, *"supposing gain to be godliness"* (LIT).

The false teachers were teaching that it was godly to get rich and that a righteous man will become rich, which is exactly what is being taught today by many big-name preachers on TV. Kenneth Hagin even wrote a small book by that very title, *Gain is Godliness*, but withdrew it after the connection to this passage was pointed out to him, but he never recanted the teaching.

There is today a man who planned to become a missionary when he was young, but he not only turned against his calling, he turned against Christianity. Do you suppose that God has blessed this man? He is today a multi-billionaire media-mogul. The man is Ted Turner who started CNN and is a partner in Time-Warner and other media companies. Can we use him as an example that God blesses a righteous man? No, actually, the opposite is most likely true, that Satan prospers those who turn from the straight way.

John Avanzini, another false prosperity preacher, said:

Child of God, as you study God's Word carefully, you will find that God's clearly stated intention is to take very good care of His children, especially those that walk in His footsteps and obey His will.

There it is, the very thing that Paul spoke out against, that God guarantees financial gain to the godly. But Paul said we should be content with food and clothing (1 Tim. 6:8). Is this what the prosperity preachers teach? Certainly not! Paul continues in the same passage we just quoted:

But you, man of God, flee from all this, [the get-rich gospel] and pursue <u>righteousness, godliness, faith, love, endurance and gentleness.</u> (1 Timothy 6:11) (NIV)

After Paul told Timothy not to pursue riches, he then told him what he should pursue. Nowhere in the list did Paul say that Timothy should pursue a big harvest of money so he can help finance Paul's ministry. If Paul really believed and taught the wealth gospel, as the prosperity preachers claim, why didn't he travel in a golden chariot pulled by six white horses, the modern equivalent of a *Bentley* or *Rolls Royce*, like the prosperity preachers do? Yes, some of them actually drive a *Rolls Royce* or *Bentley*! Paul continues in this same chapter:

> 17 Command those who are rich in this present world not to be arrogant nor to put their hope in wealth, <u>which is so uncertain</u>, but to put their hope in God, who <u>richly provides us with every-thing for our enjoyment</u>. 18 Command them to do good, to be rich in good deeds, and <u>to be generous and willing to share</u>. 19 In this way they will <u>lay up treasure for themselves</u> as a firm foundation for the coming age, so that they may take hold of life that is truly life. (6:17-19) (NIV)

Since Paul clearly is speaking out against wanting to be rich and depending on wealth, <u>he does not turn around and contra-dict himself</u> when he says God *"richly provides us with everything for our enjoyment."* He is saying that God provides our basic needs, and things that have nothing to do with the material lusts of the flesh or worldly luxury. He also provides us with things money cannot buy, such as *"righteousness, godliness, faith, love, en-durance and gentleness"* (6:11).

False teachers claim that in this passage Paul was merely say-ing that we should not trust riches, but trust God who gives us riches, so we can *"enjoy them."* NO, that is NOT what Paul said. He said we should trust in God because he provides us with eve-rything we need. Having more money is not what we need, we only need enough money to live on. Many rich people are un-happy, so money is low on the list of what is important in life.

Paul is not saying that God provides us with riches to enjoy; the riches of God are not material goods. Because riches can be so easily lost, we should trust in God who will supply us with what we need. It might be more clear in this simple translation:

> Command those who are rich with things of this world not to be proud. Tell them to hope in God, not in their uncertain riches. God richly gives us everything to enjoy. (NCV)

Since riches can be easily lost or stolen, how can we be cer-tain that we will always have plenty of those riches, like the prosperity teachers claim? Therefore, we should seek God rather than riches, because God is able to provide us with what we need.

> Better the little that the righteous have than the wealth of many wicked; (Psalms 37:16) (NIV)

The above verse says that the righteous are poor but the wealthy are wicked, just the opposite of what the prosperity preachers are teaching. Of course, not all wealthy people are wicked, but in that day, most rich people were wicked because they had to cheat and steal in order to become rich. Therefore, wealthy people are portrayed in the Bible as being unrighteous. Paul continues:

> Timothy, guard what has been entrusted to your care. Turn away from godless chatter and the opposing ideas of what is <u>falsely called knowledge</u>, which some have professed and in so doing have <u>wandered from the faith</u>. ... (1 Tim. 6:20-21) (NIV)

Here Paul said the false teachers were claiming that they had knowledge and insight that Paul and other teachers did not have. This is likely a reference to Gnosticism, but it is the very same thing that prosperity preachers are doing today, claiming they have great understanding of the Scriptures. John Avanzini also makes such claims:

> Please note I am not using the word revelation loosely. I use it in its strongest sense. What you are about to read is a body of truth I received directly from our Lord. Now mind you, it's not a new truth, it's neglected truth.

It is indeed possible to understand something that other people do not, but the passages to which Avanzini refers are not even about money, but are about the seed of the Word of God. He may have gotten it from his god, the golden calf, but it was not Jesus.

(2) Almost True Yet False Prophets

There are Christian attackers who condemn everyone who does not agree with them one-hundred percent on every doctrine. But that is absurd because no one is 100% accurate. If someone holds one doctrine slightly different from them, they condemn them as apostate and going to hell. But no religious organization or church is 100% accurate in all its doctrines. Some may be 95% right, others may be 80% or 70%, but none are 100%; which church is that? Oh, the one you attend! No, there is no church or denomination that has 100% accurate doctrine. This shows that you don't have to be 100% accurate to make it to heaven, or to be used of God in the ministry. If we must have 100% accurate doctrine to be saved and go to heaven, then there are very few actual Christians in the world, if any.

This book was written to get us closer to that 100% mark. The purpose of this book is to discover as much truth as possible, by revealing the false prophets and false doctrines found in the Charismatic Movement, which is not limited to the prosperity gospel. Because the more truth we have, the closer we are to God and his perfect will for us as individuals, and as churches. This book is for seekers of truth; who want to know the truth regarding Charismatic doctrines, especially the prosperity gospel.

Since you can be saved and delivered under the ministry of someone who teaches a few false doctrines, remember no one is completely accurate, then it means you can be saved and even healed through the ministry of a false prophet. Even false teachers teach some things that are accurate; they are not 100% wrong.

Now, you may doubt that God can use a false prophet, but God actually tells us he does in the Bible. Most people are aware that false prophets in the Old Testament are supposed to be stoned to death, but another statement will shock many people.

There are some seemingly true prophets that God works through, but God considers them false prophets because of their false doctrines. Many prominent ministers today that God actually speaks to and uses, the Bible says should be classified as false prophets. Deuteronomy describes these as almost true yet false prophets:

> "If a prophet or a dreamer of dreams arises among you and gives you a sign or a wonder, 2 and <u>the sign or wonder that he tells you comes to pass,</u> and if he says, 'Let us go after other gods,' which you have not known, 'and let us serve them,' 3 you shall not listen to the words of that prophet or that dreamer of dreams. <u>For the LORD your God is testing you,</u> to know whether you love the LORD your God with all your heart and with all your soul. 4 You shall walk after the LORD your God and fear him and keep his commandments and obey his voice, and you shall serve him and hold fast to him. 5 But that prophet or that dreamer of dreams shall be put to death, because <u>he has taught rebellion against the LORD</u> your God, who brought you out of the land of Egypt and redeemed you out of the house of slavery, <u>to make you leave the way in which the LORD your God commanded you to walk.</u> So you shall purge the evil from your midst. (Deut. 13:1-5) (ESV)

Notice that the prophets God speaks about have <u>genuine visions, dreams, and perform signs and wonders that come from God.</u> Do you suppose that they have gotten a few people healed? Surely, there are genuine results of God's power working through these ministers, <u>but at the same time these ministers are teaching damnable doctrines that lead to hell.</u> They <u>may</u> even prophesy accurately, speak in tongues, and cause you to fall down by God's anointing upon them. But the man or woman also preaches WOF false doctrines that will lead people away from the truth, including the prosperity gospel.

Why would God work through such a minister if he teaches false doctrines that will lead people away from God? According to verse 3 and 4 it is because God is testing us to find out if we will follow a man or follow what God has already told us in his Word. <u>Will you follow signs and wonders or what the Bible says</u>?

Even though God performs miracles through him or her, it does not mean that everything the preacher says agrees with what God says in the Bible. God allows this because he expects us to follow what he has clearly told us in the Bible. Even though we should listen to preachers to learn from them, in the end, we are responsible for knowing what is right and following God. Therefore, we should not believe everything that a big-name preacher teaches, or what a signs-and-wonders preacher teaches.

Millions of people have been deceived into believing the gospel of wealth merely because of the working of the Holy Spirit in the ministers who teach it. Clearly, the working of the Holy Spirit, by itself, is not proof that we should listen to or have any association with those preachers. No, the true test is not the ability to prophesy or heal people, <u>the true test is whether they teach correct doctrines</u>. He very well could be teaching something that will lead you into idolatry, or witchcraft, or divination, or the worship of angels. He could be one of the almost true yet false ministers described in Deuteronomy.

You may consider that I point out that no one teaches 100% accurate doctrine, yes, but the false doctrines mentioned here are not just any doctrines; they are doctrines that lead people away from God, such as idolatry. The Bible has warned us that <u>seeking wealth is idolatry</u>! Jesus said the truth will make you free, and that means if you don't know the truth, you are not free, but remain in bondage and could end up in hell.

Jesus gave a parable of a great field of grain, but this field also had weeds that had been put there by Satan. The workers asked if the owner wanted the weeds pulled up, but the owner of the field said not to pull up the weeds because they might pull up some of the grain along with the weeds.

This gives us one of the reasons why God does not bring down all false ministers. There are many good Christians who got saved in their meetings and even filled with the Holy Spirit, and if God were to cause all the false ministers to be discredited some of their followers who are genuine Christians would become disillusioned and turn away from Christianity. A percentage of those who are saved in the meetings of the almost true yet false prophets will read their Bibles and seek God and will eventually turn away from the false doctrines of the ministers who got them saved. I have read many such testimonies. However, the weeds are eventually pulled up, so those almost true yet false prophets will eventually be brought down.

Some of the false prophets may start out as a true prophets of God, but because they get off track by adopting the prosperity gospel or WOF doctrines, they become false prophets. So we should not support their ministries, even though they are getting a few people healed and saved! God said in his Word, "*You must not listen to the words of that prophet or dreamer.... he has tried to turn you from the way the LORD your God commanded you to follow.*" Do we really want to have any connection to the wealth gospel or WOF? No! <u>The majority, but not all, of the Charismatic preachers on TBN and other networks are the almost true yet false prophets.</u>

Chapter 4:
An Almost True Yet False Revival

We have learned that God uses preachers that teach false doctrine, like the WOF preachers. I do not fully understand why he does so, because it seems to me that it sort of endorses the doctrines of the false minister, but God knows more than I do. If he wants to use a preacher that teaches false doctrine, he can certainly do so, and has done so to start a recent revival.

Rodney Howard Brown is universally credited with bringing the laughing revival which ended up creating the Toronto Revival through Randy Clark in 1994. Brown is a WOF prosperity preacher, so you would never expect any revival that he spawns to be a true revival, and so we shall see that it is a false revival.

People are encouraged to come and get into the river of God, and enjoy the laughing and other good times they are having in the river. It is all about having some kind of experience. Derek Prince said:

> If we focus on enjoying ourselves rather than cultivating a concern for the sufferings of those around us, our spirits are far from that of Jesus. (*Protection*, 2008, p. 75)

(1) A Flood of Deception Now in USA

This is a Word from the Lord about deception coming to American churches, by Steven Dobbs (U.K.), first given in 2005:

> I received this from the Holy Spirit in early summer 2005. The Lord showed me that there is going to be a flood of deception (1) infiltrating much of the U.S church in the near future, (the gift of

discernment of spirits is therefore going to become increasingly important). Why the Lord will allow these deceptions: I was extremely disheartened by this as the U.K receives a lot of help from some good U.S ministries and there are close links between these two nations.

The Spirit then ministered to me again and showed me that God was sovereign and that this was His will. I saw that although this increase in deception will <u>test the Christians in the U.S.A</u>. It will also filter the global church from the less reliable U.S teaching ministries and reduce their influence in the global body of Christ.

Many of the world's largest and best known teaching ministries come from the U.S.A. I was shown that many were propagating <u>poor, badly emphasized or erroneous teachings</u>. The Lord showed me that He could not allow them to continue influencing the worldwide church as they are at present. This is because we will soon be entering into the end times and this season will test the faith of all of us. God therefore wants His people to be prepared for this with good teachings that have the same emphasis as found in the New Testament.

The filtering process: I was shown that the ministers that teach errors or a poor emphasis will also tend to have this reflected in their own walk with God. They will not therefore be rooted very deeply into the truth themselves even though many of them may be well known teachers or preachers. These people will therefore tend to be amongst those most open to this flood of deception. When exposed to such deception <u>many of them will start to move in increased spiritual error and folly</u> as a result. Many will get deceived as <u>they fail to discern the difference between which spiritual phenomena are of the Lord and which are counterfeit and from the enemy</u>. Their true spiritual maturity will then be revealed for all to see.

Many other Christians from around the world, those who are able to discern these things better, will then start to question the maturity and teachings of such ministries. They will start to look more closely at these teachings and notice the errors and wrong emphases that already exist, errors that they had not noticed before. People will then start to turn away from the worst teachers and listen instead to those who are teaching the full council of God in line with the whole of scripture. The overall level of teaching in the global body of Christ will improve as a result of this.

How this will realign ministries: The ministries which have the poorest levels of teaching will become less popular around the world as a result of this. Those teaching ministries that are the most mature and have the best quality teaching will become more popular than before. The overall quality of teaching ministries in the global body of Christ will therefore improve as a result of this filtering effect.

The "prosperity gospel": God showed me that one of the main teachings that He is concerned about is that which has become known as the "prosperity gospel". Although truths are taught within this I understood that errors and wrong emphases are taught as well. At present this teaching has a great deal of influence in the global body of Christ. This results in many believers around the world taking on board the errors and wrong emphases contained within it. I saw that the Lord does not want this situation to continue. We are heading into the end times in the near future and God wants us to be strong, built up with good, solid teachings that prepare us for the difficulties we are going to encounter and the sacrifices we may have to make to follow Christ.

A realigning of national churches at a global level: The Lord wants those national churches that are submitting the most to Him to have the greatest proportion of well-known ministries at a global level. The Spirit showed me that at present the U.S.A is over-represented by such ministries. This filtering process will reduce the number of influential U.S ministries on the world stage. At the same time, other ministries from other nations will become more popular and will increase in influence as a result of this.

The overall church of the U.S.A will also therefore lose some of its influence within the global body of Christ because of this filtering. The churches of some other nations, (those that have been submitting the most to Christ), will, however, see an increase in their influence in the global church.

This is God's will and the global body of Christ will be strengthened as a result. The Lord wants the body of Christ to be led by, and follow the example of, the best international ministries. He also wants the global church to be influenced the most by those national churches that are submitting the most to Jesus.

The better ministries from the U.S.A: I was then shown a picture of a vessel of milk which had cream floating to the top of it. The interpretation was that as this filtering takes place, and the overall level of deception (2) increases in the U.S church, the better U.S ministries will then come to the forefront at a global level. I understood that many of these were presently only medium sized ministries because their popularity was presently overshadowed by some larger but poorer quality U.S ministries. I saw that many of these medium sized ministries already have a better walk with the Lord and that they would therefore be less likely to be influenced by the coming flood of deception. They will be seen to be mature as they discern and avoid these deceptions. In due course this will vindicate them and earn them respect from other believers from around the world. Their ministries will then become more popular and grow in influence because of this. I saw that some of them will then start to minister and preach at the highest levels on the world stage within the body of Christ in the future.

1. I understand "deception" to mean all sorts of counterfeits of the Holy Spirit. These will include <u>counterfeit moves of God's power</u> which will come from other spirits, from <u>New Age / occult spirits</u>, counterfeit healings and miracles even, false teachings, false prophecies, counterfeit visions from the enemy, <u>counterfeit experiences of heaven</u>, <u>fake appearances of Jesus</u> and, please note, many counterfeit appearances of angels which will really be fallen angels come to deceive any believers who are open to them. Of course <u>Christians can have such experiences genuinely from the Lord</u> but there is also going to be an increase in these counterfeits as we move towards the end-times, as the enemy attempts to "deceive if possible even the elect", (Matt 24;24).

2. Concerning the U.S church, this increase in deception will have its entitlement at a national/ corporate level. We should not therefore see any deception as a judgment on individuals themselves. At a personal level some believers will be more exposed to these deceptions than others for reasons that are not necessarily their fault, e.g. if they happen to be in a church where the enemy is moving in a lot of deception. I believe, though, that <u>those whose hearts are set to follow Christ will eventually come through any serious deception if they persevere</u> in following the Lord and keep on submitting to Him.

At an international level, though, this wave of enemy deception will expose and reduce the global influence of the worst U.S ministries and will bring about the realignment of national churches and ministries that God desires. It will improve the quality of teaching and the quality of the most well-known minis- tries at an international level. This is due to God's sovereignty, and will strengthen the global body of Christ and prepare God's people for the difficult years ahead. (S. Dobbs, 30th Oct 2005)

Does this explain what is currently happening with the Char- ismatic movement? The Bible warns us in many places to beware of false prophets, yet, if asked to name one, few Charismatics could; they think they are all genuine. Pray for God to open our eyes and let us see the truth! Notice that it says it comes as a "test." This is important, we have already learned about the "test" in connection to the almost true yet false prophet. And there is more info shortly on this test.

(2) A Vision of True and False Revival

This vision is somewhat related to the above, as both are on deception in America. Patrick Ersig, in America, had a vision of what God considers a true revival, and a false revival which ap- pears to be what is happening now in the Charismatic Movement (all capitalization was in the original):

Here is the account of a vision from God that I received regard- ing true and counterfeit revival. This vision occurred on March 4th 2006.

The VISION- Everything was black and I saw one person walk- ing at a semi-brisk pace. Not fast walking, but a slight cadence above normal pace; walking with purpose. This person was walking straight and sure - upright and strong - solemn and seri- ous, like a revolutionary - a warrior - a light to darkness. I then saw a couple more people and then others in the distance and they were bright and shining against the blackness that was all around. They all walked the same way - solemn and serious and the Lord spoke and said, "These are my remnant who are walk- ing in holiness, righteousness, obedience, brokenness and utter submission to MY WILL - watch what I am doing Patrick."

Then I saw the individuals begin to unite in small groups of two to three at first and then more came and the groups grew to five and even ten and the light intensified greatly. It was beautiful like a sunset over the mountains or a sunrise on the ocean, a rose in full bloom.

What I saw next made me burst into tears and sobs to the point that I couldn't continue to describe what I was seeing. My wife kept saying "What?! what is it? What do you see?!" After a few minutes I was able to control the weeping to explain what I saw happening. As the Lord was drawing together His remnant into these small groups the power of God came down - like in the book of Acts - the lame were walking, the blind were seeing, the deaf were hearing, (literally and figuratively) and persecution fueled the fire! This end time HOLY and RIGHTEOUS remnant of serious and solemn warriors and revolutionaries walked, in the deep darkness of America and her backslidden lukewarm churches, with apostolic glory and power not seen since the book of Acts - to proclaim the true Gospel of Jesus Christ - repentance and holiness and freedom from sin!

The Lord spoke and said, "This is the revival that I am bringing about and it starts with the individuals who have been called out to personal revival and are walking straight and sure - upright and strong - solemn and serious, like revolutionaries, warriors, lights to darkness. My remnant is walking in holiness, righteousness, obedience, brokenness and utter submission to MY WILL and I am drawing them together."

Then the vision switched. Now I saw what looked like a dimly lit movie or a video shot with poor lighting. I saw clips of people dancing and shaking. I saw people falling down, shouting, jumping, and singing. There were huge multitudes rather than the few and many, many were coming in large groups that filled large auditoriums and stadiums instead of small groups of individuals being drawn together. Even some of the lights that were in the first part of the vision were drawn to this part of the vision. I saw dancing and clapping, shaking, shouting, strong and powerful emotionalism and sensationalism. Soulish and fleshy spirits claimed to be the Holy Spirit. Great miracles abounded - signs and wonders. People proclaimed, "This is the revival we have been waiting and praying for! -This is the revival we have heard prophesied! - This is the outpouring of the Holy Spirit- a great move of God!"

But the Lord spoke and said, "Patrick this is not from me, this is from Satan, it is a counterfeit! And many will be fooled and tricked by this clever deception from the enemy!"

Then the vision switched again. Now I saw both visions side by side - split screen, so to speak. They both grew in intensity at an equal rate - as the true would grow in power, the false would grow in numbers and as the true would grow in numbers, the false would grow in false signs and wonders. The Lord spoke and said, "This is not a vision of the future, but this has already begun and will grow as the days pass. I am doing this now and the enemy is coming against it at this very moment."

Conclusion: The Lord is bringing about an end times revival of which the like we have never seen and it begins with you. The Lord is calling you to be separate, to holiness and righteousness unto the Lord and to walk in obedience and utter submission to His will. Be free from sin, be perfect as your Father in heaven is perfect, be dead to flesh and alive in Christ. Walk sober and solemn and serious before the Lord with a reverent and holy fear of God. If you are looking and waiting for some big corporate outpouring of emotionalism and signs and wonders you are going to miss the coming revival. The revival starts with you! Seek the Lord and press into Him closer every day. Allow the Blood and Grace of Jesus to break the bonds of your flesh and produce Holy and Righteous living in your life. Ask the Lord to show you what it is in your life that is keeping you from that which is perfect - no matter how small or how painful; ask the Lord to expose everything that is keeping you from being closer to Him and bring Glory to Him and His kingdom and deeply renounce all that He shows you.

Live your life as a living sacrifice - a living drink offering poured out before the Lord for His glory and honor. There are many things that are cultural, societal and religious that keep us separated from God and walking in His Spirit. Pray for God to bring these things to light and put them to death no matter how hard it may be. If you don't realize that the revival the Lord is doing begins with you individually, then you are going to miss it! The Lord is calling you today, repent for your lukewarmness and your lackadaisical attitude toward sin in your own life and those who are perishing and plunging into hell all around you every day! The Lord is calling you today to allow the Blood of Jesus and the grace of God to produce holiness and rivers of righteousness in your life that you may be salt to a decaying world and light to the darkness that prevails. What will you do? The Lord is calling you right now to make up your mind to love Him with all your heart, mind, soul and strength, take up your cross, die to self and follow HIM - forsaking ALL and seeking after Him with all that you are and have. Come out and be separate in holy, righteous obedience unto God!

WARNING - DO NOT be fooled by these sensual, emotional counterfeits that are and will be popping up, that these people and churches call "revival." IT IS A TRICK FROM THE ENEMY! When you hear that "revival" has broken out in the next town or the next state or even in your own city - please remember this warning. There will be much singing and dancing and shouting and many things will sound as though they are true. There will be great surges of emotion that will cause people to fall down and jump and shout, cry and weep but this is not from God. Many will be crying out in joy, "Peace, peace." But God's Servants will have discernment above and beyond any gift, and a willingness to die than lie -despite the increase of signs and wonders from all of the counterfeit moves around them in the churches. If the revival you are in is not serious and reverent, holy and righteous, and the Love and reverent fear toward God are not the only things you see, then RUN FOR YOUR LIFE, and warn everyone you know. These spirits are strong and extremely powerful - get out of the building and don't be fooled by the signs and wonders.

Please, I am begging you to remember this, for I know that there will be many who are fooled and even (if possible) drawn away from the real to the counterfeit, but I also know that there will be some who read this warning and remember it and are spared. The true revival army will look like small bands of revolutionaries or Special Forces with an end times mission to complete and Satan's counterfeit will resemble a band of wild Indians or tribal warriors dancing and shouting battle cries.

The true revival army will attack the enemy at its stronghold, sin - their mission will be the souls of men through the power of the Holy Spirit - they will be concerned with setting people free from the bondage of sin through the message of the cross and will watch strongholds of sin topple. Satan's counterfeit will go after places and methods of sin - they will try to legislate morality and get laws changed, which results in forced morality and no salvations. God's army will seek to save that which is lost in the streets and alleys; Satan's army will try to change the laws to prevent sin but result in the salvation of no one. "Whosoever loves his life shall lose it. Whosoever loses his life for My sake, shall find it."

Satan you are on notice! God is preparing a revival army that is going to tear down the strongholds of your kingdom and Jesus is preparing a bride for Himself that is spotless and pure! God is calling to make a decision right now - what will you do?!

Could the above apply to the now gone Lakeland Revival? It seems to. But many other similar revivals are still going on. True revival is about repentance, false revival is about "bless me." True revival will cause you to die to self, false revival will make you feel happy and unconcerned.

Notice that these visions mention that God is bringing or at least allowing both of these revivals. Though a test was not mentioned, it sure sounds like a test. Will you seek after God and Biblical truth, which means repentance and sacrifice? Or will you seek after a feel good experience, unconcerned about truth?

(3) Toronto Exposed

Royal D. Cronquist (1927-1998) was a Pentecostal minister who wrote several books. I believe he *may have been* from Australia, because he is not well-known. He asked God to reveal whether the revival was from God or not, and received a shocking answer. He wrote a two page article about it called *"What Was "Toronto"?*:

This concerns the so-called "Laughing Revival" which began in Toronto, Canada, and spread throughout the nations. In all the meetings I attended, I had the sensation of embarrassment, then shame, finally leaving each meeting grieved in my inner man. I never made a final judgment, because I had to seek the Lord in prayer concerning all the negative sensing going on within me.

The founding minister of a local church where I attended some of these meetings told me I needed to go to Toronto. I prayed that if the Lord wanted me to go to Toronto, He would have to make a way without any solicitation on my part. Surprisingly, within a week I received a letter of invitation to come to London, Ontario, Canada, for a week long meeting. I agreed to go with one stipulation: they would have to take me to the Airport Vineyard Church in Toronto where the "Laughing Revival" started.

They agreed.

The hosting church took me to the Airport Vineyard on a Saturday night, which was about an hour's drive from London. In the meeting I perceived visibly a great deal of "<u>flesh" manifesting</u>.

The testimonies sounded scripturally satisfactory, but still there was a question in my heart. When it came time for ministry I expected to hear a Word, but instead the minister called all those between 8-20 years of age to come up to the front and receive a blessing. . . .

About 450 in all responded, coming forward for prayer. As prayer was made for them, all began to be "slain" in the spirit. Some very quietly went to the floor, some went laughing, and so on. My attention was drawn to a young lady who was doing something I could not make out clearly. I got up and carefully made my way through the crowd on the floor. When I arrived close to this young lady, I distinctly heard a sound coming out of her that astoundingly sounded exactly like a <u>clucking chicken</u>! I looked to my left and observed an adult woman standing over two children who I assumed were hers. One was a girl about ten years old and the other a boy of about eight. The boy had his eyes wide open in fixed gaze, not even blinking his eyes. His muscles would constrict so severely his body would fly up 18-24 inches off the floor, completely flipping around, then fall flat on top of someone else lying near him. His mother (I presumed) would pull him off to a vacant space on the floor where he would repeat the whole scenario again. This happened over and over again, at least twenty times or more.

Those praying <u>never once discerned this boy was being controlled by demon powers</u>! The same was also true of the young lady clucking like a chicken. Apparently, no one was using their ability to distinguish the evil spirits.

In spite of all I saw, I still did not make any final decisions about the so-called revival. On television, I watched as Pat Robertson and Paul Crouch interviewed ministries with doctorate degrees, each answering the questions put to them on this phenomenon going on in the churches. Without exception they were in agreement the revival was authentic, that most everything going on was of God. But I, like Paul in Acts 16:16-18, after many days had not come to a final decision within my heart whether all these things were of God or not.

I wanted to know what spirit was originating many of the unseemly noises and acts I observed.

There was enough going on which was scripturally sound, yet I still could not get rid of the negative, foreboding gnawing on the inside. People's testimonies of getting "the blessing" were good, but I cannot honestly say there appeared to be a permanently changed life in fruit, power or authority of Christ in any of them. Later, Jesus appeared to me in my room and what He said overwhelmed, shocked and surprised me:

"The manifestations presently going on the laughing revival have happened to varying degrees with every outpouring of the Holy Spirit. But in this one, we gave great liberty to Satan, commissioning him to initiate and do as he willed... [ellipsis in the original]

"We wanted to put Our people, especially Church leaders, **to the test** to see if they would "try the spirits" to see whether they were of God or not (1 Jn 4:1); to examine everything and hold fast to that which was good, and ensure that everything glorified the Godhead in attitude, motive, word or deed (1 Th 5:21); to see if the leaders would hold or keep the meetings in decency and order (I Co 14:40). Even many of the blessings and apparent miracles came from the source of Satan with Our consent." "Church leaders miserably failed the test. Why? Because they have failed to seek the counsel of the Most High (Jer 23:16-22). Therefore, in the Day of the Lord, because they have refused to grow up into Me in all aspects, I will give them over to their own lusts. I will give them a spirit of delusion whereby they will believe lies (2 Th 2:10b-11; Re 13:14a), because they have not feared the Lord nor stood in My counsel to know My ways and perform My works" (Ps 103:7; Jn 5:19-20, 30 amp; 17:18; 20:21; 14:12). (*What Was "Toronto"?*, by R.D. Cronquist) (www.isom. vnsalvation.com/Resources%20English/Christian%   20Ebooks/ Royal%20Cronquist%20What%20Was%20Toronto.pdf)

All of the Words and the vision from Jesus agree with each other. And it boils down to God is allowing Satan to enter the revival, thus creating a mixture, both God and Satan are operating. This means some people can receive from God, while other people receive evil spirits. I believe that a Christian who is 100% right with God will not receive these evil spirits, but how many of us are at that point? People who go seeking blessing rather than

God are not seeking rightly, and they will receive evil spirits.

Also notice that the first Word referred to the coming deception as a test, and the last Word also said that Jesus is allowing this as a test, but they failed the test. Remember the almost true yet false prophets described in a former chapter? The reason God uses them is a test. God uses them, yet they are false. In like manner, God can heal and save a few people in the revival, but it is still false! So I call it an almost true yet false revival.

The false spirits that are part of this revival will invade any church where they are allowed to operate, even Anglican. Derek Prince commented on the Toronto revival:

> Now, I would like to give briefly my summation of this whole phenomenon /movement/whatever-you-want-to-call-it, based partly on personal observation and partly on what I believe to be reliable reports. My summation is very simple: <u>it is a mixture of spirits, both the Holy Spirit and unholy spirits</u>. They are mixed together. . . .
>
> I have observed that the result of mixture is two things: first of all, confusion; and then division. For instance, we have this mixed message, part of which is true, part of which is false. People can respond in two ways. Some will see the good and focus on it, and therefore accept the bad. Some will focus on the bad, and therefore reject the good. In either case, it does not accomplish God's purposes. (*Protection from Deception*, page 9, 1996, emphasis mine)

Derek Prince's observation is exactly as seen above, and as I have concluded. Although a person can get healed at churches that teach the prosperity gospel, or has gold dust, or are in the revival, it is best to stay away from these churches unless you want to be deceived or get evil spirits. Prince also said:

> A mixture of good and evil yields two main results: confusion and division. . . . The recent influx in signs and wonders indicates a mixture of spirits: the Holy Spirit and unholy spirits. (*Protection*, 2008, p. 77).

And so it is that this revival is bringing both confusion and division. (Derek Prince's book, *Protection from Deception*, was first published in 1996. But either he rewrote his book before he died in 2003, or it was rewritten by his ministry staff, because the newer edition of 2008 makes no direct reference to the Toronto outpouring.)

(4) A Dream of God's Judgment

The Word from Jesus given in section 3 included this statement, "*in <u>the Day of the Lord</u>, because they have refused to grow up into Me in all aspects, I will give them over to their own lusts. <u>I will give them a spirit of delusion</u> whereby they will believe lies.*"

It is significant that one of their own actually had a prophetic dream of the Wrath of God coming upon the Charismatics, which will happen during God's judgment upon the whole world at the end of the Great Tribulation. Mike Bickle's dream of Feb. 13, 2009. Here is part of it:

> A. I was speaking at a conference in a baseball park inside a large fair ground. About 40,000 people were present. Many leaders and their people (from <u>many "charismatic" streams</u>) were present. . . .
>
> B. I preached on prayer, God's power and end-time judgment. I spoke at two afternoon sessions. . . .
>
> C. . . . I saw a token of a few of the events that John prophesied about in Rev. 12:7-9 . . . The result is that Satan will be cast to the earth at the beginning of the Tribulation. . . .
>
> D. I did not see Satan, but only demonic principalities being cast to the earth. They looked like large snakes (over 100 yards long and 50 feet thick). Each had a large head that looked like a dragon. . . .
>
> E. Every one at the conference was filled with panic. Most were terrified. <u>No one, including me, had understanding or faith that was mature enough to respond in the power or confidence</u> that I had just preached on. I ran as I felt the terror of the event. . . . All wanted to quickly get out of there. . . .
>
> G. <u>Soot or wet, muddy, thick ash was raining down from the sky. It darkened the sky as it fell on the people</u> who were running. I ran out of the vast fair grounds to the park offices (at the entrance). <u>Wet ash was all over me</u> as I ran. Many did not get out. They were bitten by the large snakes.

H. There were evil policemen at the entrance. They told me, "You have to go back into the fair grounds or we will put you in jail." . . . they were in the Antichrist's system. . . . There will be no natural way out of this crisis except by the power of the Spirit. (www.north west prophetic. com/2009 /02/mike-bickle-prophetic-dream-victorious.html)

Bickle greatly misinterprets this dream as some kind of victory, thus the title of the dream, *Victorious Church in the End-Times*. First, the events he saw will <u>not</u> take place at the start of the Great Tribulation, but at the end during God's Wrath upon the world, which means the dream shows all of the river, signs and wonders, and jerking Charismatics going through the Wrath of God. So they will miss the Rapture. It does not indicate that they will go to hell, but they will die in the global destruction at the return of Christ because their end time views are wrong. They believe in dominionism. Christians will take over, but only after a global destruction that takes place at the return of Christ.

I have a series of four books on Bible prophecy, and the fourth is titled, *The Approaching Apocalypse and Three Days of Darkness*. I show that nuclear war will precede large asteroid impacts, and both will cause a dust, mist, and murk in the sky that is deadly because the dust and mist will be full of chemicals from burning cities, and nuclear radiation from the explosions. The smoke and ash will darken the whole world and kill everyone it falls on. This is the darkness spoken about in Matthew 24. It is also the *"outer darkness"* that Jesus spoke about in other places. Other prophecies say that during this period of darkness, hordes of demons will be unleashed upon the world, so it fits perfectly with Bickle's dream.

Notice that the evil policemen (Antichrist forces) forced him to go back into the stadium and breath the poisoned air. This means Bickle and many Charismatics will die in the nuclear war and Wrath of God, unless they repent and reject the demonic deception that has entered the movement.

(5) But God Started the Revival

There is a prophecy that was given by one of those in the prophetic movement that said, *"I am going to change the understanding
and expression of Christianity in the earth in one generation."* Those in
the laughing, gold dust, "bless me" revival say that this is how
God is redefining Christianity. We should understand, though,
that God also created the Roman Catholic Church, as prophesied in Zechariah 11. Just after the prophecy of 30 pieces of silver, which refers to the betrayal of Jesus, it says:

> Then the Lord said to me: . . . 16 <u>I am raising up a shepherd in
> the land</u> who will not care for those who are perishing, nor seek
> the young, nor heal the broken, nor feed those who are standing
> still. But he will eat the flesh of the fat and tear their hoofs in
> pieces.

> 17 Woe to this worthless shepherd who abandons his flock. May
> the sword take his arm and right eye; may his arm surely wither
> up, and his right eye become blind. (Zech. 11:15-17) (MEV)

Notice that it says God himself will raise up this false shepherd. I won't go into why God created a church that is half inef-
fective (the withered arm), and has half wrong doctrines (the
blind eye), but it shows that God does a lot of things we would
not think he would do. He works through false prophets, and is
allowing a false revival to spread, WOW.

What it boils down to is, God expects you to believe what the
Bible says, not what a man says, or what a denomination says.
We must have our own legitimate relationship with God.

In Hosea it says that God rejected some of his people because
they refused to believe the truth:

> My people are destroyed for lack of knowledge. <u>Because you
> have rejected knowledge</u>, I will reject you from being My priest.
> And because you have forgotten the law of your God, I will also
> forget your children. (Hosea 4:6) (MEV)

The knowledge referred to is the knowledge of God; in other
words, the truth. The true Holy Spirit will lead you into the truth,
but the counterfeit holy spirit will lead you into deception.

Chapter 5:
False Signs and Wonders

Deception by its very nature is a mixture of truth and error. If it were all error it would be easy to spot, and few people would be fooled. So we must be diligent in examining all new teaching or new movements or new things happening in the church. Derek Prince said:

> It is lamentable how many churches specialize in the realm of the soul rather than the realm of the spirit. People in the soulish realm are carried away with little effort, setting themselves up for deception. This can be avoided only by distinguishing between the spiritual and the soulish realm. (*Protection From Deception*, 2008, page 53)

He also said, "*Those who are not rooted in Christ and are ignorant of the power and truth of God will succumb to deception and ultimate destruction*" (Ibid, p. 68). This is why the false revival is affecting people who are in the WOF movement the most. They are not rooted and grounded in the truth, but are already believing lies.

(1) Gold Dust

It may come as a surprise to many in the Pent/Charismatic movement, but there are many false prophets and false teachers in the movement, some of them perform signs and wonders by the power of Satan and his demons, or familiar spirits. These are the false ministers that Jesus spoke about when he said false prophets will "*display great signs and wonders*" (Matt. 24:24) (ISV) that will deceive many people, even almost deceiving the elect.

Many people in this group once knew the truth, but rejected it. They started out as true ministers of God, or true believers, but accepted WOF doctrines or the prosperity gospel. The Apostle Paul spoke about this in 2 Thessalonians. The signs and wonders we are seeing now are some of the powerful delusions that cause people to believe the WOF doctrines and end up in hell:

> The coming of the lawless one will be in accordance with the work of Satan displayed in all kinds of <u>counterfeit miracles, signs and wonders</u>, 10 and in every sort of evil that deceives those who are perishing. They perish because they **refused to love the truth and so be saved**. 11 For this reason **God sends them a powerful delusion** so <u>that they will believe the lie</u> 12 and so that all will be condemned who have not believed the truth but have delighted in wickedness. (2 Thess. 2:9-12) (NIV)

God allows the false signs and allows people to be deceived who have rejected the truth. This very much fits the WOF group of preachers. In all likelihood, the majority of the churches that have gold dust or any other type of strange manifestation, are either WOF or they at least teach the prosperity gospel. However, the Toronto Blessing / river revival movement includes even mainstream churches. (Even though the context of the passage above refers to the followers of the Antichrist, it is not limited to them.)

What are some of the strong delusions that will lead them to destruction? Signs and wonders such as deceptive dreams and visions, teeth and rosaries turning to gold, gold dust, gems, glory clouds, feathers, weeping statues, visits from angels giving false doctrine, etc. The Catholic Church has had this sort of thing for hundreds of years, but now they are happening in WOF and prosperity gospel churches. (Not everyone who believes the prosperity gospel is WOF, but all WOF believe the prosperity gospel.) Derek Prince said,

> It is also important to realize that signs and wonders neither guarantee nor determine truth. Truth is established and unchanging; it is the Word of God. . . .
>
> <u>True signs attest the truth</u>; <u>lying signs attest lies</u>. Many Christians assume that every supernatural sign must be from God, forgetting that Satan, or the devil, is completely capable of performing supernatural signs and wonders. (*Protection*, 2008, p. 7)

Beware, these strange things are taking place because they are actually false signs, designed to deceive people. People who desire riches will be deceived. <u>People who seek signs and wonders will be deceived</u>.

Many Charismatics believe that all supernatural spiritual experiences are signs from God, and so they follow the false ministers and believe whatever these ministers teach. There are times when the gold dust, gems, and angel feathers are faked, but there are many occasions when it really happens, but is caused by familiar spirits or even demons.

If you are not aware of the gold dust phenomenon, it is tiny specs of what looks like shiny gold dust that appears on the skin and hair of people. Usually it appears on people when they attend a church service of some WOF or prosperity preachers, then it can happen to them anywhere, or even on someone standing near them.

Perhaps the first person to have gold dust was a lady in Brazil who came to visit Ruth Ward Heflin's church. Then the gold dust started happening in Heflin's church, then Bob Shattles visited Heflin's church and it started happening with him. *Charisma Magazine* reported on the death of Bob Shattles:

> The pastor emeritus of Souls Harvest Worship Center in Douglasville, Ga., had experienced the gold flakes phenomenon for two years after attending a meeting led by revivalist Ruth Heflin. (Sept. 2001).

The false spirits of sorcery and divination appear to be easily transferable, just like a virus. I originally believed that the dust was faked, but there is now significant evidence that the gold dust came from familiar spirits.

Both Heflin and Shattles died of cancer within a year of each other: Heflin (10-2000), and Shattles (7-2001). This is <u>not</u> proof that it is <u>not</u> of God, but it is a major warning we should not ignore.

Here are two emails that were sent to the owner of a website that speaks against the gold dust. I do not believe the persons who sent the emails had any reason to make up a story. Email of June 17, 1999:

This is really wild. My assistant and I went to this evangelist's house. The evangelist is not in the gold thing and believes that it is a bewitching spirit. The evangelist's daughter came into the room and joined the conversation. The daughter is not saved and was smoking a cigarette and drinking wine. Suddenly, gold dust began to appear on the unsaved daughter. It was on her face, hair, chest, shoulders and rounded her eyes as if she had put on gold dust eye-liner! Look, she's got that gold dust all over her, my assistant said. The girl said, "What are you talking about?" We took her to the mirror and she was shocked. No one had ever told her about the gold dust before.

We took her to Ruth Heflin's [web] page and showed her Silvania's gold falling out of her hair. This unsaved girl said, "Look, I am not a holy person and I do not want to be a kook, what can I do to get this stuff off me?" The Next day, I went to see her. "Is the gold still there?" I asked. "No," she replied, "but I've been as sick as a dog all night. My nose is stopped up and my throat is sore. Every time I move my head, it feels like my brain is floating." I asked her, "How did you get rid of the gold?" "I washed it off. That thing is not a holy thing from God." she said. I know this sound wild, but it really did happen. (http://amighty wind.com/ golddust/caution.htm)

Email of July 15, 1999 from London, England:

The gold dust phenomena has arrived here. I was just watching a news item on one of the main stations (ITV) with the most respected news reporter in the UK today, Trevor McDonald about the gold dust experience.

It seems people in one of the suburbs (Surrey) are experiencing their dental fillings turning to gold. Others are experiencing the gold dust on their body.

. . . The people who are going through this experience seem very excited and all but a Church of England Vicar thinks it is God and it is a miracle. (http:// amighty wind.com/ golddust/ caution.htm)

Even though some people claim the gold dust was tested and showed real gold, some of the dust was tested and the results showed that it was plastic, and the feathers were chicken or bird feathers. *Charisma Magazine* had two samples of the gold dust from Heflin and/or Shattles analyzed by U.S. Geological Survey in Washington D. C., and the results showed plastic. As a result,

John Arnott of the *Toronto Airport Christian Fellowship*, now *Catch the Fire Toronto*, canceled meetings with the lady from Brazil because of the findings. Yet he actually prays for the fillings in teeth to turn to gold.

In more recent years, a preacher named Joshua Mills claims that he entered an elevator that had three people in it and he immediately became covered with lots of gold dust. All three of the other passengers converted right there. And the amazing thing was, all three had walked passed a street-preacher outside, but ignored him. But the gold dust made them want to convert. Mills promotes the prosperity gospel. So if the gold dust really did appear, <u>since the prosperity gospel is false, this tells me that the gold dust is strong delusion to ensnare those who reject the true gospel</u>. Mills tells his story on an episode of *It's Supernatural* with Sid Roth.

People claim that it is bringing people to God, but they are being converted to a false gospel. Another preacher can be seen on a Youtube video praying for the gold dust to appear, not in a church service, but just for the video, and it appears (*Gold Dust Under a Microscope*, Dominion Fire Church). This is the mark of familiar spirits because God cannot be manipulated in that manner, but familiar spirits can (discussed below).

Someone may want to argue that Elijah prayed that God would stop the rain, and that God would send fire to consume the offering. But I believe he did not do those things on his own initiative, but was led by God to do them. And they had a purpose other than to inspire awe or excitement, so they were totally different from the signs and wonders we are seeing today.

Jesus said, *"<u>This is an evil generation. It seeks a sign</u>"* (Luke 11:29) (NKJV). That statement strikes me as though Jesus was a bit angry when he said it. This generation of Charismatics and Pentecostals are seeking after signs, but the Bible says God has already given us a sign, which is the tongues and interpretation of tongues, which rarely happens anymore because of all the false doctrines, idolatry, and worldliness. And people who seek after signs are many times more likely to be deceived.

How can you tell if something is a false sign or a true sign? A false sign may excite the human imagination, but otherwise have no practical purpose. It may be awe inspiring, call attention to itself or to a person, but does not otherwise indicate that it is actually from God. To understand true signs we should first read what Jesus told us about the signs that will follow believers, which are signs such as casting out demons, speaking in tongues, not being hurt by snake bites, healing the sick (Mark 16:17).

Other examples of true signs are when Peter was miraculously released from prison by an angel, or when Philip was transported away after baptizing the Ethiopian. Therefore, true signs are practical signs of ministry, or miracles that a minister might perform while spreading the gospel. Christian history is full of examples of true miracles, but nowhere are there any examples of emotionally excitable stuff like gold dust, except with the Roman Catholic Church which has rosaries turning to gold, weeping statues, etc. Jesus did not say that gold dust will follow those who believe.

A true sign will edify the church (1 Cor. 14:12) or otherwise be part of the fivefold ministry, or gifts of the Spirit. Gold dust and gold teeth are not such signs. Gold dust and other similar signs cause wonder and make people think that the minister of that church is somehow something special. It edifies man, not God or the body of Christ. It causes people to go seeking after the signs, rather than God and are most likely done by familiar spirits.

(2) Gold Teeth and Familiar Spirits

Fillings in teeth began turning to gold many years ago, then in the 1990s it began happening in John Arnott's church in Toronto (he preaches the prosperity gospel), and it has happened many times. Has anyone ever heard of God putting an artificial hip into someone with a bad hip? How about an artificial heart valve into a heart? No, God only gives new parts, so God would merely give you a new tooth, or heal the decayed one.

The teeth being filled with gold fillings are not even bad teeth that need a filling, but teeth that already have regular fillings. Therefore, no one is getting a bad tooth filled; no healing or even improvement by getting a gold filling, just changing normal fillings into gold, thus <u>causing wonder and excitement</u>. But teeth turning to gold happens in other settings:

> Toronto dentist Robert Clark says he has heard similar stories of fillings turning gold in the past, but they were from a New Age rather than a Christian context. One woman told him a few years ago about silver fillings turning to gold, but "what she was describing didn't sound like anything tied to a movement of the Holy Spirit." ("Dental miracles" the latest to hit Toronto, by Debra Fieguth. Christian Week, V. 12, No. 24. May 1999)

This sounds like the sort of thing that could happen by the power of a spiritual shaman connected to several other false religions. Similar gold miracles also happen to worshipers of Mary at Medjugorje, Herzegovina:

> On June 24th 1987 one lady stated that her rosary had turned gold while she was visiting Medjugorje, Yugoslavia [a site of Marian visitation]. . . This same woman claims that over forty people whom she ministered to have had their <u>rosaries turned to gold</u>. This phenomenon is not at all unusual.... thousands have come back from Medjugorje testifying that their <u>rosaries turned to gold</u> ... the chain or <u>beads often turn to gold</u> immediately during a prayer service in the presence of hundreds of witnesses. (*Voices, Visions and Apparitions*, by Michael Freze S.F.O., p. 61)

Teeth that are filled with <u>anything but God's original enamel is counterfeit</u>, and helps people believe the false teachings in the churches where it occurs. Therefore they are false signs and wonders done by familiar spirits to deceive those who refuse to believe the truth and be saved.

The teeth are not even filled with gold spontaneously, at least not at Toronto, because John Arnott actually prays for teeth to be filled with gold. Why not pray that God will cause the teeth with regular fillings to be filled with natural enamel? Because it would not happen. The reason it would not happen is because that would be a real miracle, and familiar spirits do *not normally* perform real miracles, only fake ones. By fake I mean, not from God.

People can actually watch the fillings in teeth change into gold. This too is evidence that it is a false sign and wonder. God does not perform magic tricks, he prefers to do his miracles out of our view, at least most of the time. This is why most angels appear as average humans and seldom identify themselves as angels. Even when Jesus performed a great miracle by feeding 5,000 people with a few loaves and fishes, it was not obvious. He did not cause several hundred baskets of food to appear before everyone's eyes.

Of course, there were healings that took place, like the withered hand that straightened out, and Lazarus being raised from the dead, so some things cannot be done quietly.

But you are not likely to see a bag of food appear on your table. Although there is a chance that you may find one sitting there, it will not appear before your eyes. But the most likely thing to happen will be the milk in your jug does not decrease in volume, or the number of cans of beans in your cabinet does not decrease, even after weeks of pulling out cans of beans. Though God does do noticeable miracles, he specializes in these almost unnoticeable miracles.

One prosperity preacher claimed that an angel appeared and gave him a big stack of cash, but that was not a false miracle, it was just a bold faced lie. Do I believe that John Arnott knowingly prays to familiar spirits? No, but when you pray for something like that, it is against the Bible, so that is why familiar spirits show up.

Have you ever watched those magicians on TV do incredible "magic tricks"? Some of them are tricks, but some of them are done by familiar spirits. Back when I was a teenager, a friend of mine was interested in magic tricks so he read a book on magic. He told me that to do a certain trick, the instructions said to do this and this, and then *"wait for the spirits to show up and finish the trick."*

I have seen magic "tricks" on TV that must have been done by familiar spirits. One fellow stopped two girls on the street and borrowed a cellphone from one girl and a scarf from the other. Then he proceeded to pull the entire scarf through the face of the phone and out the back, as though it had a slit in it. The girls freaked out. But, you say he may have switched phones using sleight of hand.

But there have been many other tricks that cannot be mere tricks, like taking an object from someone and then it is found inside of another solid object. Like when a magician had someone choose a playing card, then it was signed, and the magician reaches over and picks up a basketball and cuts it open to find the card inside.

One fellow held in his hand two Rubik's Cubes that each had all four sides the same color. Then he handed one Rubik's Cube's to someone and told her to turn the cube many times to mix up the colors on each of its four sides. The other cube he put behind his back. When she was finished she held up the cube, and the magician brought out his cube and both cubes were exactly the same on all four sides. There are 43,252,003,274,489, 856,000 different configurations on a Rubik's Cube. And he was holding it with just one hand, so he could not have turned the cube even once.

Sorry these could not be in color, but you can see them in color with a Google search.

Probably every summer you can see a magician, sometimes called illusionists, on the TV show *America's Got Talent*. Some of them do magic "tricks" that are clearly impossible without the use of familiar spirits. Sometimes you can even see the magic. You can still watch these magicians, just go to youtube.com and search for "America's Got Talent Magic" and videos of those magicians will come up.

Most people do not know what familiar spirits are. Most demon spirits try to influence people. There are demons of anger, jealousy, hate, murder, deception, lying, and many more. But familiar spirits will do what people ask them to do. This is why they are called "familiar," because they associate with humans in a nonthreatening way. The Bible forbids God's people from having anything to do with them:

> Give no regard to mediums and familiar spirits; do not seek after them, to be defiled by them: I am the Lord your God. (Leviticus 19:31) (NKJV)

As mentioned previously, no minister or movement is 100% accurate in all of his or her doctrines, who would that be? Also, no two ministers agree on every single point of most doctrines of the Bible! Therefore, God does work through ministers who teach false doctrine, but how false can a minister get and still be used of God? How far away from the truth can a movement get and still be safe to associate with?

(3) Bethel's False Signs and Wonders

Bethel Church in Redding, California, pastored by Bill Johnson, is very famous because of the many signs and wonders that are appearing, such as the glory cloud, gold dust, feathers, etc. But surprise, surprise, surprise, it is also a WOF church with all sorts of strange teachings. Students in the school of the supernatural go to the graves of dead preachers and lay on a grave in an effort to absorb some of the anointing of the dead person. This is called "*grave soaking*" but critics call it "*grave sucking.*"

The adults and even the children are taught how to make field trips to heaven, which is nothing but astral projection that is part of the New Age Movement. They supposedly have tried to draw energy from the earth called "earthing." This has nothing to do with any part of Christianity, it is New Age.

Bill Johnson and his wife are openly bringing in many practices and beliefs from the New Age Movement, not even trying to hide it. They have a book out called *The Physics of Heaven* which is full of New Age teaching. Co-authored by Johnson's administrative assistant, Judy Franklin, its contributors include Johnson and his wife, while the foreword was written by Kris Vallotton, a lead pastor at Bethel. The book's other co-author, Ellyn Davis, said the book's contributors *"all agree that there are precious truths hidden in the New Age that belong to us as Christians."* She even moved to Sedona to investigate the New Age:

> I saw healings and mystical experiences and revelations to rival anything I had seen or experienced in the church. . . .
>
> At that time, I could not find a single Christian leader who shared a similar interest in finding out if there were truths hidden in the New Age. Now we are beginning to hear more and more revelation that is in line with what New Agers have been saying all along and we are hearing more and more teaching about Christians "taking back truths" from the New Age that really belong to citizens of the Kingdom of God. (*The Physics of Heaven*, Destiny Image, 2015, chapter 2)

I originally believed that the Holy Spirit was at work at Bethel, like it says in Deut. 13, where God works through false prophets, but there is evidence that Satan is also at work. Johnson says he specifically <u>sought after signs and wonders</u>, but Jesus told us not to seek for signs. So the mere fact that he was seeking signs could have opened him up to false signs, like the Mormons.

Mormons have a lying sign which is a burning in the bosom. When Mormon missionaries go into a home they instruct people to ask God to prove that Joseph Smith is a true prophet and the Book of Mormon is genuine Scripture. The proof they say will be a burning sensation in the chest. This has been a part of Mormonism from the very beginning (Moroni 10:4), without which there would not have been so many converts. Many foolish people do as instructed and ask for the sign, and low and behold they get the burning sensation in the chest. <u>This is a lying sign</u>, do not believe it. Mormons specifically tell people to ask for the sign, but it is done by familiar spirits.

I was shocked to see something similar on video. I saw a young fellow connected to Bethel, who met a nonChristian on the street and prayed this prayer: *"Holy Ghost I ask you to send your power all the way up his arm as a sign of your love."* This is so close to Mormonism, but the Holy Spirit cannot be manipulated the way familiar spirits can.

Here is some important evidence: Annika was a member of many different churches, but none of them felt like home, so she left Christianity and became a witch, then joined a coven. She writes a blog called *"Born Again Witch."* She took a few of her friends to Bethel because she wanted to get healed. She did not get healed, but she did get prophesied over by four people. What is shocking is what the prophecies said. One prophecy said that she needed to start writing to tell her story, to help others on a similar journey!

> Yes, I feel Jesus saying that you have been a part of many communities. So many! Different churches and ministries. But none of them really felt like home, did they? . . . I see a community that you are in now and it is different. . . . This one is your home. All of the other ones were temporary . . . This community is where Jesus wants you, . . .

Jesus wants her in a coven of witches? Each person who prophesied over her did not know what the other had said. Another one said:

> . . . No, there is no doubt, I do see you playing sacred music, now and in the future. Music that pleases God. But your audience isn't Christian. . . . But the music is sacred. . . . The images I get are very strong, but I can't see how they make sense. . . .

Annika said, *"She was so confused! To me, however, her words made perfect sense."* Another person prophesied:

> God is really proud of you, I just want you to know that. He will bless your community, your writing, and your music. . . . God will give you abundance and you will have time to focus on your ministry. (www.patheos.com/blogs/bornagainwitch/2015 /08/ christian-prophecies-for-a-witch/)

Does that send a chill up your spine? Think about what those people prophesied, which supposedly came from God. But that is not all. Another person said:

> . . . there are many people telling you that you are now going the wrong way. But God knows it isn't true. He wants you to know that He is proud of you. <u>God knows that you are walking with Him and He is so proud of your faithfulness</u>. (www. patheos. com/ blogs/ agora /2015/ 07/born-again-witch-witches-at-a-pentecostal-church-healings-and-prophecies/)

Annika said, "*Then she looked into my eyes, repeated how important it was for me to know that <u>God approved of how I lived</u>, and implored me to <u>keep doing what I was doing</u>.*" Would God have encouraged her to continue to be part of a coven of witches? NEVER! Some people will want to defend Bethel by saying that they just got it wrong. All four of the people merely missed it? Did you notice that one of them said that she was getting "*very strong*" images? No, they did not miss it, the god they worship was speaking, but <u>it was not Jesus or any other part of the Trinity</u>. It was the god of the golden calf speaking.

The Holy Spirit would have said something like, "*Daughter, what you are seeking is not found in religion, but in me.*" You do not have to actually cast spells on people or worship Satan, to operate in witchcraft. Whatever disagrees with the Word of God, the Spirit of God, or the character of God it is falsehood.

Bill Johnson tells about the time when he apparently became demon possessed, but of course he does not see it that way:

> After one such trip in 1995, I began to cry out to God day and night for about eight months. My prayer was, "God, I want more of You at any cost! I will pay any price!" Then, one night in October, God came in answer to my prayer, but not in a way I had expected.
>
> I went from being in a dead sleep to being wide awake in a moment. Unexplainable power began to pulsate through my body. <u>An extremely powerful being seemed to have entered the room</u>, and I could not function in His presence. My arms and legs shot out in silent explosions as this power was released through my hands and feet. The more I tried to stop it, the worse it got. I heard no voice, nor did I have any visions. This was the most

overwhelming experience of my life. It was raw power. It was God. He had come in response to the prayer I had been praying. (Bill Johnson: *Going Face to Face With God*, 5/5/2015, www.charis mamag.com/spirit/supernatural /23062-going-face-to-face-with-god)

Combining different reports of the same incident, his arms and legs were flailing uncontrollably for about an hour with only his head not moving. He was not seeking after more truth, or more understanding, but more signs and wonders. Randy Clark said, *"Bill has pursued signs and wonders and healing more than any-body I know"* [*]. So here is an almost true yet false prophet, because he is a WOF prosperity preacher, seeking signs and wonders. So it should be no surprise that he gets false spirits. * (*The Truth About Bethel's Bill Johnson*, Jennifer LeClaire, 8/26/16 www.charismanews.com)

Johnson has said that people should *follow signs and wonders*, as if Jesus never said that false Christs and *"false prophets will arise and show <u>great signs and wonders to deceive,</u> if possible, even the elect"* (Matt. 24:24) (MEV). So should we follow signs and wonders? NO, definitely NOT.

Did you notice that one of the two golden calves were set up at "Bethel." Yes, Bethel had a golden calf, now Bethel Church is worshiping the golden calf, and is a major center for deception and demonic spirits.

I am sure that Bill Johnson really believes he is following God, but he does not know that he is an almost true yet false prophet. You may question whether he is really WOF or not, but he invited Benny Hinn to speak at his church in Jan. of 2017, so that should settle it. He also teaches that Jesus was born again, which is a WOF doctrine.

Bethel gets many visitors from around the world each week, with thousands more watching online, all because of the signs and wonders and miracle healings. I was watching myself online one Sunday when a fellow said he asked God why he chose Bethel to pour out such signs and wonders, and the golden calf said, he did not choose the church, but the pastor. So here we see that these signs and wonders are not glorifying God, but a man. I have seen Bill Johnson speaking on Sunday mornings online and he frequently brings glory to himself by talking about the feathers and other things that happen to him personally, as well as in the church, because of him.

In 2016 I bought Bill Johnson's latest book, not knowing all of this about him. I found myself writing "wrong" in the margins several times, and stopped reading before I got halfway through. I decided to do some research on him, and found that he is WOF. So that explains the wrong teaching in his books. Jeremiah said:

> Behold, I am against those who prophesy lying dreams," declares Adonai, "and tell them, and so lead My people astray with their lies and with their reckless boasts. Yet I never sent them or commanded them. Nor do they benefit this people at all." . . . (Jeremiah 23:32) (TLV)

This passage says that the false prophets were not giving any benefit to the people, which must have been the opposite of what they were claiming. This certainly describes the WOF and revival movement today which has many people making all kinds of claims, such as, *"You too can make frequent trips to heaven."* No, that is lie. <u>Even if</u> one person does actually make frequent trips to heaven, it does not mean we all can! And I would doubt that such a person is powered by God, but familiar spirits.

(4) A Genuine Example

Now, having said all of that, it is not a contradiction to now present an example of genuine gold dust appearing. The reason it is genuine, and not counterfeit, is because it did not bring glory to any person or any church, but merely ministered hope to a prisoner in North Korea.

Kenneth Bae was born in 1968 in South Korea, then moved to the U.S. when he was a child. He graduate from high school and college, and in 2006 began leading tours from China into North Korea as a secret missionary. He was caught and required to stand in a very cold prison cell:

> The room remained uncomfortably cold. It was warmer than it

was when I had arrived a couple of days earlier, but it still wasn't over fifty degrees. As I had the first night, I shivered from the cold. But suddenly, my left hand started getting warm. Standing absolutely still, I slowly opened my hand. <u>I saw something sparkling like gold dust</u>. Then, the warmth spread from my hand and up my left arm. I did not know what was happening.

I heard the Lord speak in an unmistakable way. *The Holy Spirit is holding your hand, his Spirit said to my spirit. You are not alone. The Holy Spirit is standing next to you, holding your hand. Do not worry about anything. No one will harm you through this. Do not worry about what you are to say. I will speak through you, because I am with you and I will never leave you. No one will be harmed. Don't worry about anyone. Just tell the truth.* (*Not Forgotten: The True Story of my Imprisonment in North Korea*, Kenneth Bae. Thomas Nelson, 2016, p. 29-30)

Kenneth Bae is not even a Pentecostal / Charismatic Christian, but is a licensed minister with the Presbyterian Church of America (PCA), and ordained as a Southern Baptist pastor. So this is a genuine occurrence of gold dust. And just because it genuinely appeared once, it does not mean that every appearance is genuine.

There may be a few occasions when gold dust genuinely appears in the United States, but I would seriously question any gold dust appearing regularly on people at churches that teach the prosperity gospel, or that are part of the Toronto Blessing revival movement. But the above example shows that it can genuinely appear.

Chapter 6:
Look at the Fruit

(1) Bad Fruit

When I was questioning God about this revival, asking whether it was true or false, God said, "*Look at the fruit.*" Jesus said a good tree does not bear bad fruit, so let us examine the fruit. Some of the fruit can be seen by reading firsthand reports coming in for many years now.

Some of these testimonies are very long, which is why I had to shorten them. Here is part of Kati's testimony of *Escaping the Fire*:

> I wasn't able to attend church one Sunday and our daughter came home three hours past when she was supposed to arrive with mascara running down her face from her tears. She was telling me how "wonderful" church was because there was preaching all about stepping into the river . . . and of course, they did an alter call and craziness broke out. There was one lady close to my mom's age who would always laugh hysterically. One day during church she simply placed her hand on my daughter's leg causing my daughter to loose complete control of herself laughing in a way we had never heard before. It was then that she began to fail her college classes and backslid majorly. . . . I started digging and researching and my eyes began to open wide as the truth became revealed to me. (https://thenarrowingpath.com/2016/09/19/personal-testimony-escaping-the-fire/ & https://kimolsen.net/category/dominionism/)

Here is Corissa's story of deceiving signs and wonders:

> I've seen this gold dust. It always happened during "praise and

worship." I remember the first time I was being encouraged to pray for it. I was <u>told to pray for it</u> and receive it, and I opened my eyes to see my hands sparkling as if gold glitter was on them. There was no one walking around sprinkling this stuff on people. It was real! That is why so many are attributing it to God just because it really does happen. The problem is that it is 100% a sign and wonder, but it is not one of God. I experienced this in my quiet time at home, and anywhere I prayed. In fact, I first witnessed this when a girl at my school invited me to youth group. She was holding out her hand, and you could see it just shimmering. I asked her what it was and she said, "You get this when you have Jesus." Mind you, I was not saved at the time, but the Lord was already drawing me, and apparently Satan was hot on my heels, too. . . .

I used to follow the likes of Todd Bentley, Benny Hinn, Joyce Myers, Joel Osteen, Paul and Jan Crouch, Kenneth Copeland, Creflo Dollar, Marlyn Hickey, Jesse Duplantis, TD Jakes, Crystal Cathedral, Paula White, and so on. How did God get me to see the cold-hard truth? First, He showed me that Joel Osteen was twisting Scripture. That was a hard pill to swallow, but even though, it was bitter tasting in my mouth, I digested it with humility. I then began to question teachers for the first time in all the years that I was saved. Pride was being chiseled away and I was actually becoming teachable!

I found a Christian forum, which God used to show me the truth about the signs and wonders movement also known as the hyper-charismatic movement. I fought it tooth and nail; debated with the Moderators of the forum and was really defensive in the apostasy sub-forum. During this time, my church was holding services which were being influenced by Todd Bentley's Lakeland Revival. I knew something wasn't right, but couldn't put my finger on it. I believe the forum debates had planted seeds in my stubborn heart and I was finally given just enough discernment to detect something very off.

I remember one day, my husband was watching GodTV and Todd Bentley was running his marathon. If I remember correctly, that was all that was on for 24 hours a day. I may be wrong. Anyway, I felt a really familiar and <u>unsettling presence filling the room</u>. I immediately went to the computer room. What was that, and why did I feel the need to leave the room in a hurry? If it was of God, then the presence would not have been so oppressive.

I decided that I would actually research about Todd Bentley. . . . I watched the videos exposing the movement and became convinced that this man was either a con-artist, or he was an escapee from the mental institution. . . .

One video led to another, and finally, a video exposing the Kundalini practice in Todd Bentley's "revival." . . . I sat there for hours with my mouth gaping, wondering what to make of it because the very things that were being exposed were, coincidentally, were what I experienced, accepted, and participated in.

I'll admit, I didn't want to believe it at first. I prayed to God. I kicked and screamed and cried, "<u>do I have to give up my precious experiences</u>?" I pleaded with God. I didn't want to let go, but the truth was cracking the foundation upon which this lie stood on. It took weeks for this all to sink in. I read the Bible more, I sought out teachings, and inside felt like a part of me was dying with each blow of truth. It was like someone picked up a rock and threw it at the mirror which shattered the reflection that I had been staring at. It was all just an illusion. . . .

I got saved in a church built on lies and I was spiritually starved. I had to go back to the milk of the Word. God used this time of despair to show me the truth. I was ripe to receive it and was ready to surrender my experiences for the truth. God opened door after door once I gave up those experiences. They were like carved images that I worshiped. They were my chronicles of truth built on sand! (https://kimolsen.net/page/30/?)

One of the bad things about this "revival" is that people are now beginning to believe that all "experiences" are from false spirits, but they do not know the truth of old-fashioned Pentecostalism, and even the Charismatic Movement before the false revival began. God does move and touch people, he does slay them in the Spirit, even give them dreams and visions, which are all Biblical. Just because Satan has a counterfeit anointing, does not mean we should reject God's genuine anointing. But what is happening, as seen in this book, is a counterfeit. The book of Acts refers to the presence of God:

Therefore repent and be converted, that your sins may be wiped away, that <u>times of refreshing may come from the presence of the Lord</u>. (Acts 3:10-20) (MEV)

Notice that it refers not only to the *"presence of the Lord,"* but to how his presence can bring "refreshing" to you. This is the genuine presence of God in many church services and music today, which is wrongly classified as from Satan merely because the counterfeit is felt in the "river" churches. Notice also that the first step is to "repent." This does not reflect what happens in the "Holy Ghost party" churches, where people go, not to repent and be refreshed, but to party in the river of God; or so they believe.

A fellow was talked into going to Bethel, to his regret (all capitalization was in the original):

> He began to tell me about how the presence of God permeated and saturated the campus at Bethel. He RAVED about the school. He RAVED about the music in the worship services. He RAVED about the teachings of Bill Johnson and Kris Vallatton. He raved about everything from the prayer tower to the coffee shop. After about an hour and a half of what could've EASILY qualified to have been a top notch infomercial, Dan made me an offer that two weeks later I found out."I couldn't refuse." Dan told me that he was so confident that my walk with Christ would intensify by leaps and bounds by going to Bethel, that if I agreed to go, NOT ONLY would he pay my transportation there, he would also PAY THE $9000.00 Tuition required to attend the School of Supernatural Ministry.

> . . . I succumbed. I said okay Dan, I'll go check it out. . . . The next day I was off to Redding. Set up with a nice motel, I found my way to Bethel the next day, and this would be the beginning of the road to my NIGHTMARE. Please note though, it didn't start out that way.

> When I attended Bethel for the first time it was LOVE AT FIRST SIGHT!! And that "love" would continue for the next two months. I immediately called Dan to tell him how right he was about everything. I even went on to tell him that he UNDERSTATED his description. I SWORE that I had died and gone to heaven. People seemed to really love Jesus. The view from the top of the mountain was ABSOLUTELY BREATHTAKING!!! There was something going on ALL OF THE TIME, LITERALLY 24/7. Being one that's GREEDY FOR GOD, it was the perfect milieu for me and my insatiable appetite for HIM. There were ubiquitous house

groups within the community and I loved attending them. It reminded me of the New Testament church in Acts.

I went to EVERY possible function that I could, and there were "ZILLIONS". During a house meeting I was offered a place to stay, for FREE. And that was just in the nick of time as I began running out of money. A few days later, I began living with students from Bethel's school. Still floating on a cloud, I just seemed to see God's hand moving at every turn I made. . . .

So to make a long story short, I absorbed everything Bethel offered. I dove in seven days a week. . . .

Also, I found it strange that I couldn't even communicate with people even about simple matters like the weather or a basketball game without them jerking, shaking or convulsing, these convulsions were so profuse within the cult that for me it QUICKLY became overkill.

Another idiosyncrasy was the constant belting out of the phrase, "WHOA" OR "WOE." [*They say "WHOA" when the false anointing hits them strongly.*] This is heard constantly. . . .

Later, I started noticing a LOT of name dropping from the pulpit (mostly from Bill Johnson) of false prophets and wolves like Bob Jones, Patricia King, Todd Bentley, Heidi Baker, and a plethora of others. This was constant, and when these names were mentioned, cheers went up with the fervor and magnitude of a Super Bowl touchdown reaction. . . . I might add that NEVER ONCE did I hear salvation, repentance, holiness, righteousness, judgment, or wrath preached, neither from the pulpit nor when I'd travel the streets with them. The whole business plan (because it's NOT a ministry) is to focus on LYING signs and wonders, impotent magic tricks. I've always wondered why Bill would rave about all of these so-called and UNDOCUMENTED "miracles" happening through Bethel around the world, YET, when it comes to home, we never get to see any of em' manifested. For instance, Bill and his wife both wear prescription glasses, where's the healing?? Bill had a hernia surgically removed, WHAT??? No miracle?? Bill's son Eric is deaf and has a speech impediment . . . but no "supernatural" intervention has taken place, yet all of this GREAT stuff is happening EVERYWHERE ELSE EXCEPT HOME ON BETHEL'S TURF!!! Gimme a break!

The real thing that got me though was the death of little J.C. the infant of two dear Korean friends of mine. He died from cancer at two years old. Prayers went out for him every second of the day. People jerked, shook, laughed, convulsed, spoke in (FAKE/ DEMONIC) tongues over him, the works, and when he died, we were left with feeble excuses like "God needed him more" kind of CRAP!!! Around this time I had already stopped going to the church. When I first got there, for the first two months, because God gifted me with charisma, celebrity looks (and I don't say that arrogantly) and the ability to draw people, I instantly became EXTREMLEY popular. By the time I left Redding, I was considered a pariah in some circles and cliques within. Even though I lived with Bethel students, I began to expose Bethel, Bill Johnson, Kris Vallaton, Danny Silk, and ALL of the celebrity WOLVES within their evil and deceptive cabal. People that used to "love" me (so they said), snubbed me on the streets. . . .

When I stopped going to the church and began staying home and listening to REAL MINISTERS OF GOD like Michael Boldea and Mike Hoggard, Paul Washer and David Eells, I got flack from my roommates saying that those guys were mad and didn't know God. They asked me not to play their sermons. But I'd ignore their comments and continued to feed on what was REAL GOSPEL. I would often challenge my roomies and other Bethel "robots" on Bill and Kris' theology and their twisted new age "sermons" WITH SCRIPTURE and it ceased to surprise me anymore that they'd rebuttal my challenges with quotes from one of Bill or Kris' books. IMAGINE THAT!!! They ALWAYS tried to refute GOD'S WORD with quotes from books written by their false teachers. Can you say MIND CONTROL?

So after 2 months, I stopped going. I continued to live with the students because it was a "phat crib" OR, a nice house for those who are linguistically challenged in "SLANG", LOL :) I was paying rent by this time in a new home and different students. The landlord approached me one day while shooting ball in the yard and told me that if I didn't start attending Bethel and doing what they call "SOZO" classes (which is simply /new age mysticism/ chanting/ contemplative prayer or "soaking" kinda stuff) that I would have to find somewhere else to live. It was my 4th month in Redding and that was my "Q" to leave. . . .

There was a class held every Sunday called "Fire Starters" birthed out of the Toronto Blessing movement. This class was supposed to, get this, "TEACH" PEOPLE HOW TO PROPHESY, LOL!!! Yes, I laughed too!! So anyway, every class people were randomly called to the front of the room, they were lined up, and asked to pick someone in the room and give them a word of knowledge... BUT THERE WERE RULES... WHAT EVER YOU SAID HAD TO BE SWEET, KIND, AND MAKE THE PERSON "FEEL" GOOD. Those are the rules verbatim!!!

After weeks of seeing this nonsense and people stating the obvious and touting it as hearing from God, out of frustration, one Saturday night, I decided to MAKE UP, FABRICATE a "word of knowledge" just in case I would be picked out to prophesy in tomorrow's class. And whaddaya know, I get picked. When my turn came, I shared my FABRICATED "word." It was this, "there's someone here who's been strategizing suicide, and the devil is tormenting you. If you'll raise your hand, we can pray for you and you can be released." Much to my surprise, a hand went up, WOW, I'm like okay God, you used my prank to REAL-LY get someone's attention. "Praise You".

But I was about to get an even BIGGER surprise, because, I immediately thought the room would shut down and people would bombard this poor girl who planned to take her life, so they could pray and labor over her soul, but NO!!! That's NOT what happened. Instead, I got reprimanded by Kevin Dedmond, one of the "leaders" (you can see his crap on youtube w/Sid Roth), and I was told that I'm to only say things that make people feel good. And they resumed right back into letting people perform their exercises of divination, cause that's what it REALLY is.

More upsetting is that when class dismissed, out of a room of about 150ppl, I only saw 2 people (excluding myself), a couple go minister to that girl, everyone else??? Well, they were too anxious to go through the FRUITLESS "fire tunnel" so that they could appease their flesh, and so they did, THEY LAUGHED, THEY JERKED, THEY SHOOK, THEY CONVULSED, THEY WRITHED ON THE FLOOR, and to this very day, they call it GOD. . . .

God Bless You, Shofar (http://jesuscultureawakening.blogspot. com.au/2012/06/god-delivers-another-from-cult-of-jesus.html#.WPEnH2krJEZ & https://closingstages.net/)

Think of what happened; how could anyone who is saturated with the genuine presence of God every day even contemplate suicide? The mere fact that a person was thinking of suicide in that environment, is a red flag. This means it was a counterfeit feeling of God. (Even if the person suffered from mental illness, given the conditions that are <u>supposed to exist</u> at the church, it would seem unlikely that such a person would desire to commit suicide.)

Another lady got involved all the way into the Bethel church, and spent lots of time "soaking:"

> Then something happened that completely opened my eyes. At a church gathering . . . We started talking about all the amazing anointings and manifestations that were happening overseas, like the gold dust, glitter and jewels and how we wanted these things to start happening in our church. We longed to go and attend these conferences and receive "more".
>
> Then it happened. She started telling me about this amazing "anointed" man of god, who received the glory of god. His name was Joshua Mills. At his conferences were all the same manifestations, she started telling me that the glory of god was so strong on this man that he had oil that drips from his body as a show of his anointing. She was amazed by this. But I suddenly started to realize that something wasn't right. In fact there was something very wrong with this.
>
> I felt very uncomfortable with this. I had been raised in the Catholic church, before I became a born again believer. When I became a believer God opened my eyes very clearly to the satanic influence in that church. The Catholic church is full of visitations from "mary", oil dripping from their own "anointed" people, the stigmatas etc. So when my friend started telling me about Joshua Mills and his oil dripping from this body as a sign of the glory of god, alarm bells starting ringing inside my heart!
>
> As soon as I got home I started looking up Joshua Mills to find out more about this. Joshua Mills is part of the Elijah List, a list of special "prophets". On this list included Bill Johnson, Kim Clements, Rob De Luca, Randy Clark, Cindy Jacobs, Rick Joyner, Todd Bentley, Patricia King, Rodney Howard-Brown, Carol and John Arnott and so on. Joshua Mills was a man who ran conferences and teaching classes (<u>which you pay huge amounts of money to attend</u>). He ran these classes so the students could receive from him and take home his special anointing. And sure enough, just as my church friend had said, Joshua Mills was producing oil from his skin, that was a <u>sign of the glory of god</u>

upon him. And if it wasn't bad enough – he was collecting his drips of oil on rags and selling it, so that people could buy and get his special anointing from the rag.

All of a sudden, like a lightning bolt, I realized what I had got myself involved [in].

She had tried to get her husband involved, but he would not get involved:

He told me that he had been praying to God intensely for Him to reveal to either one of which of us was wrong. God answers prayer and He came through for us! (http://jesus culture awakening. blogspot. com/2011/03 /my-testimony-of-deliverance-from-signs.html#. WPEzS2krJEY) (of https:// inerrant word. word press.com/)

Here is a testimony from a fellow who was born into the Prophetic Movement that is part of the Toronto revival "river":

I was born and raised in the "Prophetic Movement" (which is now in the process of morphing into the "New Apostolic Reformation"), and I grew up completely oblivious to what Biblical Christianity is meant to look like. Some of the leaders who had an influence on how I perceived what the church is to look like, have included John and Carol Arnott of the "Toronto Blessing" . . . Kim Clement, Benny Hinn, Chris Harvey, Todd Bentley, Bob Jones, Randy Clark, Patricia King, Georgian Banov, Bobby Conners, Mike Bickle, Lou Engle, and Bill Johnson.

In the fall of 2002 I ended up moving to Redding, California to get "plugged-in" to Bethel Church, which Bill Johnson (a self-proclaimed "apostle") oversees. It was here where I ended up jumping into and entertaining the supernatural phenomenon, signs and wonders, and mystical experiences (which were falsely attributed to God) in a much greater way then I did when I was a kid growing up. I soon got involved in the youth group, which was heavily influenced by Lou Engle who heads up "The Call" and Mike Bickle who heads up "IHOP" (International House Of Prayer). I later enrolled in Bethel's School of Supernatural Ministry in 2006, and went through the whole three-year program. I was heavily engaged and supportive of many of the things, which were being taught and practiced. When Todd Bentley and his, "Lakeland Revival" began to take place, I jumped on board with that as well, and became a full supporter and advocate for it. I was gladfully defending it against all the, "Religious Pharisees" (or so I called them at the time). It was also at this time that I noticed the, "Toking the Ghost" movement and became a "Toker" myself, and a full supporter of John Crowder and Ben Dunn.

However, when Todd Bentley's affair was made public (August '08), I ended up becoming grieved by what happened and by the poor response that was to follow. Shortly after the crash of the "Lakeland Revival" I received some severe rebukes for being involved with John Crowder's and Ben Dunn's "Toking Mania", and so I withdrew myself from this aspect of the chaos. It was also at this time, while I was in my third year internship with Bethel, that I was starting to notice that things didn't line up and I began to question the legitimacy of the Prophetic Movement.

First off, before I share my testimony of how God saved me and brought me out of this movement, I want to explain why I believe that <u>Bethel is a cult, and not just on the charismatic fringe</u>. Labeling someone or a group a "cult" is not a thing to take lightly and so I hope to explain why I believe this to be true with the Word of God. The following statements are examples of the beliefs and practices of Bethel, . . . I hope to bring some awareness to the dangers that this movement possesses, and bring encouragement to those of you who are praying for friends and loved ones who are entangled in this deception.

Bethel has a really high view of man, and is extremely man centered. My understanding after being involved with Bethel for almost seven years, and after going through three years of their school of ministry is that they teach that man is basically free to choose good or evil, and that man isn't all that bad. . . .

Among one of the more common and heavily embraced practices would be that of getting "drunk in the Spirit". This is where you lay hands on each other, pray for each other, or ask the Lord to get you "hammered", in which people (including myself) would have experienced spiritual bliss, joy, and ecstasies. People would react differently to these experiences, some would fall down and not be able to stand, others would stumble around as if heavily intoxicated with alcohol, some would shake violently, and others would experience the blissful side of this but not necessarily exert any physical manifestations. . . .

Another common practice is for people to hear the Lord "speak to them prophetically". In this movement and at Bethel in particular it is taught that the Lord is always and continually speaking to you (apart from the Scriptures), and all you have to do is "tune" in to the right station (like an FM/AM radio) to be able to hear from the Lord. . . .

It is believed and taught at Bethel that the Lord is revealing new truths apart from what has already been revealed to us in the Scriptures. Bill Johnson has said, "The Lord wants to give revelation at a measure that has never, I don't think has ever happened in the world before. The spirit of revelation is being released upon the church . . ." . . .

While I was involved in the Prophetic Movement it was my experience that many people (yet not all) didn't bother to read their Bibles on a regular basis, which was also the case for me. From what I observed I believe this was the case because it is believed that we need fresh words from the Lord, and the Written Word of God is not enough, and it is believed that you <u>can't walk in the fullness of your relationship with the Lord using the Scriptures alone</u>. . . .

The worst and most horrifying thing in all of this is that there is <u>no gospel being preached</u> at all! It is all about the signs and wonders and the stories of supernatural encounters and experiences. This creates a spiritual frenzy, that promises health, wealth, supernatural encounters and experiences, for anyone who "presses in". . . .

At Bethel there is no preaching on the Justice and Righteousness of God, and how God can't let the guilty go unpunished. There is no preaching of the sinfulness of man, and how everyone has violated God's standard. There is no preaching on the eternal conscious torments of Hell. There is no preaching of Christ and Him crucified. There is no preaching of Christ's substitutionary death on the cross paying the full penalty of the sins of those He died to forgive, that is penal substitution. <u>There is no preaching of repentance and faith in Jesus' name as the only basis for which one is justified and declared righteous in the sight of God. Bethel preaches a gospel that is deficient, useless, and powerless to save</u>. . . .

While I was involved in the Prophetic Movement I was entertaining and practicing all these things and I <u>had many supernatural experiences and encounters (which I falsely attributed to God)</u>, which at the time I perceived to be absolute evidence and proof that I was truly saved. In reality I was not saved at all; the fruit in my life was testifying to the contrary that I was actually saved. I was living a continual and habitual lifestyle of sin, without remorse, regret or genuine repentance. I was heavily involved with pornography, and watching it several times a week, if not at times daily. As well I had an ongoing struggle with rage and anger, which at times got violent. . . .

The following March (2009) while I was still questioning the validness of the Prophetic Movement someone posted a video sermon of Mark Driscoll (whether or not you agree with everything that Mark says and does, there are good fruits coming from his ministry, regardless of the errors) . . . While I was listening to the sermon I realized that I had never heard preaching like this before, where it was straight bible, verse by verse, truth bluntly told. I was then hooked, and began to listen to several of Mark's sermons a day (later on I found out about other ministers like John Piper, John MacArthur, and Paul Washer). It was around this time or soon there after that God saved me, that the Lord drew me to repentance and saving faith in Jesus' name.

Never before this have I ever been told that I was really, really sinful. Never before did I hear of Original Sin, or the radical depravity of man and how everyone has violated God's Holy and Righteous standard, and is thus fully deserving of God's righteous and just wrath being poured out upon them. . . . I was involved in the "church" for nearly twenty-two years, and I never heard the gospel fully preached! . . .

The fact that I never heard the gospel before, even though I was heavily involved in a movement that professes to be Christian, was completely shocking and devastating to me. (www.face book.com/notes/bethel-church-and-christianity/saved-from-the-deception-of-charismania/160778463948581)

In the church I grew up in, the gospel was preached on a regular basis, in the Sunday school lessons and in the preaching. Derek Prince said, *"One ministry of the Holy Spirit is convicting us of sin. Where conviction is lacking, the work of the Holy Spirit is most likely lacking, as well"* (*Protection*, 2008, p. 57). These churches claim to have a great move of the Holy Spirit, but there is little to no preaching on sin and salvation. That should tell you something about the nature of the spirit that is moving. Here is the personal story of deception by Hope Wingo:

My story involves the New Apostolic Reformation and GOD TV. . . .

In light of my story, you need to know that I did not have a computer until the end of 2011. As far as Christian programming, I was at the mercy of cable TV with TBN, Daystar, and a few other channels. Whenever I discerned a red flag in one of the programs, I'd just switch the channel to another pastor with another sermon. That was all just part of watching Christian TV. I didn't know the term Word of Faith, much less the New Apostolic Reformation. I only knew that I loved the Lord and craved all of Him that I could get. What I did not realize was that I was the perfect candidate to fall into deception. I matched Tozer's qualifications perfectly, in that I fervently craved more of God and would not settle for lukewarm Christianity! I wanted everything that I could get!

In 2008 I was introduced to GOD TV (a New Apostolic Reformation channel) and I quickly became addicted to it. . . . Quite frankly, I couldn't get enough of it. Their worship music seduced the viewers into a deep spiritual experience with captivating repetitions. The pastors spoke of deep, prophetic things that they had heard from God. It wasn't long before I had completely abandoned the other channels for GOD TV. I was totally blind to its influence.

The red flags were there from the start. I noticed that spiritual experiences seemed to dominate most of the sermons while repentance and the importance of a personal relationship with Jesus were not being mentioned at all. There were stories of angelic encounters, oil dripping from the speaker's feet, feathers and gold dust falling on the worshipers, rain falling inside of the buildings, and supernatural gems being found all over the church. Due to my strong Christian upbringing, I knew that those things were not coming from God, but I was so intrigued with it all that I kept watching it. It was exciting compared to the money -grabbers and fake healers that were on the other Christian channels. . . .

Let me pause here to say that, by allowing this programming to continue, I gave satanic deception an open door. When I initially noticed the red flags, I should have rejected this false doctrine.

However, I chose to ignore the warnings . . .

Another night after work, I turned on the TV to find a woman introducing a special training program that was available through her ministry. . . . Having surrounded myself with deception for months, I thought, "Surely this must be from God". I ordered the series. A few days later it arrived in the mail and I began to listen to the CDs. When I got to the middle of the series and realized what it was all about, I was literally shocked. It was demonic. It was angel worship. It was astral projection in the name of praying for others. Yep, we could go to them! We could also hover over other countries as we prayed for them. We could leave our bodies and enter into the "third heaven". It was purely satanic.

Instead of throwing the garbage away, I decided to listen to the CDs again. Then I listened to them again; then over and over. I had become intrigued by them. A few weeks later, having gone through the lesson several times, I tried to do what they suggested, by inviting an angel to appear in the room, even though I knew that the Bible warned against it. I listened to the music that they had provided as I tried to experience "going to heaven" with them. I also imagined my spirit going into another person's house to pray for them.

Shortly thereafter, I began to experience many vivid dreams and daytime flash-visions. I saw angels. I heard voices. Even though I knew better, I tried to convince myself that these were Godly manifestations that I had somehow missed in my earlier Christian walk.

On the physical side, flocks of vultures began to hover over my house. If I stood outside, they would circle over me and cast their shadow on me, one by one. One day, when returning from town, while I was still about 1/2 of a mile away from my house, I saw a flock of about 100 of these birds hovering directly over my house. Another time, I heard a crash outside of my back window as an entire flock [had] crashed a tree limb in my back yard. I later learned that birds often represent demonic spirits.

One day, as I was about to enter my front door, I felt a swat on my back side as if a parent had just swatted a child. This frightened me terribly as I realized that I had just entered a realm that I didn't want to be in. Demonic spirits had actually been allowed to touch me. At that point, I knew that it was only going to get worse, so that very day, I threw away all of the materials that I had received from that ministry. I also cleaned house and threw away most of my contemporary Christian music CDs. . . .

I desperately called on the Jesus that I had known as a child. Even so, it took months, and I mean months, to get back into a right relationship with the Lord. It still frightens me when I think about how I allowed this deception into my life. After all, I had been grounded in biblical truth since childhood.

Let me backtrack a little to add that when I threw the CD lessons in the trash, it <u>sparked an attack of satanic rage that lasted for the next several months</u>. I started seeing demonic faces in clouds, in trees, in bushes, in reflections, and in almost every-thing else, all day long, day after day. These were harassing spirits. They were relentless and tormenting, and they robbed my mind of all peace. I learned to keep music on all the time to block out the mental noise, especially when I attempted to fall asleep. I was worn down to my wit's end, both mentally and physically.

The torment eventually began to subside through the process of fully submitting myself to Jesus again. I could do nothing else but to throw myself into the verse, "Submit yourselves therefore to God. Resist the devil, and he will flee from you." (James 4:7) In my efforts to make that happen, I made a conscious decision to resist the devil by literally ignoring the harassment. . . . I prayed constantly. Then, finally, one day it occurred to me that I hadn't seen them for a while. It had taken months, but they were gone. Completely gone! . . . (https:// kimolsen. net/ category/ testimonies/)

Notice that she threw away her music CDs. As mentioned previously, God can work through false prophets, and not every-thing they teach is even wrong; therefore, I believe we can accept the music, as long as it is God-honoring. I have heard a lot of their music and it genuinely worships Jesus and is anointed. If it starts to include lyrics that refer to false doctrines, or gold dust, then I would reject it. However, some of the music I have heard coming from Bethel is what I would call, "dark." The lyrics seem ok but the singers actually sound emotionally depressed.

Here is an anonymous testimony from the UK:

The music was getting louder and people were exhibiting bizarre manifestations. Suddenly I was pinned to the floor. I couldn't get up and I was <u>being transported through the clouds at breakneck speed</u>. I knew this was <u>astral projection</u>, as I used to do in my occult days. So I cried out to the Lord to save me and I came back from the astral projection and I could get off the floor. I told some others about this and they said it was great that the Lord was taking me through the Universe and I should just go with it.

As the years went on we were told from the front of the church that these things were normal. People were thrown off chairs. <u>We were told to take our heads off and not think any longer</u> but to "drink in the Spirit" and to "jump into the river". So we did. Chaos had come into our church. Our real introduction to "it" came when we got drunk -- not on alcohol but on the manifestations which we experienced. . . .

I saw the guest speaker sitting on a metal stool, blind drunk -- a "drunkenness in the spirit". His face was puffed out, really large. He was waving his arms at a man outside on the street shouting at him with unintelligible words. When he pointed his hand at people in the room, they did somersaults backwards and ended up on the floor unable to move, drunk with this "spirit". Others <u>slithered across the floor</u>. I thought to myself "The answer is to not look at this man", because as soon as his eyes met yours you were gone. It wasn't just pointing - it was eye contact. So I decided not to look at him.

Others were convulsing all around me. Some were shooting each other with bows and arrows. There were no chairs so I had to sit on the floor. <u>People were rolling fast across the floor</u>. I ended on my back when our future Pastor rolled over my neck with his body. I cried out to the Lord as I thought I was going to break my neck. I didn't, but it hurt. One lady was <u>beating her chest like King Kong</u>. At the time I thought, "what is she doing?". She was beautifully dressed and behaving like an animal. I could see some women were very shy of all of this because they had dresses on and ended up indecent.

It was then that I made a mistake. I accidentally looked at him and he looked at me. He then said "Let her have it Lord!". Within seconds, I was a gibbering wreck, unable to walk or talk. My body felt like it was swelling up. I started to laugh uncontrollably and everyone was rolling over me -- arms, faces, legs. I knew enough to be cross inside that it had happened to me, but I could do nothing about it. Eventually, I crawled to the door to try to get out. Outside it was dark and I saw the headlights of a car coming towards me. I thought "I'm going to be killed and there is nothing I can do". I was rescued by my future pastors, who took me home. They were thrilled that I could get under the "anointing" so quickly. It lasted for days.

Then, on Sunday my husband got 'zapped' by this man. At this stage, it was popular for them to zap the soles of your feet with the microphone. People went under quicker through the feet. That night, my husband drove us home with his head on his steering wheel totally drunk. From now on, it was easy to get into this experience. If anyone pointed their finger or laid hands on us, we were gone.

It was at this time that we installed the Christian Channel Europe in our home. There was programme after programme where you could get zapped if you were already under this power. From then on we were completely initiated into the "Toronto blessing". It was August 1994. (www.spiritwatch.org/ fireriversurvivor.htm)

This is not Pentecostalism, it is not Charismatic, it is not even Christian. It has nothing to do with the gifts of the Holy Spirit, it is demonic! The above lady also suffered enormously from spiritual abuse from her pastors, who threatened people by saying anyone who left the church would die within weeks, and actually put a curse on her and her husband when they did leave. Witchcraft and idolatry are all about control, or manipulation. They were also instructed not to "think" about whether the manifestations were of God or not, but to just accept them. This goes against what the Bible says:

Examine all things. Firmly hold onto what is good. (1 Thes. 5:L21) (MEV)

Paul Gowdy was a pastor at another Vineyard church in Toronto and took part in the revival at the *Toronto Vineyard*, which became *Toronto Airport Christian Fellowship*, and is now *Catch the Fire Toronto*. Here is part of his testimony, which he wrote in an article titled, *"The Toronto Deception:"*

It has taken me nine years to actually come to the place where I would write this story. Part of the reason was because I was not fully convinced that it is appropriate to speak out against weaknesses in the body of Christ publicly. Another reason is because it has taken years of soul searching to become convinced that what happened in the Toronto Airport Church was actually all bad or at least more bad than good!

For the past number of years I have called it a <u>mixed</u> blessing. I think James A Beverly called it this in his book *Holy Laughter and the Toronto Blessing* 1994. Today I would call it a mixed curse concluding that any individual good that came from this experience is far outweighed by much harm and satanic deception. I suppose that therein has been my dilemma. I have tried to live my life in the fear of the Lord and Jesus told us that the unforgivable sin was the blasphemy of the Holy Spirit. Attributing to Satan what was in fact a work of God. If pressed as to whether or not the Toronto blessing is all God or all Devil I will still be hedgy, but I am <u>convinced that Satan has used this experience to blind people</u> to the historical doctrines of God, to produce fruit in keeping with repentance, to <u>failing to test and discern the spirits and failing to test prophecy</u>.

After three years of being in the thick of the Toronto blessing our Vineyard assembly in Scarborough (East Toronto) [we] just <u>about self-destructed</u>. We <u>devoured one another, with gossip, backstabbing, division, sects criticism etc</u>. After three years of 'soaking,' praying for people, shaking, rolling, laughing, roaring, ministering at TACF on their prayer team, leading worship at TACF, preaching at TACF, basically living at TACF we were <u>the most carnal, immature and deceived Christians that I know</u>. I remember saying to my friend and senior pastor at Scarborough Vineyard Church in 1997 that ever since the Toronto Blessing came <u>we have just about fallen to bits</u>! He agreed!

My experience has been that the manifestation of spiritual gifts mentioned in 1st Corinthians 12 was much more common in our assembly, before January 1994 (when the Toronto blessing started.) than during this period of supposed Holy Spirit visitation.

During 1992-1993 when praying for people we would experience what I believe was genuine prophecy, deliverance and much grace and favour from the Lord. After the Toronto Blessing started, all ministry time changed, the only prayers were 'More Lord MORE', the shouting of 'Fire' the jerky shaking of the body with the 'ooh ooh OOH WOOOAAH' prayer. (I kid you not!)

On January 20th 1994 about 15 people from our church traveled over to Toronto Airport Vineyard in order to listen to Randy Clark, a Vineyard pastor from the USA. John Arnott had called our senior pastor to invite us. He communicated that Randy had been to the Rodney Howard Browne meetings and that the stuff had broke out in his church in the following weeks. John was hoping that something might break out with us too. We were only too happy to travel over. We were a church plant out of the Toronto Airport and we started in 1992. In those days there were three Vineyard Churches in Toronto. One Down Town church, Scarborough vineyard church to the east and the Airport Church. We were one big happy family. Because we were small in number we did special meetings, conferences etc, together.

The year before most of our leadership teams joined and had headed to Nicaragua for a short term missions trip. We had genuine love and fellowship with each other. Since leaving the Vineyard churches I have read a fair bit of analysis from the critics. Some make out that the Toronto Blessing was one huge conspiracy to lead the body of Christ into heresy. Heresy and apostasy I suspect may well be the result, but none of these destinations were intentional.

I am honestly convinced that the leaders in the Vineyard churches are genuine born-again Christians who love the Lord, but have fallen into deception. They have not loved the Lord enough to keep His commandments. They have failed to obey the scriptures and have been led astray by our longing for something bigger and brighter and more exciting and dynamic. I am guilty of this sin also. I have preached renewal in Korea, the United Kingdom, the USA and here in Canada. I am genuinely repentant and in writing this story I would ask you the bride and body of Christ to forgive me.

. . . In hind sight I look back and think how could I have been so blind? I laughed at people acting like dogs and pretending to urinate on the columns of the TACF building. I watched people pretend to be animals, bark, roar, cluck, pretend to fly as if they had wings, perpetually act drunk and sing silly songs. How I thought that any of this was from the Holy Spirit of God amazes me today. It was loud irreverent and blasphemous to the Holy God of the Bible. . . .

John [Arnott] would defend the chaos by saying that we ought not be afraid of being deceived, if we have asked the Holy Spirit to come and fill us then how could Satan come and deceive us? This would make Satan very strong and God very weak! He said that we needed to have more faith in a Big God to protect us than in a Big Devil to deceive us. This sounded very convincing but was totally contrary to scripture for Jesus and Paul and Peter and John all warn us about the power of deceiving spirits and especially so in the last days. Again we did not love God enough to obey His Word and the result was that we opened ourselves up to lying spirits. May God have mercy upon us!

Finally the penny dropped for me as I was rolling around one night 'drunk in the Spirit' as we would say. I started singing and as I rolled around the floor the Nursery Rhyme 'Mary had a little lamb its fleece was white as snow.' came to mind. I sang this in a mocking spirit and instantly my heart told me this was a demon. Instantly I repented and was in total shock. How could a demon get into me? Did I not love God? Was I not zealous for the things of God? Was I not nuts about Jesus? I knew that an unclean spirit had just manifested through me and I was guilty of great sin. After this experience I stayed away from TACF. I did not go back there any more. I did not possess the conviction to denounce the whole experience but thought that we were failing to pastor the Blessing well enough.

Even after I stopped going over to TACF, I had to pastor the fruit of it. One example was when some of our people returned from a meeting there asking us if we had all received the golden sword of the Lord? I asked them what they were talking about thinking that it was some prophetic reference to the Holy Scriptures but they said, 'no, it's not the Bible, it's an invisible golden sword that only the really pure can receive. If taken in an unrighteous fashion then the Lord would kill you. But if you are holy enough to receive it then you can wield this sword and it will heal Aids, cancer etc. and bring salvation. How one wielded this sword was by pretending to have this invisible sword in your hand and motioning to strike people with it when in prayer! I thought while even in deception at this time that the TACF had become Looney bins! This was purportedly first received by Carol Arnott and then given to the ones holy enough to receive it!

Another thing was the golden fillings in the teeth. We had people in our assembly peeping down one another's throats looking for the gold fillings that God had placed there to show how much he loved them! <u>In all my time there I only heard one message on repentance</u> given by a visiting speaker from Hong Kong named Jackie Pullinger. <u>It went over like a lead balloon. We were not there to repent, we were there to party in the Lord!</u> After one year into the blessing I spoke out at a pastors meeting and said "guys we have shaken, rattled, rolled, laughed cried and bought the tee-shirt. But we have no revival, no salvation, no fruit and no increased evangelism so what's the deal?" I was soundly rebuked - who was I to expect to see fruit when the Lord was healing his broken people? We had been legalistic long enough and God was spending this time restoring his wounded and freeing us from legalism I was told not to push the Lord and the harvest would come in his time.'

I knew this was wrong because the Lord had commanded us to go into all the earth and make disciples! Not, that everyone should take a sabbatical for who knows how long, while God does some strange new thing! . . .

So there is my story. I could go on and document much excess, folly, sin and latter day reign teaching that manifest from the prophetic end of this Blessing but others have already done that. We sang about Joel's army and the billion soul revival as if it were one of the Ten Commandments, and as always it was just around the corner. Next month, next year etc. Jesus said that when the son of man returns will he find faith upon the earth? And if he does not return when he does no flesh would be saved but for the sake of the elect he comes. This is a far cry from the domionism that is being taught all through the vineyard / prophetic/ spiritual warfare movement. I honestly think that they think they are going to take over the whole world! While in the Vineyard I embraced a life verse from the Apostle Paul the phrase do not go beyond what is written! . . .

To those in the river I would say swim out, there are things living in the water that will bite you real good! . . . I would call on all who read this to pray that the Lord would open the eyes of all who have been involved in this deception. Whether leader or follower, we are loved and the Lord is a forgiving God. He says if we confess our sins he is faithful and just to forgive us our sins and purify us from all unrighteousness. I believe we are like the church in Laodicea, we think that we are rich, have prospered and need nothing, we do not realise that we are wretched, pitiable, poor, blind and naked. We must take the Counsel of Jesus and buy gold refined in the fire (which is his suffering, not a false spirit!) white garments to clothe our shameful nakedness and salve for our eyes that we might see again. Jesus is calling us to repentance and thank the Lord that he is, for it will lead us to true restoration with our Father! If God has forgiven me and opened my eyes then he can do it for all those caught in deception too. I will finish with a warning from Paul, he says if you think you are standing firm be careful lest you fall. (www.apostasy alert.org /vineyard pastor.htm)

The evidence just keeps piling up. Notice that he was in the thick of it and says there is not much fruit. Sure, some people get healed of emotional wounds, but we know that God works through almost true yet false prophets, so this is an almost true yet false revival.

We cannot just accept anything that looks like it might be, perhaps, from God, but must do as the Bible says and test the spirits by the Word of God. Churches in the "river" do not have to totally reject any move of God, but they need to repent of allowing demons to operate and ask God to free them from those spirits, but still desire God to move among them.

Why are so many people falling into this deception? It is because they are much too willing to embrace whatever looks like God, and they are very hesitant to question it.

An article appears on Charisma Magazine's website that provides more insight and evidence. One of the pastors at one of these churches reports what happened when he preached on hell and the judgment of God:

Today we have meetings that are focused intently on the glory, God's presence and the river. Healings, signs and wonders are primary. They can no longer be primary if we want to avoid allowing darkness and deception to thrive in such an environment.
. . .

God instructed me to preach with great unction and urgency on the cross, hell, holiness and the blood of Jesus. This ended the Holy Ghost parties and opened the door to Holy Ghost conviction.

This led to many rushing to the altars to allow God to break them, heal them and set them free.

Sadly, and disturbingly, there were previous Holy Ghost, glory meeting dancers <u>who soundly rejected that message</u>. One supported lesbianism and was convinced that God would never send homosexuals to hell. Another <u>was involved in sexual New Age practices</u> and rejected the theology of eternal separation from God entirely. Others told me they didn't affirm a definition of God that included judgment or anything negative. One of the most passionate young people in the church said that she <u>doesn't know the God associated with that message</u>! (*A Holy Ghost Party Can Be Dangerous Without This Key Element*, John Burton, 7/14/2016 www.charismamag.com)

If <u>preaching on hell and judgment ended the Holy Ghost parties</u>, then it was not the Holy Ghost, but a counterfeit. Without preaching on the cross, sin, and hell there is no conviction of sin. If there are no changed lives, then it is not the Holy Spirit at work.

(2) Kundalini Spirit

In Andrew Strom's book, *Kundalini Warning*, he reports that a lady sent him an email about her experience with the Prophetic Movement that is part of this false revival. She attended many conferences by Jill Austin and Patricia King, and was even a prayer person in some, then she bought a teaching by Todd Bentley:

I was in my living room laying on the floor listening to the teaching on how to visualize the third heaven and what to say and was getting caught up into his teaching and all of a sudden I began to shake uncontrollably and jerk and groan, and no sooner had this taken place I <u>became frozen stiff</u> – I could not move any part of my body and I knew this was a demon trying to take hold of me – and so with all the effort I could muster I cried out, "God save me, Jesus help me," and as soon as I cried out to the Lord my body went limp. God spared me that night and I will be forever grateful.

I spent much of the night in tears asking God to forgive me, and renouncing all the hands laid on me and all the awful deception I had opened myself up to . . . (*Kundalini Warning*, page 49-50)

Another person who experienced this revival wrote:

> I inadvertently got prayed over by some people who had received "The Toronto Blessing." I ended up that night with **uncontrollable flopping** and shaking of my limbs, being drunk in spirit and uncontrollable laughter. At the time it felt right. But later as time went on, these manifestations came at inopportune times and were uncontrollable. My arms and legs would shake when trying to pray for people or when just sitting in church. My legs would give out and I would have to catch my balance just to stand upright while worshipping. It soon became clear to me that this was not the Holy Spirit and so I repented of allowing myself to receive this spirit and asked God to take it away from me. Praise Him, He did! (Ibid, page 22)

In a previous chapter we read how Bill Johnson had a major episode of arms and legs flopping around, which he thinks was from God. The above example shows that it was not of God. A lady named Sherie wrote to Andrew Strom to report what she experienced:

> I was desperate for God to move in my life and change situations and heal hurts and was very open to ministry, I had many in this movement touch my forehead and experienced the manifestations you describe – drunkenness, laughing and crying, shaking. I got dreams and visions and just before I left the structure (church) I had a vivid dream of a huge python that came through the back door and attached itself to my car, and also to rooms in my home. I was very disturbed and sought the Lord for an answer. It took 6 months before I was delivered . . . (Ibid p. 24)

She felt a snake in her spine, and when she finally got deliverance, a "kundalini" spirit was identified and cast out of her. If allowed to continue, there will be an increase in the Kundalini spirits like those found in Hinduism. Here is a story of a man who had a full Kundalini Awakening:

> One of the most dramatic instances of classic kundalini awakening was experienced by Gopi Krishna (1903-1984), of India, who meditated for three hours every morning over seventeen years. On Christmas Day, 1937, he had his explosive awakening with kundalini pouring up his spine. By his personal account, he rocked out of his body and was enveloped in a halo of light. His

consciousness expanded in every direction, and a <u>vision of luster</u> unfolded before him; he was like a small cork bobbing on a vast ocean of consciousness. This extraordinary experience occurred once again, and then Krishna was plunged into twelve years of misery, during which he "experienced the indescribable ecstasies of the mystics . . . and the agonies of the mentally afflicted." Following twelve years his body apparently adapted to the new energy and stabilized, but he was permanently changed. Everything in his <u>vision was bathed in a silvery light</u>. He heard an inner cadence, called the "unstruck melody" in kundalini literature. Eventually he could <u>experience bliss just by turning his attention inward</u>. He became, as he said, "a pool of consciousness always aglow with light." His creativity soared allowing him to write poetry and nonfiction books. . . . A.G.H. (www. themystica .com/ mystica/ articles/ k/kundalini.html)

Derek Prince said, "*There exists a counterfeit holy spirit—one example is the "holy spirit" propounded by adherents of the New Age movement*" (*Protection*, 2008, page 38). Pray for the Christians caught up in this deception.

(3) An Example From History

You may be surprised to learn that the same sort of manifestations that are taking place today have taken place MANY times throughout history. I will present just two examples. The first one is from *Origins of Pentecostalism and the Charismatic Movement*, by Paul Fahy. This example is about the Jansenists / Convulsionaires of France (1726-1790):

This group was a French ecstatic sect which claimed miracles, and was originally formed in opposition to the Catholic revival known as Ultramontanism. It was rejected by Roman Catholicism and hated by the French court. Upon the death of one of their deacons, Francois de Paris, in 1727 the miracles intensified through prayer meetings at his grave.

Invalids from all over France began to be brought seeking cures while women went into ecstaises [trances].

Four years later followers who touched his tomb, in the cemetery of St. Medard, received his experiences and were apparently healed of blindness, paralysis and cancers and many started to have convulsions (tetanic spasms) and violent contortions. It is said that they fell like epileptics, groaned, shrieked, whistled, spoke in tongues and prophesied.

These convulsionaires spread so that whole streets were full of convulsing men and women and while in this state they appeared to be invulnerable to their many tortures with metal rods, chains, timbers, hammers, knives, swords and hatchets (administered to shake them out of the state). It is recorded that some Convulsionnaires had received from six to eight thousand blows daily without danger. At one point there were large numbers of people involved as volunteer medics in helping over 800 convulsionaires in Paris. Some were even able to levitate while witnesses tried to hold them to the ground while other women were clairvoyant (similar to the word of knowledge). Others would become rigid and during this state they could be hit with sledgehammers or be used to hammer nails into wood A famous example is that of a woman bent backwards over the sharp point of a peg. A fifty pound stone was dropped from a great height on to her over and over again. Just the falling stone would have usually crushed a person, but she left without a mark on her! These events were seen by thousands of witnesses.

. . . In the end the movement indulged in the grossest immorality in their secret meetings and moderate Jansenists condemned the Convulsionaires. The French Revolution finally 'shook the structure of this pernicious mysticism'.

All this degenerated at length into decided insanity. A certain Convulsionnaire, at Vernon, who had formerly led rather a loose course of life, employed herself in confessing the other sex; in other places women of this sect were seen imposing exercises of penance on priests, during which these were compelled to kneel before them. Others played with children's rattles, or drew about small carts, and gave to these childish acts symbolical significations. One Convulsionnaire even made believe to shave her chin, and gave religious instruction at the same time, in order to imitate Paris, the worker of miracles, who, during this operation, and whilst at table, was in the habit of preaching. Some had a board placed across their bodies, upon which a whole row of men stood; and as, in this unnatural state of mind, a kind of pleasure is derived from excruciating pain, some too were seen who caused their bosoms to be pinched with tongs, while others, with gowns closed at the feet, stood upon their heads, and remained in that position longer than would have been possible had they been in health. Pinault, the advocate, who belonged to this sect, <u>barked like a dog some hours every day</u>, and even this found imitation among the believers. (JFC. Hecker, *The Black Death and The Dancing Mania*, from Chapter 4.)

A thorn in the side of the hierarchy, they were formally condemned by the Pope in 1864 and the King of France, Louis XV, had the tomb of the leader walled up to prevent people reaching it. (*Understanding Ministries*, 1998, pages 17-18)

Of course I disagree with Fahy's thesis that all of these historical groups were "origins" of modern Pentecostalism and Charismatics. For them to be an origin, there must be a direct link. They are not even origins of the modern "river" manifestations, even though they are similar, except that the same demons are involved.

(4) Another Example From History

An eyewitness account of the Kentucky Revival was written in 1807 by a man who was there at the start of the revival; it was published in 1808. The revival began with great repentance, and God moved in great ways, but it got infected with false spirits which were accepted as from God. It was the early years of the Second Great Awakening:

The general gift of exhortation was to search out the state of the sinner, convict him of sin, and warn him to fly from it; and they often came so pointed, even to naming out the person and publicly arraigning him for specific crimes, that often evil spirits, whose work it is to cover iniquity, and conceal it, were stirred up to great fury; and those possessed with them, would come forth in a great rage, threatening and blaspheming against the author of the revival, and bold as Goliath, challenge his armies to an encounter. Could nature, without bloodshed and slaughter, overcome beings so fierce? Or must it not be something supernatural?

To see a bold Kentuckian (undaunted by the horrors of war) turn pale and tremble at the reproof of a weak woman, a little boy, or a mean African; to see him sink down in deep remorse, roll and toss, and <u>gnash his teeth, till black in the face</u>; entreat the prayers of those he came to devour, and through their fervent intercessions and kind instructions, obtain deliverance, and return in the possession of the meek and gentle spirit which he set out to

> oppose: who would say the change was not supernatural and miraculous? Such exorcisms, or casting out of evil spirits, are justly ranked among the wonders which attended the New-Light. (*The Kentucky Revival*, McNemar, p. 35)

They cast out the demons from a man who rolled on the ground and gnashed his teeth. It appears that they had all the gifts of the Spirit in operation except unknown tongues and prophecy. People were even slain in the Spirit at home, while walking down the road, or plowing a field. There are reports of as many as three thousand people being slain in the Spirit at the same time. And sinners were also struck down when they came to mock:

> These public testimonies against the work, particularly by ministers, were a means of stirring up and encouraging those who were openly wicked, to come forth and mock, oppose, and persecute; but even such, were often unable to withstand the power, and sometimes in the very act of persecuting and afflicting, were struck down like men in battle; and so alarming was the sight, that others on foot or on horseback, would try to make their escape and flee away like those who are closely pursued by an enemy in time of war, and be overtaken by the invisible power, under which they would be struck down and constrained to cry out in anguish, and confess their wickedness in persecuting the work of God, and warn others not to oppose it. Thus, many who were openly profane, were taken in the very act of persecuting the work, and like Saul of Tarsus, made the happy subjects and zealous promoters of it; while bigoted professors [of Christianity], who had hissed them on, remained like the heath in the desert, that seeth not when good comes. (Ibid, p. 28)

There was a group that broke off from the main body of the Kentucky revival in what was called a "*grand schism*." Richard McNemar says that in this other group, additional gifts such as prophecy, dreams, visions, and trances took place. But he said bizarre manifestations also took place in that group. I did not notice in the book, but I believe the schism was probably caused by the many strange manifestations that began taking place. One group accepted them as from God while the other group did not:

> But there were moreover in the schismatic worship, a species of

exercises of an involuntary kind, which seemed to have been substituted by the Great Spirit, in the room of the falling, etc., which had been among the New-Lights. The principle of these, were the <u>rolling exercises</u>, <u>the jerks, and the barks</u>.

1. The rolling exercises which consisted of being cast down in a violent manner, doubled with the head and feet together, and rolled over and over like a wheel, or stretched in a prostate manner, turned swiftly over and over like a log. This was considered very debasing and mortifying, especially if the person was taken in this manner through the mud, and sullied therewith from head to foot.

2. Still more demeaning and mortifying were the jerks. . . . The exercise commonly began in the head which would fly backward and forward, and from side to side, with a quick jolt, which the person would naturally labor to suppress, but in vain; and the more anyone labored to stay himself and be sober, the more he staggered, and the more rapidly his twitches increased. He must necessarily go as he was stimulated, whether with a violent dash on the ground and bounce from place to place like a football, or <u>hop around with head, limbs and truck, twitching and jolting in every direction</u>, as if they must inevitably fly asunder. And how such could escape without injury, was no small wonder to spectators.

By this strange operation the human frame was commonly so transformed and disfigured, as to lose every trace of its natural appearance. Sometimes the head would be twitched right and left to a half round, with such velocity, that not a feature could be discovered, but the face appear as much behind as before. And in the quick progressive jerk, it would seem as if the person was transmuted into some other species of creature. . . .

3. The last possible grade of <u>mortification</u> seemed to be couched in the barks, which frequently accompanied the jerks, nor were they the most mean and contemptible characters, who were the common victims of this disgracing operation, but persons who considered themselves in the foremost rank, possessed of the highest improvements of human nature; and yet in spite of all the efforts of nature, both men and women would be forced to impersonate that animal, whose name, appropriated to a human creature, is counted the most vulgar stigma [dog]. Forced I say, for no argument but force, could induce any one of polite breeding, in a public company, to take the position of a

canine beast, <u>move about on all fours, growl, snap the teeth, and bark</u> in so personating a manner, as to set the eyes and ears of the spectator at variance. It was commonly acknowledged by the subjects of these exercises, that they were laid upon them as a chastisement for disobedience, or a stimulus to incite them to some duty or exercise to which they felt opposed.

Hence it was very perceivable that the quickest method to find release from the jerks and barks, was to engage in the voluntary dance; and such as refused, being inwardly moved thereto as their duty and privilege had to bear these afflicting operations from month to month, and from year to year, until they, wholly lost their original design, and were converted into a badge of honor, in the same manner as the first outward mark of human guilt. Although these strange convulsions served to overawe [strike them with awe] the heaven-daring spirits of the wicked, and stimulate the halting Schismatic to the performance of many duties disagreeable to the carnal mind, yet in all this, their design was not fully comprehended . . . at least these kind of exercises served to show that the foundation was not yet laid for unremitting joy, and that such as attached themselves to this people, must unite with them as a body destined to suffer with Christ, before they could reign with him. (Ibid, p. 61-63)

It must have been because of this group that the term *"holy roller"* originated. According to the Merriam-Webster dictionary online, the first known use of the term *"holy roller"* in print was in 1841. So it did not originate with early Pentecostals, though it was attributed to them.

This was more than just roaring or barking, this was bodily control like nothing I have ever heard of before. Some people had their head jerked around so fast that the facial features were a blur, yet no injury occurred. They did not understand why the barking and rolling occurred. The rolling was at first seen as a humbling experience from God, or a chastisement, especially when someone was forced to roll in the mud. It happened to people from all walks of life. But a few years later their view changed and it was seen as a badge of honor.

Yet, after what we have learned about the modern revivals with similar manifestations, it is evident that God was allowing those spirits into the revival. If they had rejected the manifestations *en masse*, and repented of allowing the spirits, then the people would have no longer been controlled by those spirits.

These strange manifestations went on so long that many people grew up and lived most of their lives in churches that were having those manifestations. And it only stopped when some people tested the spirits and worked hard for many years to convince them that it was not of God. Derek Prince said:

> Anything ugly – in a spiritual sense – does not proceed from the Holy Spirit. Twelve key words associated with this type of ugliness should identify anything they describe as being unholy: degraded, degrading, flippant, indecent, insensitive, rude, self-assertive, self-exalting, sham, silly, stupid, vulgar. These words never apply to the Holy Spirit. (*Protection From Deception*, 2008, p. 39)

Rolling on the floor, barking, clucking like a chicken, and much more, certainly fit *degrading*, *silly*, etc.

(5) Negative Manifestations

I have seen on video what I believe are *negative manifestations*. By that I mean that God is causing some of them as a sign or a warning to us that what is happening is of Satan. Let me explain.

I saw a video clip on YouTube of a WOF camp meeting of 1997 that showed Kenneth Hagin sticking out his tongue and flicking it like a snake. Therefore, I believe that when he flicked his tongue like a snake, it was an <u>involuntary manifestation</u>. God was trying to tell us that something was wrong. When Hagin touched people who were sitting down, some of them slithered to the floor like a snake. I copied the video and put that clip into the video I made for this book.

God caused it to happen to warn those of us who are discerning that the teachings of this group are of the Serpent. God is saying, *question what is happening, question the doctrines*. I believe the Holy Spirit can be so strong on you that you cannot stand or even sit, but how they slithered down, and how Hagin flicked his tongue, tells me they were negative manifestations.

Is it possible that God gave *"great liberty to Satan"* to cause strange manifestations because God does not like the doctrines that are being taught in those churches, and therefore the barking and other things become, in effect, negative manifestations. God is trying to tell us, question the doctrines, because they could lead you astray, like the prosperity gospel.

What about the fact that all churches have some doctrine that is false, otherwise they would all be in agreement? These strange manifestations are not happening in all churches today that teach false doctrine, true, but the prosperity gospel and other equally dangerous doctrines are being taught in false revival churches; another chapter discusses the WOF doctrines.

(6) Brownsville?

As strange as it may seem, some Pentecostals and Charismatics were against the Pensacola Outpouring at the Brownsville Assembly of God, in Pensacola, FL, in the 1990s because a few people had manifestations, such as mild head-shaking. The Holy Spirit can and does cause head shaking, body shaking, quivering, etc. But only when the Holy Spirit is upon someone.

I personally visited Pensacola and saw none of those manifestations which must have been a one in 10,000 event, or they must have ended by then, because I was there for several weeks. So those were rare and nothing compared to Toronto.

Having attended a Pentecostal church while growing up that regularly had a move of the Spirit, I was able to recognize a very strong presence of conviction of sin inside the Brownsville Assembly of God church. The conviction was present regardless of who was preaching; and even when there was no preaching sinners would run to the altar and repent. Only the Spirit of God can or would do that. The church also preached against the prosperity gospel, which is very much contrary to the other revivals of the last twenty-five years.

Another great part of the Brownsville Revival was the worship music. The worship part of the service literally lasted four hours, before the preaching ever started, yet it seemed like thirty minutes, and many people agree.

Chapter 7:
The False Lakeland Revival

(1) A False Prophet and a False Revival

Todd Bentley, who got his "anointing" at Toronto, sparked a revival in Lakeland, FL in April of 2008. He did not grow up attending church and the first books he read after getting saved were books from the false Word of Faith preachers. Even though a few people got saved and healed, the revival in Lakeland was a false revival because Bentley holds to many false doctrines, such as the idolatrous wealth-gospel. He is also connected with gold dust, gold teeth, and the Prophetic Movement. He even practiced astral projection of the New Age movement, which the Prophetic Movement is calling third heaven visitations. I do not believe that anyone has made any third heaven trips out of their bodies except by the power of evil spirits. Only God can cause this to happen, we cannot.

Bentley claims he saw a vision of the angel of finance and visited heaven's treasure room where he began filling his pockets with gold coins. He was stuffing the coins in everywhere he could put them, even in his pants and shirt. He asked the angel what he (the preacher) was doing and the angel said he was taking the offering, at which time he tried even harder to stuff even more coins onto himself:

> "After I heard that answer, I made a conscious decision (in this experience) to get even more gold. Now I was collecting more, stuffing as much as possible anywhere I could fit it, even my ears!" (www.freshfire.ca).

Because he had not even been saved very long, he did not realize how deceived that vision was. He did not know how far away from sound Biblical truth it was. The Bible is clear that greed is idolatry. Therefore, he was leading people into idolatry and he must be classified as a false prophet, at least at the time of the revival. It seems the worship service was very anointed, but not the speaker. But those healings may actually be from Satan; remember, the Egyptian magicians also performed the same miracles that Moses did. This means Satan's false ministers can also perform signs and wonders.

The Lakeland Revival was the "next big thing" until it crashed and burned after only about 4 months. Todd Bentley was just another spawn of Toronto. It had the usual barking and other satanic manifestations, false claims of miracles, etc.

The short-lived Lakeland revival generated strong opinions in those who were for it or against it. It was broadcast live over God TV and endorsed by all the big leaders in the Charismatic Movement. Then it crashed because Todd was abusing alcohol and cheating on his wife. Andrew Strom opposed the revival from the beginning and wrote this about Todd Bentley:

> But why am I opposed to this "Healing Revival" so soon after it has been announced? It is because I already know Todd Bentley's ministry all too well, and this whole thing centers around him. . . . I myself have heard the tapes of Todd Bentley's "Third Heaven Visualization" teachings, and I want to tell you, they are straight out of the New Age handbook. Terrible stuff. And yet so widely accepted by thousands of Christians today. . . .
>
> [Bentley] is a leading proponent of strange "Angel" encounters (and I do mean "strange"). Todd has openly promoted these encounters for years, in fact he is well-known for leading others into contact with these "angels" too. This has been a big part of his ministry for a very long time. And it is really no different now. (*Kundalini Warning: Are False Spirits Invading the Church?*, page 64-65)

We have already learned how God is allowing false spirits to be a part of the meetings of those connected to the Toronto Blessing. But you can see that it is much more than that, because these ministers are knowingly leading people into New Age practices. Rather than *Third Heaven Visitation,* the New Age movement calls it Astral Projection, where your spirit is supposed to be able to leave your body and travel to wherever you want to go. There is nothing Biblical or Christian about it, it is satanic deception. Here is one person's testimony:

> I went to Lakeland 3 times. I was so drawn to go there. I really thought it was of God. . . . I had so many supernatural experiences – to seeing a mystical Jesus with a third eye, angels talking to me, visions, being transported. I had one experience with my daughter being in the room and her experiencing it too. I was roaring like a lion, had gold dust and many other experiences. The worst thing that happened to me is that it got sexual. This false Jesus was approaching me sexually and I fell into it. I still to this day do not understand how I could have been so deceived. I have been a Christian since the age of 16. I am 49 now. . . . I fell right in . . . hook, line and sinker. When I came home that last visit I became aware it was demonic, and I was surrounded and covered with demons literally, it was so horrible, all that I went through, you cannot imagine. . . . I was seeing demons and being touched sexually and torment[ed] constantly. . . . it has been 1 ½ years and I am still battling these demonic spirits. I cry out to the Lord everyday for total deliverance. It has been horrible. I have renounced and repented, but still fighting. How do we get free of this? (Ibid, page 71)

Other people have also had problems getting free from these demonic spirits. It is *possible* that those who have problems getting free may hold to beliefs such as the prosperity gospel, or Word of Faith doctrines. It is possible that believing those doctrines will hinder getting free. (I suggest reading *Pigs in the Parlor* by Frank Hammond.)

Ed Tarkowski wrote an article on *Finding Freedom From The Spirits Of "Revival."* Another person posted a comment below the article:

> If someone was in church and was praying at the front of the church and they fell out and were levitating off of the floor, what would you think of that? Why would that happen? The person was unaware that this had happened and the elders of the

church reported this took place. (ChrissyGS9288, February 14, 2016) (https://mkayla.wordpress.com/freedom-from-false-spirits-of-revival/)

Clearly, this is not anything that has ever taken place in historic Christianity, but it has taken place in Eastern religions like Hinduism.

(2) Spiritual Effects

Here are a few online posts of some of the spiritual side effects of being prayed for by Bentley at the Lakeland Revival:

He [Todd Bentley] said recently, "This man has just received the anointing for prophecy." The man was <u>on his hands and knees barking like a dog</u>. (http://gordwilliams.com/monthlymessagesc 162.php)

Another post about Lakeland states:

A personal friend of mine, very stable mature woman who goes to our church, married with kids and grandkids, very outgoing . . .went to a Todd Bentley meeting in Orlando back in January. Has hands laid on her by Bentley.

Soon after, she <u>began having panic and anxiety attacks</u>. She sought medical help, but the attacks always came back. She started going to the Lakeland meetings. Her symptoms worsened. She was an emotional wreck. We, her pastors and her husband did not understand what was going on.

While researching Bentley, really wanting to see if the meetings in Lakeland were truly a revival I came across this from Andrew Strom's website: www.revivalschool.com/florida.html:

"A Spirit-filled pastor that I know from the UK who has been following Todd Bentley's ministry closely for some years wrote to me about what he himself has observed since the year 2000: 'When Bentley conducted a healing meeting in a large charismatic church here in England in 2005, he laid hands on many people who were apparently healed. I know of at least one instance where a pastor's wife with cancer was prayed for by Bentley. <u>Soon afterwards she heard voices in her head telling her to 'drown herself</u> just like her father did'. The poor woman <u>ended up in a mental hospital</u>, I believe she still has the cancer.'"

Things started to add up. I myself, after watching the "revival" several times, started "seeing things" in my home. It seemed as if someone was slowly turning just outside my peripheral vision. When I turned to look, nothing [was] there. I told my wife who in turn told me she had been experiencing the same thing. She said she was also seeing things "scurrying" across the walls.

This went on for two weeks. In that time I was also having nightmares and weird dreams with 'angels' and Bentley himself. The woman from our church I was telling you about, she too was seeing things in her home. She was also seeing spider-like creatures scurrying across the wall, but when she would turn to look, they would be gone.

I got a testimony from a minister friend who told me of a woman who engaged in an affair with her 20 something year old personal trainer after coming back from the Lakeland meetings. <u>She broke off her years long marriage to her husband to "run-off" with the young man</u>. According to my minister friend, this woman has been <u>in a state of emotional confusion since the meetings</u>.

Two other ministers I know have been experiencing severe pain in their legs and hips. One man had hip replacement surgery months ago, was recovering really well and without complications. <u>After attending the Lakeland meetings he began experiencing bad pain and having severely demonic nightmares</u> (extremely unusual for this gentleman).

The other fellow, a long time follower and supporter of Bentley has been having difficulty walking (extreme pain) since going to the meetings (I thought this was a 'healing' revival?). . . .

Did you hear his comment Saturday night about the "angel" that stood around his pulpit that would heal you and COME INTO YOU if you were up there? What crazy weirdness is that? This is lunatic! (http://forums.charismamag.com/viewtopic.php?f= 25&t= 2452).

During the revival, other testimonies like the above appeared on numerous websites. It is surprising that anyone would ever defend this guy after reading testimonies like this.

Even watching the videos online can have similar results as those described above. The revival would not have gained the notoriety it did but for God TV that showed the services live and even online. God TV is another WOF network like TBN.

(3) A Leader Speaks Out

There were great claims of healings at Lakeland but they cannot be verified, because few people actually got healed there. Robert Ricciardelli, a member of Peter Wagner's International Coalition of Apostles, who has written for *Charisma Magazine*, denounced the Lakeland meetings online in June / July of 2008:

> "Truth is there are very few people being healed in Lakeland. I have worked with Charisma Magazine editor Lee Grady in discovering how many false reports have been released as facts. These are our brothers and sisters involved in this, but this move of God has been <u>a move of men with God still touching some</u> who come to seek Him." (posted on www.revival school.com)

He also wrote at another website:

> Charisma reporters and a few others like myself have tried to get these [claims of healing] verified and cannot. At one point, I was told that [it] is God's job and not the ones reporting these [to be] invalidated and now some have been found out to be fraudulent claims.

> We actually had offered to help, because any news of a resurrection in my opinion is world news if it can be validated. But then when the totals continued to mount which led to hype and embellishment, they began to ask us to stop asking questions. Hmmmm?

> Friday night, Todd Bentley said that God said there were 1000 people that were to give $1000, and they were to receive a 1000 fold blessing. The one hour drama on this giving subject was so deceptively evident that it was embarrassing to watch. On top of that, those that would give that money were able to come to the platform to be recognized.

> <u>I know that there is mixture</u>, I know that God is still touching despite the deception and manipulation of people, but results do not equal righteousness. Remember Jannes and Jambres producing snakes to come against Moses. . . .

> There is far too much of man's negative influence and character that is far from Him, for me to endorse Lakeland. But I will endorse a God who will touch people, and is touching people in the midst of deception, manipulation and the marketing of His glory. I will continue to pray for all of us who represent Him, and repre-

sent each other to the world. (http://stevehickey. word-press.com/ 2008/06/05/)

Ricciardelli stated in another posting:

> The biggest thing about Lakeland is the lack of the fear of our Awesome God, lack of repentance and humility. Many have exchanged the truth for a lie and chosen experience over content. Angels, trances, and 3rd heaven focus has replaced the gospel as a focus. . .

> It is my opinion that it was man orchestrated and <u>demonically influenced from the very beginning</u>. The worship has been good and Roy Fields is an awesome worship leader, so many in the worship and even watching from afar can sense God in the worship of His people. The truth is God has been engaged in the worship and has touched and healed some. This is why it has been so confusing to some. <u>I have heard that Roy Fields has stated a few times that when the worship ends, God's presence leaves the platform</u>, and then Todd Bentley operates void of His presence. That is why most all of what they have claimed cannot be verified, because it just is not happening.

> We have heard a few people getting well, being touched and so on. There is a church here in North Carolina that brought 27 sick down there for a week. Some with cancer, leukemia, diabetes and such. None got healed and <u>most were worse when they came back</u>. The emperor is not wearing any clothes and the truth must be known. Many are claiming that Bentley is the new thing that God is doing. The fact is he is still operating in the old thing, and operating with less integrity and character than the previous one man shows.

> God is about nameless and faceless people who are operating without any agenda but the Lord's. Preaching about the King and His Kingdom, and moving supernaturally after Him, and as they do, signs and wonders follow. The problem in Charismania is that they seek the sign, they seek the thrill, . . . gold dust, feathers and gems. They may get the chills and frills, but l<u>eave with nothing more than goose bumps and really little spiritual change</u>. When they seek the King, the Kingdom of God and His righteousness, you begin to see transformation take place at the heart level. This is God's way and always has been.

> (www.revivalschool.com)

Did you notice that Todd Bentley was trying to get one million dollars in one offering? Wow. How greedy can you get? The 100 fold return was not big enough, so he invented the 1,000 fold return! The falsehood just keeps getting worse. Since you cannot serve both God and money, who is the one behind this guy's ministry? I think the evidence is clear.

Attempts were made to bring correction to him while the revival was still going on, but he refused to believe the truth and chose to follow false spirits and angels of deception. Then finally his private behavior became known, and public antics became too much, and the revival ended.

We must stay away from any preacher who teaches the wealth gospel and the Toronto revival because he or she will eventually end up in gross deception, like Bentley.

Preachers take warning, you must stop following the blind leaders of hype and false doctrine, and follow what God says in his Word. He will not hold you guiltless simply because you are just teaching what many others are teaching.

Flee from anyone who teaches the prosperity gospel. Flee from anyone who teaches third heaven visitations. Flee from anyone who has gold teeth or gold dust appearing. (After the revival ended, Bentley reportedly went through restoration at the direction of Rick Joyner and Bill Johnson!)

It is more than interesting to note that many of the big names in the Prophetic Movement flew to Lakeland to endorse the revival and prophesy great things over Bentley, just weeks before it crashed. This shows a great lack of being able to hear from God, or use discernment.

Chapter 8:
False WOF Doctrines

WOF teaching says that Christians should not suffer, it shows a lack of faith. Derek Prince said:

> Suffering is a reality of the Christian life. God uses it to shape us. Anyone who expects or promises only good things is a false prophet or a misled individual. (*Protection*, 2008, p. 146)

(1) Apostate Doctrines

The prosperity gospel is so widespread that it seems a minority of Pent/Charis Christians are spiritually mature and wise enough to reject it, the same as most of the false doctrines which are discussed below. It is sad that so many of them believe the false doctrines being taught, and the problem is getting worse, so I cannot cover all of them here, or in great detail. There are other books that discuss the theology of the WOF movement, but I will briefly discuss the most horrible doctrines.

I previously discussed 2 Peter 2 where he predicted the coming of false prophets preaching how to get rich. I want to briefly discuss part of verse 1:

> They will secretly introduce destructive heresies, even denying the sovereign Lord

The Word of Faith movement was founded in the books of E. W. Kenyon which he wrote in the early 20th century. Then later an Assembly of God minister named Kenneth Hagin came across his books, and those of Charles Capps who was also influenced by Kenyon, and began teaching the same doctrines in his books, tapes, on radio, and in his Bible college. Then Kenneth Copeland learned Hagin's teachings. These preachers influenced TBN to become WOF, and so you have the WOF doctrines being broadcast into the homes of Pentecostals and Charismatics for several decades.

So how does that show that they secretly introduced heresies? Hagin did not start his own church in which he taught his WOF doctrines, then send out missionaries and evangelists to gain converts to his heresy, like the Mormons did. No, he taught it from within Pentecostalism and the Charismatics. The result of this being what amounts to the <u>infiltration of WOF doctrines</u> into Pentecostalism and the Charismatic Movement.

And yes, they deny the Lord Jesus, because they claim he was a mere man who became a God. As will be shown in this chapter, the WOF doctrines are so twisted and messed up that they are much closer to Gnostism or Mormonism than historical Christianity.

(2) Jesus Died Spiritually and Went to Hell

WOF says that when Jesus died on the cross, he went to hell because he had to die spiritually, because the death of his body was not enough to pay for our sins, so he was tortured for three days in hell and then was born again in hell and became a God. Here are some heretical quotes from Kenneth Copeland:

> Satan conquered Jesus on the Cross and took His spirit to the dark regions of hell. (*K. Copeland Bible*, Reference Edition, 1991, Page 129)

> <u>It wasn't a physical death on the cross that paid the price for sin</u>... anybody can do that. (*What Satan Saw on the Day of Pentecost,* audiotape #BCC-19, side 1.)

> He [Jesus] allowed the devil to drag Him into the depths of hell.... He allowed Himself to come under Satan's control... every demon in hell came down on Him to annihilate Him.... They tortured Him beyond anything anybody had ever conceived. <u>For three days He suffered</u> everything there is to suffer. (Ken Copeland. *The Price of It All*, page 3.)

> Jesus had to go through that same spiritual death in order to pay

the price. Now it wasn't the physical death on the cross that paid the price for sin, because if it had of been any prophet of God that had died for the last couple of thousand years before that could have paid that price. It wasn't physical death anybody could do that. (*What Satan Saw on the Day of Pentecost*, audio tape)

"Any O.T. prophet could have atoned for our sins if they knew what Jesus knew." (Substitution and Identification)

Nowhere in the Bible does it say that the death of Jesus' spirit paid for our sins. Here is what the Bible does say:

And according to the law almost everything must be cleansed with blood; without the shedding of blood there is no forgiveness. (Hebrews 9:22) (MEV)

For you know that you were not redeemed from your vain way of life inherited from your fathers with perishable things, like silver or gold, but with the precious blood of Christ, as of a lamb without blemish and without spot. (1 Peter 1:18-19) (MEV)

It also says, "*Be shepherds of the church of God, which he bought with his own blood*" (Acts 20:28a). This is very clear, that it was the shed blood of Christ that paid for our sins. Ken Copeland claims that it was not his death on the cross that paid for our sins. Therefore, he does not teach the historic Christian faith. It is another gospel, which makes Ken Copeland and ALL WOF preachers heretics. WOF is in the same category as Mormons and Jehovah's Witness. Here is another Bible passage:

. . . by setting aside in his flesh the law with its commands and regulations. His purpose was to create in himself one new humanity out of the two, thus making peace, 16 and in one body to reconcile both of them to God through the cross, by which he put to death their hostility. (Ephesian 2:15-16) (NIV)

Notice that Copeland said Jesus was in hell and was tortured by Satan for three days. But what does the Bible say? On the cross, Jesus spoke to the thief and said:

"Truly, I tell you, today you will be with Me in Paradise." . . . And Jesus cried out with a loud voice, "Father, into Your hands I commit My spirit." Having said this, He gave up the spirit. (Luke 23:43, 46) (MEV)

Apparently, Satan did NOT drag Jesus into hell, as Copeland claims. About Luke 23:43, they twist the verse to say that *"truly I tell you today, you will be in Paradise."* This is a bold-faced altering of what the Greek literally says. They remove the words, *"with me."* There is no evidence that can justify such a change to the Word of God. Not only did Jesus go to Paradise, he also went to Abraham's Bosom and released the captives there:

> For Christ also has once suffered for sins, the just for the unjust, so that He might bring us to God, being <u>put to death in the flesh</u>, but made alive by the Spirit, 19 by whom He also <u>went and preached to the spirits in prison</u>, 20 who in times past were disobedient . . . (1 Peter 3:18-20) (MEV)

So there you have it, we know without a doubt where Jesus went, and it was not to hell! But his spirit did NOT need to be born again, because he was and is God. In spirit Jesus was GOD, and so he did not die a spiritual death or become born again in hell. <u>GOD CANNOT DIE</u>! Jesus did NOT become God in hell, he was already God!

> In the beginning was the Word, and the Word was with God, and the Word was God. 2 He was in the beginning with God. 3 All things were made through him, and without him was not any thing made that was made. (John 1:1-3) (ESV)

But the Wolves of Falsehood (WOF) are not disturbed by verses that clearly contradict their twisted doctrines. Jesus was not a mere man, he was the sinless Son of God, therefore, the death of his body on the cross paid for our sins. Here is what Joel Osteen had to say:

> I can imagine when Jesus bowed His head and died on that cross, that Satan and all those demons, they gathered in hell for a great victory celebration. . . . You can see them giving high five's and jumping around, shouting with great excitement, We did it! . . . Can't you see Jesus looking right into Satan's eyes and saying, "Satan, I hate to spoil your victory party, but I think you're celebrating a little bit too soon" . . . Satan says, Listen, Jesus, you're on my turf now. . . . Jesus says, "Look, Satan, I'm down here to take care of business." . . . Jesus went into the very depths of hell. Right into the enemy's own territory. And He

did battle with Satan face to face. . . . <u>He went over and ripped</u> <u>the keys of death and hell out of Satan's hands</u>. And He grabbed Satan by the nap of his neck and He began to slowly drag him down through the corridors of Hell. (E, Sermon CS-002, 4/23/00, posted on his Web site, 5/2004)

What a joke! First, Satan never had the keys to death and hell. Satan does not have total power of death. If he did, then he would have killed all the Jews long ago. But Hebrews 2:14 says, *"by his death he might destroy him who holds the power of death—that is, the devil."* Barnes Notes says:

> I understand this as meaning that the devil was the cause of death in this world. He was the means of its introduction, and of its long and melancholy reign. This does not "affirm" anything of his power of inflicting death in particular instances - whatever may be true on that point - but that "death" was a part of his do-minion; that he introduced it; that he seduced man from God, and led on the train of woes which result in death.

Jesus took possession of the keys to death and hell, which means he personally conquered them both. He did not need to go to hell to conquer hell. And Satan is not in hell, nor does he rule over hell. It is not his kingdom. Some angels are bound there in chains (2 Peter 2:4; Jude 6), but Satan is not there. This is just one of many examples that prove these false teachers do not know the Bible.

They also quote Acts 2:27 that says, *"For you will not abandon my soul to Hades, or let your Holy One see corruption"* (ESV). Barnes Notes says:

> . . . The meaning probably is, "Thou wilt not leave me in Sheol, neither," etc. The word "leave" here means, "Thou wilt not resign me to, or wilt not give me over to it, to be held under its power."

> . . . The Greek word "Hades" means literally "a place devoid of light; a dark, obscure abode"; and in Greek writers [sic] was ap-plied to the dark and obscure regions where disembodied spirits were supposed to dwell. It occurs only eleven times in the New Testament. In this place it is the translation of the Hebrew Sheol. . . .

> While, therefore, the word does not mean properly a grave or a

sepulchre, it does mean often "the state of the dead," without designating whether in happiness or woe, . . . the meaning is simply, thou wilt not leave me among the dead. This conveys all the idea. It does not mean literally the grave or the sepulcher; that relates only to the body. This expression refers to the deceased Messiah. Thou wilt not leave him among the dead; thou wilt raise him up. It is from this passage, perhaps, aided by two others (Rom_10:7, and 1Pe_3:19), that the doctrine originated that Christ "descended," as it is expressed in the Creed, "into hell"; and many have invented strange opinions about his going among lost spirits. The doctrine of the Roman Catholic Church has been that he went to purgatory, to deliver the spirits confined there. But if the interpretation now given be correct, then it will follow:

(1) That nothing is affirmed here about the destination of the human soul of Christ after his death. That he went to the region of the dead is implied, but nothing further.

(2) . . . All suppositions of any toils or pains after his death are fables, and without the slightest warrant in the New Testament.

So Acts 2:27 means "*you will not leave my soul in the place of the dead, or my body in the grave.*" In other words, body and soul will be brought together again in life, by resurrection. There is no evidence that Jesus went to the place we understand as hell. He went to the place of the dead to release the captives (Ephesians 4:8) who were the Old Testament saints, nothing more.

All they have to do is believe what the Bible says, and also consult a good Bible commentary like *Barnes Notes*, which is free online and with the free eSword computer Bible study program.

Joyce Myer's teaching is also messed up and confused:

"Do you know something? The minute that blood sacrifice was accepted, Jesus was the first human being that was ever born again. . . . Now it happened when he was in hell." (video)

So, if he was in hell being tortured by Satan and his demons for three days, as they all claim, then it took God three days to accept Jesus' blood sacrifice! LOL lunacy. But this contradicts the WOF teaching that it was his suffering in hell that paid for our sins. How can God accept Jesus' blood sacrifice if his death on the cross did not pay for our sins? Which is it Myers? Fred Price says:

> Do you think that the punishment for our sin was to die on a cross? If that were the case, the two thieves could have paid your price. No, the punishment was to go into hell itself and to serve time in hell separated from God. (Frederick K. C. Price, "If Christ Did Not Rise, What Then?" *Ever Increasing Faith Messenger* (June 1980, p. 7)

Guess what Fred, Jesus was not the only one in hell. If his death on the cross did not pay for our sins, his torture in hell would not either, because the thief also went to hell! So couldn't the thief have suffered in hell for us?

(3) Jesus Became United With Satan

They also quote 2 Corinthians 5:21, "*For our sake he made him to be sin who knew no sin, so that in him we might become the righteousness of God.*" So they claim that Jesus became literal sin, and became united with Satan:

> Jesus had to "accept the sin nature of Satan." (*What Happened from the Cross to the Throne*, side 2.)

Here is what a good commentary on 2 Cor. says:

> The Heb. word for "sin" (hatta't) and consequently the LXX hamartia "sin", Paul's word here, are occasionally used for "sin offering" (e.g. Lev. 4:24), and it is probable that this is Paul's meaning here. Christ's death is frequently spoken of as a sin-offering (e.g. Rom. 8:3; Heb. 7:29; 9:12; Jn 1:29; Is. 53:6, 10) . . . Paul is <u>careful to avoid any suggestion that Christ became sinful or a sinner</u> . . . and explicitly asserts that He had no sin." (David J. A. Clines. *2 Corinthians*, New International Bible Commentary Based on the NIV Translation. Zondervan, 1979, p. 1399-1400)

Moses lifted up the serpent in the desert, which was seen as a type of Christ; therefore, they claim it means that when Jesus was lifted up on the cross he became like the serpent, Satan (Numbers 28:3-4). But it is not literal, but figurative. When Moses lifted up the serpent, people looked to it and were healed. Likewise, when people look to Jesus they can be healed.

What's worse, the Wolves of Faith claim that God told them

about the serpent, and Jesus becoming united with Satan. Take careful note of this, because they make similar claims about other horribly apostate doctrines, which shows that they are NOT listening to God, but Satan.

(4) Jesus Was Only A Man, We Are Gods

All the Word of Faith teachers teach the same messed up pile of stinking garbage. They teach that Jesus became God when he was born again in hell, and when we are born again we too become gods:

> Man was created on terms of EQUALITY with God, no inferiority. (Hagin, *Zoe: The God Kind of Life, 1989*, p. 36.)

> God turned to a man [Jesus] and called him God. He is in a higher position now than he was before He headed to the cross. (K. Copeland, *What Really Happened from the Cross to the Throne*. Tape, side 2)

> I am a little god! . . . I have His name. I'm one with Him. I'm in covenant relation. I am a little god! Critics, be gone! (Paul Crouch, TBN July 7, 1986)

> God draws no distinction between Himself and us. God opens up the union of the very Godhead, and brings us into it. (Paul Crouch, TBN, November, 1990)

> Let's say, "I am a God-man." . . . This spirit-man within me is a God-Man. (Benny Hinn, TBN, December 6, 1990)

Here is what Copeland teaches:

> [T]he spirit of God hovered over you, and there was conceived in your body a holy thing identical to Jesus . . . And there was imparted into you zoe, the life of God. (The Abrahamic Covenant, tape side 2)

> You don't have a god in you, you are one! (K. Copeland, *The Force of Love*, Audiotape, 1987)

Here is what the Bible says:

> Jesus answered them, "Is it not written in your Law, 'I said, you are gods'? 35 If he called them gods to whom the word of God came--and Scripture cannot be broken ... (John 10:34-35) (ESV)

The WOF teachers read that passage and take it literally, but it is speaking figuratively. WOF preachers actually think that they are literal Gods. Here is what Copeland said: "*When I read the Bible where He* (Jesus) *says, 'I AM,' I say, 'Yes, I AM too!'*" (Copeland Crusade meeting, July 19, 1987).

God has given us a certain amount of dominion and power over the world and even over some other people, so that we have the power of life and death; in this sense we act as little gods. When you feed a starving person, you give them life, in that sense you become like God to them. God said that Moses would be like God to his brother Aaron (Ex. 7:1; 4:16). The *Epistle of Diognetus*, long attributed to Justin Martyr, agrees with this interpretation:

> But if a man will shoulder his neighbor's burden; . . .by sharing the blessings he has received from God with those who are in want, he himself becomes a god to those who receive his bounty – such a man is indeed an imitator of God. (Arnold, *The Early Christians in Their Own Words*, page 181)

We are God's hands and arms here on Earth to do good and show God's love to the world, that is all it means. This simple explanation is enough to prove the little god doctrine is totally false. So this teaching about us being a race of little gods, able to speak things into existence, and create things, is a bunch of worthless nonsense. If WOF preachers are little gods, why don't they have the power to do more than take offerings? And if they are gods, why would they even need to take offerings? A commentary says about John 10:34-35:

> It is now known that it was widely held in the ancient orient that kings were the image of God, that is, that they were the god's representatives on earth and governed the earth on his behalf. This is clearly the idea here, with one great change, namely, that every human being, male and female, not just the king, is God's representative who governs the rest of creation on God's behalf. (Gordon J. Wenham, *Genesis*. Eerdmans Commentary on the Bible, 2003, p.33)

(5) More on Little Gods

Copeland said:

> Jesus is no longer the only begotten Son of God. (*Now We Are In Christ Jesus*, 1980)

He means by this that he too is a begotten Son of God.

> You are not a spiritual schizophrenic - half-God and half-Satan - you are all-God. (*Now We Are in Christ Jesus*, 1980)

> You have the same creative faith and ability on the inside of you that God used when he created the heavens and the earth. (*Inner Image of the Covenant*, Audiotape)

> God's reason for creating Adam was His desire to reproduce Himself. I mean a reproduction of Himself. He [Adam] was not a little like God, he was not almost like God, He was not subordinate to God even. (*Following the Faith of Abraham*, tape # 01-3001)

> Don't be disturbed when people accuse you of thinking you're God. The more you get to be like me [Satan speaking, though he says it's God], the more they're going to think that way of you. (*Voice of Victory*, Vol. 15, No. 2, 2/87)

Kenneth Hagin said:

> You are as much the incarnation of God as Christ was.... The believer is as much an incarnation as was Jesus of Nazareth. (K. Hagin, *Word of Faith*, December 1980)

> "[Man] was created on terms of equality with God, and he could stand in God's presence without any consciousness of inferiority... [The] believer is called Christ.... That's who we are; we're Christ." (K. Hagin. *Zoe: The God-Kind of Life*, 1989)

But because Hagin believed in the gifts of the Spirit, his WOF aberrant teaching was accepted and spread. But WOF is not Christianity. Here is an interesting quote:

> But you saw something of that place, and you became those things. You saw the Spirit, you became spirit. You saw Christ, you became Christ. You saw the Father, you shall become Father. So in this place you see everything and you do not see yourself – and what you see you shall become. . . . But one receives the unction . . . of the power of the cross. This power the

apostles called "the right and the left." For this person is no longer a Christian but a Christ. (*Nag Hammadi Library*)

This sounds like something Hagin could have said, but it was
taken from a book of Gnostic falsehood called the *Gospel of Philip*, section 2, 3:61. Early Church father, John Chrysostom, spoke
about the idea of multiple gods:

> . . . they do not have any power, and they are not gods buy only
> stones and demons. . . . For although they may be so-called
> gods, since they are gods in word only, not in reality. . . . Paul's
> argument has been directed against idolaters to show that for
> Christians there is no multiplicity of gods. (John Chrysostom,
> quoted in Judith L. Kovacs, *1 Corinthians by Early Christian
> Commentators.* Eerdmans Publishing, 2005, p. 135.)

Here is what the Bible says against it:

> . . . there is no one besides Me. I am the Lord, and there is no
> other . . . (Isaiah 45:6)

> See now that I, even I, am He, and there is no god besides Me .
> . . (Deut. 32:39)

Here is a quote from a Theological Dictionary that speaks
against the idea of little gods:

> The OT basis for the description of humans as gods is slight,
> and in passages like Ps. 82:1; Ex. 21:6 the reference is to judg-
> es as God's representatives. The rabbis resist strongly the pa-
> gan pretensions of human deity (cf. Dan. 11:36-37). Where the
> OT calls heavenly beings Elohim, the LXX usually has angels or
> sons of God. This is part of the great polemic against the idea
> that the idols of paganism are gods in any true sense. . .
> (Gerhard Kittel and Gerhard Friedrich. *Theological Dictionary of
> the New Testament,* abridged. Eeradmans Pub., 1985, p. 327)

Walter Martin spoke against the teaching of little gods:

> The faith teachers do not speak of the believer's "deification" in
> the sense merely of the Holy Spirit's indwelling presence, since,
> as Copeland says, "You don't have a god in you. You are one."
> Of course, the Orthodox church and the [early Church] Fathers
> judged this very same teaching (Gnosticism) as heresy. (Walter
> Martin, "Ye Shall be as Gods." *The Agony of Deceit: What Some
> TV Preachers are Really Teaching.* Michael Horton, Moody Press,
> 1990, p. 93)

(6) Faith Comes by Hearing?

Kenneth Hagin said faith comes by literally hearing someone preach or teach, because of this verse; "*So faith comes from hearing, and hearing through the word of Christ*" (Romans 10:17) (ESV). Hagin says, "*The reason they are saved by hearing words is because faith cometh by hearing . . . You can't believe without hearing.*" He says in order to be saved we must literally hear the Gospel preached.

This is an example of how stupid Ken Hagin was. If this were true, deaf people could never be saved! It is true that you can acquire faith by hearing someone teach from the Scriptures, but the only reason it says "*faith comes by hearing*" is because most people of the first century could not read, so the Scriptures had to be read to them. Also, they did not have printing presses, so few copies of the Scriptures existed. One copy had to be read out loud for the whole congregation to hear.

> Blessed is the one who reads aloud the words of this prophecy, and blessed are those who hear . . . (Rev. 1:3) (ISV)

Today, you don't have to hear it, you can read it for yourself. Hagin's interpretation is evidence of his great lack of wisdom and understanding. So don't think that you must buy anyone's expensive teaching tapes or CDs and listen to them in order to build your faith, just read the Bible for yourself.

(7) King's Kids

WOF also teaches, "*You are the King's kids, so you should have the best.*" Such teaching causes Christians to develop pride and great desire for material things, especially if they are poor. The Bible says God gives grace to the humble but opposes the proud (1 Peter 5:5; James 4:6). This means God opposes Christians who think they are something special.

> The proud are those who have an inordinate self-esteem; who have a high and unreasonable conceit of their own excellence or importance. (Barnes Notes)

Religious pride has not just infected the Charismatics, but

many evangelicals and fundamentalists as well. Does this pride come from our wealth or because we think we know so much more than the church down the street? It is hard to be humble when you live in a huge home with plenty of money in the bank. The Bible says that pride goes before a fall, therefore, we need to repent of pride and seek humility.

What's more, Jesus said the greatest in the Kingdom will be servant to all here on Earth, so I guess that means a rich TV preacher will become a street sweeper in the Kingdom. While prayer warriors and food servers will be rulers.

(8) Saying Confessions

The Scriptures do not teach the doctrine of saying confessions to make things happen. You cannot create your own reality. You cannot make things happen by the power of your own words. This teaching originated from the Theosophical Society, which became the New Age Movement. Joel Osteen teaches the very same things, which is why he is so well liked by Oprah and other New Age gurus.

You cannot make money come to you, that is false doctrine from hell. This leaves the will of God out of the picture, which is the reason most confessions do not come to pass. *"Unless the Lord builds the house, its builders labor in vain"* (Psalm 127:1) (NIV). But if you think you are a god, I guess this doctrine makes sense. I believe in taking authority over evil and standing on God's Word, but that is different from confessions.

Kenneth Hagin wrote a small book titled, *You Can Write Your Own Ticket With God.* He claims that Jesus appeared to him and told him to write down what Jesus was about to tell him. Then Hagin claims that Jesus told him *"If anybody anywhere will take these four steps and put these four principles into operation, he will always have whatever he wants from Me or God the Father."* Even nonChristians! Talk about a magical formula!

> You can have what you say. You can write your own ticket with God. And the first step in writing your own ticket with God is: Say it. (K.H. *How to Write Your Own Ticket*, p. 8)

All you have to do is, 1) Say it, 2) Do it, 3) Receive it, 4) Tell it. In another booklet he said:

> Believe in your heart; say it with your mouth. That is the principle of faith. You can have what you say. (K.H. *You Can Have What You Say.* 1979, p. 14)

Hagin says if you want a particular house, just confess *"That house is mine."* How do you know what will or will not happen tomorrow? The day after you buy the house there could be a flood or fire that destroys the house. You should pray and ask God if it is within his will for you to have that house. Perhaps God is planning to tell you to take a job in another city, and you go and buy a house without even asking him. Wow! Or you might get transferred or laid off from your job. You cannot know these things in advance, but God does, therefore, you should always ask God about anything you do:

> 13 Come now, you who say, "Today or tomorrow we will go into this city, spend a year there, buy and sell, and make a profit," 14 whereas you do not know what will happen tomorrow. What is your life? It is just a vapor that appears for a little while and then vanishes away. 15 Instead you ought to say, "If the Lord wills, we shall live and do this or that." (James 4:13-15) (MEV)

Like all their other false doctrines, this is a doctrine that they have made up that cannot be proven in the Bible. It is another doctrine that is CLEARLY proven false in the Bible. But the WOF preachers ignore these verses and say the exact opposite, that we should not ask if it is God's will to do this or that, just say it if you want it to happen, because God wants you to have whatever you want. Only God knows what is best for you, you do not! Many good Christians have gotten themselves into trouble by pursuing their own desires, rather than seeking God's will.

> O Jehovah, I know that the way of man does not belong to man; it is not in man who walks to direct his steps. (Jeremiah 10:23) (MKJV)

> "I am the LORD your God. I teach you what is best for you. I lead you where you should go." (Isaiah 48:17) (GW)

There have been many cases of God choosing a person's wife or husband. He has also chosen cars and places to live. Though it is not the norm, I believe God is showing us through these examples that we must seek his advice and will when it comes to making important life decisions. God may in fact allow you to have or do certain things you desire, provided you inquire of him, and are willing to accept his will. When you presume to determine your own way through confessions, you are saying, *I don't need God's guidance, I can make my own decisions.* This is one step away from rebellion. You must be willing to live in accordance with God's plan for your life, not your plan. God may allow you to get into trouble to teach you a lesson. Don Basham said:

> God will allow us to have our own foolish way simply because it's often the most effective way of teaching us that His ways are better. (*The Way I See It*, Basham, p.102)

There is a proper way to say confessions, which is to make them into a prayer. For example: "*I am delivered from alcohol, in Jesus' name*" or "*Thank you, Father, for a good job.*" This way you are not trying to make something happen by the power of your own words, but you are in fact saying a prayer from a position of faith, but always in accordance with the will of God for your life.

For example, it is always God's will to be delivered from alcohol or cigarettes.

We don't always want what God wants for us, but often we have no choice in the matter. Joseph had to suffer in slavery and prison before ruling Egypt. It was not Joseph saying confessions that brought him out of prison and to the throne; it was the will of God for him. The dreams he had from God gave him the faith to believe that even though things were bad, God would eventually deliver him and place him in a position of authority over his family. What resulted was far more than Joseph anticipated! He was placed over a whole nation.

The faith teachers say that if you have enough faith and say your confessions, that nothing will ever harm you, that no disaster will ever hit you. They quote Psalm 91:

> You will not fear the terror of night, . . . nor the pestilence that stalks in the darkness, nor the plague that destroys at midday. A thousand may fall at your side, ten thousand at your right hand, but it will not come near you.... no harm will befall you, no disaster will come near your tent. For he will command his angels concerning you to guard you in all your ways ... (Psalm 91:5-7, 10-11) (NIV)

The Bible contains many such sayings, but you have to consider everything the Bible says, not just a few verses. God is God, and he can do whatever he wants (Exodus 4:11), and he can allow whatever he wants to happen. He can put you through trials and testing, and frequently does.

It rains on the just and the unjust, it also floods on the just and the unjust. Show me one house where the water stands up around it without touching it, and I will believe every word that comes out of the mouths of the WOF teachers. Otherwise, buy flood insurance because if you live in an area that could flood, next time it floods, your house will flood too!

> Many are the afflictions of the righteous, but the LORD delivers him out of them all. (Psalm 34:19) (ESV)

This passage does not say that God delivers us FROM afflictions, it says we will indeed have many afflictions but God will see us through them. The letter of Barnabas, which was not included in the Bible, said:

> "So they," says Christ, "that will see me, and come to my kingdom, must through many afflictions and troubles attain unto me." (Barnabas 6:15)

Do not get me wrong, I believe that God can protect us. But that does not mean he will always keep us from accidents. There are many reports of people being saved from accidents, but there are just as many reports of angels being with people after a car wreck or other accident. The doctors often say they should have died, but the angels kept them alive, but did not keep them from having the accident.

My mother was a hard working woman who was raised by Spirit-filled parents on a farm in South Eastern Oklahoma. My mom became Spirit-filled as a young married lady, after she had married the wrong man. She tells us that one day when she was in her 30s, my dad drew back his fist and was about to hit her with all his strength, when suddenly his expression changed to one of fright, like he had seen a ghost, and he turned and ran out of the house. My mom believes that he saw an angel standing behind her. But many God-fearing Christian women do get abused.

I have my own story of protection. When I was twenty years old I was driving a truck delivering fruits and vegetables to restaurants and convenience stores throughout Southwest Oklahoma. It had started to rain and I did not notice that it was turning to ice. I left a restaurant a little after daybreak and headed south out of a town called Marlow. Back then, the highway between Marlow and Duncan was just two lanes with no shoulder, and a ditch on each side of the road.

I pulled onto the highway and had accelerated up to 40-45 miles per hour when I topped a hill and saw a car that was going very slow, perhaps 20 mph. I just touched the brake and immediately started sliding. The rear of the truck slid to the left, thus turning the truck until I was facing the opposite direction. Yet I was still moving south on the highway and in the other lane. So I was now going south, backwards, and in the northbound lane. I continued moving south and passed the car, while going backwards. I will never forget the look on the faces of the elderly couple.

I continued traveling backwards until I was well clear of the car and then suddenly I swished across the road right into the entrance of a farmer's field, and still facing north. The car slowly passed me and the couple still had the astonished look on their faces. I restarted the truck and made a U-turn and headed south again, this time much slower.

When I got home my mother said, *"What happened?"* I said, *"Nothing, just almost had a wreck . . ."* She had the gift of intercessory prayer and the Holy Spirit moved upon her to pray for me at the time I was in danger.

Another time I was living in a house that had a crop of brown spiders every year that were over an inch across. God warned me that I was in danger of losing an eye, so I prayed about it. And one night, while I was sleeping on my right side, I woke up just enough to detect my right hand moving up by itself. My right hand came in contact with my pillow next to my face, and then did a sweeping motion away from me. I felt something against the palm of my hand and surmise that it must have been a spider that was only an inch or two away from my eye. It would have bit me next to or on my eye. God is good.

Though I have endured all kinds hardship, God has saved me from the worst of what I could have suffered. So it was not saying confessions that saved my mother or myself, because neither of us believed in saying confessions; God answers prayer.

(9) God's Will vs "If"

These false teachers have been teaching for many years that we should not seek God's will for our lives, that we create our own reality by speaking things into existence and commanding angels to bring us money, and so we decide what we want and bring it about by speaking those things into existence with faith. This is why they teach that we should never use the word "if" when asking God for anything. Using "if" shows a lack of faith, say the faith teachers, and if we use it we will not get what we ask for. But a man with leprosy asked, *"Lord, if you are willing, you can make me clean." Jesus said, "I am willing. . . Be clean!"* (Matthew 8:2-3) (NIV). This passage shows that the man did not have much faith, because he doubted whether Jesus would heal him. *"Maybe he will and maybe he won't."* It also proves that you don't need big faith. The man only needed enough faith to ask if Jesus would heal him, Jesus did the rest.

The get-rich preachers teach that the will of God has nothing to do with whether we get healed or get rich; that God wants us to be rich and healed so we should never say, *"if God wills"* about anything we ask for. They say it is not according to the will of God but according to our faith. They use this verse:

> Then he touched their eyes and said, "According to your faith will it be done to you"; 30 and their sight was restored. (Mat. 9:29-30) (NIV)

They teach that everything is totally up to us. Fred Price says this about the above passage:

> If you've got one-dollar faith and you ask for a ten-thousand-dollar item, it ain't going to work. It won't work. Jesus said, "according to your faith," not according to God's will for you, in his own good time. If it's according to his will, if he can work it into his busy schedule. He said, "According to your faith, be it unto you." (*Charismatic Chaos*, 1993, page 349)

In the passage, Jesus was not acknowledging that the person had a lot of faith. He was saying, *"because you have faith, it will be done."* Of course we need faith to receive anything from God, but to ignore many other passages and create a theology that says the amount of material goods or healing we get is based on the amount of faith we have, is worse than stupidity, it is a *doctrine of demons.* We do indeed need faith to receive what God wants for us, but the Bible does not teach that it requires great faith, or that we can even have great faith, or that we should have faith for luxuries.

The will of God is the primary factor that determines the life of a Christian. Paul said even the Holy Spirit intercedes for us *"in accordance with God's will"* (Romans 8:27, NIV). Is your faith more powerful than the prayers of the Holy Spirit? The Holy Spirit only wants God's will for us, but when you want something that is not God's will for you to have, then you are going, not only against God's will, but against the prayers of the Holy Spirit.

The Holy Spirit ONLY prays according to God's will for us, but Satan's preachers say that we should pray according to our own will, not God's will. The will of God for each person is the focus of 1 John 5:14-15:

> And this is the confidence that we have toward Him, that if we ask anything according to His will, He hears us. 15 And if we know that He hears us, whatever we ask, we know that we have the petitions that we desired of Him. (MKJV)

According to this passage, God does not even hear our requests unless they are in line with God's will for us! In other words, it is not what we want that is first priority, but what God wants. Perhaps it is the will of God for you to be healed, and perhaps it is not. It is very possible that by your death many other people will be brought into the Kingdom, so if you proclaim yourself healed and be healed by the power of your own faith, it could cause people to never get saved, because they would not hear the gospel at your funeral. Only God knows what is best for us, we do not.

Likewise, your illness could end up making you a better person, or perhaps you will meet a nurse God wants you to minister too, or even marry; God knows what is best. We need to learn to seek his will, then accept it. But of course if we seek his will and we believe that it is not God's will to die from an illness then we should claim God's promises and pray for victory; and if in fact it is God's will, then you will be healed. It does not require mountain-sized faith to be healed, but it does sometimes require a lot of prayer, and sometimes also fasting; there is more than faith involved.

To get around this obvious interpretation and make it fit the get-rich message, the money-loving preachers say there is a comma in the wrong place in that verse. They say that the passage should read, *"if we ask anything, in accordance with his will he hears us."* This would make it say that if we ask for anything, it is his will to at least hear the prayer, and if we have big enough faith, then we get it. But there is no comma in the original Greek. The best translations into English have a comma in the same place as the KJV, or word it to say the same thing, *"we are sure that he hears us if we ask him for anything that is according to his will"* (GNB).

(10) The Truth About Faith

We already know that Kenneth Hagin was stupid, so it should be no surprise that he said that Jesus did not heal the woman who had an issue of blood in Mark chapter 5, that it was her own faith that healed her, *"Daughter, thy faith hath made thee whole..."* Hagin said:

> He didn't say that His power had made her whole. When I saw this I knew then that if her faith made her whole, then my faith could make me whole.

But what does the verse actually say?

> ... she thought, "If I just touch his clothes, I will be healed." ... At once Jesus realized that power had gone out from him.... He said to her, "Daughter, your faith has healed you." (Mark 5:28, 30, 34) (NIV)

The text clearly shows that she was healed when power left Jesus' body and went into her body. So it was the power of Jesus that healed her, but because of her faith. She was healed when she touched him, not when she believed. She believed long before she touched him. She made a great effort to reach him because she believed she would be healed by touching him; she believed in his power. If it was the power of her faith that healed her, she would never have needed to get anywhere near Jesus. It is truly amazing that such a stupid man could become a successful, popular teacher with his own Bible college. But it was Satan who was directing him and making him successful.

If faith alone could heal, then faith in Buddha could heal. Faith by itself can do nothing; it must be attached to something with power in it. If you were floating in a lake, weakened from trying to save yourself, holding onto a life-line would do you no good unless the other end was attached to a boat with someone who could pull you in. This is why faith in an idol is worthless or faith in your own words or in your own faith; the lifeline by itself cannot save you.

Faith is also like a length of electric wire. With one end attached to a light-bulb, the other end must be attached to a power source. The wire does not light the bulb, it is the power flowing through the wire that lights it. Faith in God is the wire, the power of God is the electricity. Faith in your faith is expecting the wire to light the bulb! All you have to do is have faith in God, he will heal you or not heal you, depending on his sovereign will. This is why you don't need a large amount of faith. A mustard seed-sized wire is more than enough to connect with God; his power will do what is needed.

> And the Lord said, "If you had faith like a grain of mustard seed, you could say to this mulberry tree, 'Be uprooted and planted in the sea,' and it would obey you." (Luke 17:6) (ESV)

Jesus was likely referring to the size of the mustard seed, not to the fact that a mustard plant can grow large from a small seed. It only takes a small amount of faith to connect with God, because it is the power of God that flows through faith that does the work. As long as you have faith, that is the main point. Some people just don't have any faith.

Faith comes from the Word of God, true, but how much? God has given everyone a *"measure of faith"* (Romans 12:4), but obviously not mountain moving faith. The false preachers spend a lot of time trying to get people to have great faith. There is not one Scripture that says anyone can have great faith. Perhaps we can pray to God for more faith, but God is the one who decides whether we have mountain moving faith or not. If many Christians had mountain moving faith, they would do more than heal the sick and raise the dead with it, they would use it like a genie in a bottle. So only the most spiritually mature, knowledgeable, and wise will ever have that kind of faith.

God wants you to have faith and he wants you to trust him, but he understands people and knows that they will occasionally doubt. The false teachers say you must have nothing but faith, and the moment you doubt, everything stops and you have to start all over again. False! If Abraham never doubted that Sarah would have a child he would not have had sex with a servant girl. That proves he did doubt. Did he have to start over? No. Some people who do not even believe that God can or will perform miracles have been healed; which is proof that you will never be able to completely figure out God.

However, the more you know about God, the more God expects from you. God performed many miracles for the Hebrews, such as delivering them from the Egyptian army, yet they did not have the faith to believe that God could win the battle against the Canaanites. Doubting cost them more than a delay of weeks, months, or years. None of those who doubted were allowed to enter the Promised Land, regardless of how much they repented afterwards, or how much their faith grew during the 40 years in the desert. So in this case, their disbelief did not delay the will of God for them, but totally shut off the plan of God for that whole generation. Joshua and Caleb were the only ones that made it into the Promised Land. We don't have to have mountain-moving faith, but we must have at least some faith in God.

(11) Word of Faith and Healing

As a former Pentecostal - Charismatic, now Full Gospel, I have seen people genuinely healed and delivered; what I oppose is the false doctrine of the WOF group that says you will always be healed, if you have enough faith. And so if you are not healed it is your fault for not having enough faith.

Two of the main false prophets of this movement, E.W. Kenyon and Kenneth E. Hagin, both died of disease, which is completely contrary to their teachings. Kenyon died while in a coma caused by a malignant tumor at only 81. Hagin said people should live to be very old and then just die, but he died at 86 from heart problems while in intensive care at a cardiac care facility. My grandmother lived to be nearly 100, and my mother was 90. Why did both of the big faith-claimers die of disease, in a hospital? Why did another big one, Billy Joe Daugherty, die of cancer at age 57? Is God poking this movement in the eye, and trying to wake us up at the same time?

In addition, Kenneth Hagin's sister died of cancer; and his son-in-law, Buddy Harrison, founder of the WOF book publishing company *Harrison House Books*, also died of cancer. Kenneth Hagin's son is also a Word of Faith preacher, and admitted that his own son had "*a brain tumor that required immediate surgery*" but made no mention of divine healing (*Christianity in Crises: The 21st Century*, Hannegraaf, page 421).

Another giant in the Word of Faith camp was John Osteen, Joel Osteen's father. He started Lakewood Church, but he died of a heart attack while in the hospital undergoing dialysis for kidney failure, at age 77. Yet, instead of people saying, "*he spoke it, believed it, and yet he died, so it must not be true,*" people are following his son like a pied piper.

While reading the local newspaper, I frequently read obituaries of people who died before their time of cancer or some other disease, and guess who performs the funeral? A local WOF pastor.

I have my own testimony on this subject. I want to relate a story that helped opened my eyes. When I believed the WOF stuff I stepped off a high porch and twisted my ankle. It hurt somewhat so I stopped walking and began confessing that I am healed and proclaiming that I am healed and thanking God for healing me. I then began walking again and the pain went away.

I was very happy and was praising and thanking God for the healing. I said to myself, "*This WOF stuff really works,*" then suddenly the pain came back with a vengeance. It felt like I had been stabbed by a huge knife, but I kept on confessing and rebuking the devil and kept on walking and believing, but the pain only got worse. Eventually I was unable to walk at all on that foot and I was by then over a block away from my apartment. I had to hobble back home in great pain. Every step was excruciating.

When I got home I called an ambulance and was taken to the hospital where I was x-rayed. I had a hairline fracture in my angle bone and had to walk on crutches for several weeks. This was one of the events on my path to the truth, that the Word of Faith teaching is false.

Many more examples could be given, but this is enough to prove the Word of Faith stuff is false; it does not work most of the time. Sure, there will be times when people get healed by declaring themselves healed. There are also people that win the lottery, but that does not mean that you can expect to win the lottery!

(12) Eternal Security Proven False

Like the prosperity gospel, the doctrine of Eternal Security (ES) has spread beyond its roots and is being accepted in parts of the Charismatic Movement. And why should we be surprised? It is one of those ear ticking doctrines; one of those yummy tasting doctrines that Americans love so much. Even though I could write a whole book just on Eternal Security, I feel one passage is so powerful that it cannot be factually refuted, only ignored or twisted. So I will mainly discuss that passage.

This is a doctrine that was once the domain of the Baptists, but thanks to Jack Hayford and Pat Robertson who have taught it for decades, it is growing in the Charismatic Movement, including the WOF. After all, if you think you are a god, how can you lose your godhood, LOL? Therefore, WOF is a perfect group for Eternal Security (ES). So now WOF preachers like Joseph Prince are also teaching it, but it is just another false doctrine that should be exposed.

Given that there are verses that *seem* to support ES and some against it, let us focus on one of Christ's parables, because ALL other passages must agree with what Jesus said, since the Bible does not teach contrary doctrine. This parable by itself proves the doctrine of ES is false.

There is an old saying that goes, *a picture is worth a thousand words*. This is probably one of the reasons that Jesus gave us parables, they contain information that would take a lot more words to say, and cannot be altered without altering the story itself. So the truth is certain to reach us, if we are not blinded by false doctrine when we read the parables. William Barclay's commentary on Matthew 13 says this about parables:

> . . . the parable conceals truth from those who are either too lazy to think or too blinded by prejudice to see. It puts the responsibility fairly and squarely on the individual. It reveals truth to him who desires truth; it conceals truth from him who does not wish to see the truth. (www.studylight.org/commentaries/dsb/matthew -13.html)

Now, do you believe that an apple seed can produce anything but an apple tree? No, an apple seed can <u>only produce</u> an <u>apple tree</u>. But do you really believe it? Likewise, we should believe the words of Jesus Christ the Son of God when he gave us the parable of the SEED OF THE WORD OF GOD.

One of the most important parables Jesus gave is of the seed that fell on different types of ground, and Jesus tells us that the seed is the "<u>Word of God</u>." The ground represents the hearts of men and women who hear the Gospel. The condition of the person's heart determines whether the seed is able to produce fruit. Jesus said:

> "But other seeds fell on rocky ground where they did not have much soil, and immediately they sprang up because they did not have deep soil. 6 But when the sun rose, they were scorched. And because they did not take root, they <u>withered away</u>. . . . But he who received the seed on rocky ground is he who hears the word and <u>immediately receives it with joy</u>, 21 yet he has no root in himself, but endures for a while. For when tribulation or persecution arises because of the word, eventually he falls away." (Matthew 13:20-21) (MEV)

This plant is an illustration of a man or woman who hears the gospel message and is full of joy at finding the truth: *"Praise God I've been born again!"* Some people make quick decisions without thinking things through, but they have not counted on the high cost. They are not informed that they will likely suffer greatly for being a Christian.

There can be no doubt then, that the plant that sprang up represents a newborn Christian, but because the plant did not put down roots by being fully discipled, including feeding on the Word and prayer, it was not able to stand up against outside forces, which was the heat of the sun. The plant is persecuted or suffers trials and tribulations, and renounces its faith in Christ.

Those who teach ES would have you believe that the root represents Christ, and since it had no root then it means <u>that it was never actually born again</u>. So the doctrine of ES says that the SEED of the WORD OF GOD produces FAKE Christians! No it does NOT. <u>The seed of the Word of God can ONLY PRODUCE real born again Christians</u> the same way that an apple seed can only produce an apple tree!

It is true that some apple trees will not produce fruit, and some of them will be sickly and small, while others will be strong and produce much fruit, the cause is the soil and water a seed may get. But in this doctrine of ES, when we look at the parable, it is the <u>nature of the Seed that is in question</u>, not the soil into which it is planted.

The doctrine of ES says if you are truly born again then your spirit can never die because it is not up to you, but up to God to sustain you. But this is false doctrine, if only because it does not agree with this parable. The only thing, physical or spiritual, that cannot die is God, otherwise, your spirit can indeed die again for lack of spiritual nutrients.

Such a person as in the parable is a baby in the Lord and has not been properly discipled, so when faced with trouble for being a Christian, he *"withered away."* You have heard that one cannot fall if he was never standing. So <u>he cannot die if he was never alive</u>! In this case, if he withered away then he had to have been alive; he had to have been a real newborn Christian plant, the product of the <u>Seed of the Word of GOD</u>! You cannot fall away from the truth if you never had the truth. This is proof that he was in fact a "saved" Christian.

Notice that in this parable at least, the plant did not die because it did something wrong, it died because it was a young plant that was not strong enough to stand against persecution. It takes more than being born again, but it also takes growing strong spiritually. A baby Christian needs to grow.

Sin can also kill a plant, but not one sin by itself. Sin is like putting rocks in the soil. The more rocks there are, the less nourishment the plant can get, and eventually the plant will die of starvation. Another way of looking at sin is as bricks that are laid to build a wall. Each <u>unrepented</u> sin builds the wall a little more until the wall separates you from God.

Yes, the Holy Spirit gives life (John 6:63), and brings forth the increase (1 Corinthians 3:7.), but if you don't keep drinking from the water of life you will die. One drink will not keep you alive for eternity! We are only alive if we keep drinking of the Spirit, and <u>when we stop receiving this nourishment, then we will die</u>, plain and simple.

Those who teach ES say it is nonsense to suggest that you sin and get saved again, over and over. Yes, indeed. I have never heard anyone teach such nonsense. This is what is called misrepresenting the doctrines of other churches. One sin or even two will harm your relationship with God, but many sins will choke off the life-giving nourishment. So will intentionally renouncing your faith in Christ, like so many have done who grew up believers but were fed poison in the form of false New Age teaching or atheism. So the poison killed their plant, it killed their spirit by stopping the plant from soaking up the water of life.

To suggest that once a person becomes born again, that they cannot die again, is utterly ridiculous and not biblically supported:

> 7 Some seeds fell among thorns, and the thorns grew up and choked them." . . . 22 He also who received seed among the thorns is he who hears the word, but the <u>cares of this world</u> and the <u>deceitfulness of riches</u> choke the word, and he becomes unfruitful. (Matthew 13)

Here again the Word of God, which is the life of the plant, is choked off by outside influences such as false doctrine or compromise, which causes the plant to die!

It will come as a shock to many Baptists who oppose the

WOF movement and the teaching about becoming little gods, but the doctrine of ES is almost exactly the same as the WOF teaching of little gods. How so? ES teaches that once you are born into the family of God, you cannot loose your salvation, *"How can you become unborn?"* But only a god cannot die. So THAT is the only way you will never die and live forever; unless you have life-inflow from the Holy Spirit. The Holy Spirit is what gives us life. If you cannot die then you have life-sustaining ability within your own self, so you are a little god and could go off and create your own universe if you were not locked inside a physical body. So, which is it? Do you become a god and so have life in yourself, or do you live because of the power of God in you? I believe it is the latter.

You see, the Holy Spirit can be choked off, and it can depart. If you allow a root of bitterness to grow inside of you, it can choke off the life-giving flow of the Holy Spirit. You can become filled with hate, even toward God, even though you were once saved. I know, it almost happened to me.

There are many more passages that support the belief that you can lose your salvation, but they have been preached on many times over the centuries, but ignored or twisted by people who are blinded by false doctrine.

Like the prosperity gospel, the ES doctrine leads to even more falsehood. The teachers of ES even claim that if you do not believe in ES you are not even saved! Yes, they actually teach that, because if you do not believe in ES then they claim you are trying to earn your salvation by living right, LOL.

Requiring that you believe a doctrine beyond the Gospel message in order to be saved is a sure sign of a false doctrine. They do not realize how stupid that doctrine sounds, and is. In other words, if I resist temptation because I do not want to sin, I commit the sin of trying to earn my salvation by works and I am, therefore, not saved. Which means, in order to be saved I must yield to temptation and commit sin to prove I am saved. LUNA-CY! Of course no one will ever actually teach the full results of that belief openly, but that is what it amounts to.

Teachers of ES claim that God has already forgiven you of every sin you will ever commit, therefore, you never have to repent of any sin you may commit in the future. This goes against the clear teaching of Scripture that says if you confess your sins, *God is faithful and just to forgive us* (1 John 1:9). John was not speaking to sinners, but to those who were already born again.

It takes enormous amounts of what is called knowledge filtering to read all the passages in the Bible that are against the teaching of ES and not see what it says. Believing a false doctrine blinds you to what the Bible actually says against that doctrine. The hardest people to reach with the truth are not those who have never heard the truth, but those who think they already have it, but don't.

So it is false to say that you are guaranteed eternal life just because you said a sinner's prayer once. Total falsehood.

Derek Prince (1915-2003) was a balanced Charismatic teacher. I agree with most of what he taught. Here is a short excerpt taken from a video of him speaking:

> [A deliverance session] lasted five hours, but we had a woman in Chicago who was a friend of ours, now we know her personally, who was delivered from, one lady sat there and counted, wrote the names down, she counted 72 different spirits that came out. This is her count not mine. But in the middle of this, these spirits are all speaking out of this woman, in the middle one said, "I'm a seducing spirit." Well, I said, "Come out in the name of Jesus." It said, "I'm the seducer of the faith." I said, "Still come out in the name of Jesus." Then it said, "I'm the chief one." Well I said, "Still come out." And then it said, "I have many roots." So I said, "Come out with all your roots." And then, this happened in the Conrad Hilton Hotel in Chicago. And I have a little tablet with the Conrad Hilton name on the top. After about four of these spirits had come out, I suddenly realized that these were the roots of error coming out. So I grabbed this tablet and wrote them down. Now I may upset you, you can get mad, you can stand on your head, but I'll tell you some of the names of them. One of the first was "Jesus Only." . . . Another . . . you must know this one, "Eternal Security." (https://youtu.be/aHFiR ifC0YI)

So that is why so many people are blinded by this doctrine, demonic deception is involved. I realize that a large volume of theology has developed to support ES, but it is false, the same as the prosperity gospel.

(13) The Prophetic Movement

Andrew Strom of New Zealand was very much a part of what is termed the Prophetic Movement, but because it got off track and mixed up with New Age false spirits, he left the movement and wrote the book, *Why I Left the Prophetic Movement*, while living in the U.S. in 2007. The Prophetic Movement began in Kansas City in the 1980s but is now global, with many well-known prophets. But it became infected with the operation of false spirits because they embraced the "Toronto Blessing," so they are now doing things that are closer to the New Age movement and witchcraft than Christianity. (It is likely that some of them are WOF and some are not.) Andrew Strom writes:

> People are getting all kinds of counterfeit spiritual experiences. There seems to be almost no discernment at all.

Andrew urges people to get out of the movement before it gets worse and that there should be a totally new, genuine, prophetic movement to take its place.

> It is actually worse than I ever imagined. . . . We are talking here about a movement where it is encouraged for people to interact with "Orbs of light" that come hovering down (- a major prophetic ministry does this) or to pay money for personal "dream interpretations". We are talking about a movement that teaches people how to "visualize" their way into the 'Third Heaven' and sometimes holds 'Presbytery' days where you can book a half-hour personal appointment with a prophet for a hefty fee. We are talking about a movement that majors on 'manifestations', "portals" and weird 'visitations'. In every way it more closely resembles the New Age movement than anything Christian. In fact, more and more I am seeing that this movement is utterly dominated by a spirit of DIVINATION and fortune-telling. (Ibid, p. 14-15) (Emphasis in the original)

The book was originally an article he wrote wherein he announced that he was leaving the movement, and many people sent him emails telling about their experiences in prophetic meetings. Here is an email from someone identified as MS:

> "I read your article, *"Why I left the Prophetic Movement,"* and it was so similar to an experience and a reaction that I had at a recent "Prophetic" conference last year. Every observation you had is exactly what I observed! These so-called prophets and worship leaders were <u>ushering in lude and familiar spirits, worshipping angels and opening and going through ungodly spiritual portals</u>. I have never been so grieved and disturbed by anything in my life! And nobody else seemed to notice or care other than my fellow peers/disciples who discerned this also! I was so upset I strongly considered confronting .[the big-name leaders].
>
> The disturbing thing is that other respectable leaders were not able to discern and bring to correction what was going on. The weirdest part about everything is that one of the spirits that was <u>causing some creepy laughter</u> at the conference followed us to the mall after we left the conference and caused a girl working one of the little booths that sells stuff in the middle of the mall to <u>manifest when we walked by</u> and laugh the same exact way. God showed me that the only reason some of the other leaders could not discern this is that <u>they accepted money</u> and thus the <u>spirit of mammon</u> had blinded their eyes to see what was going on. . . . (page 27-28, emphasis and brackets in the original)

Notice that *"creepy laughter"* had occurred at the conference, which is not the same as normal laughter. Andrew states:

> It is very dangerous for Christians to seek anything but a deeper and purer relationship with Christ Himself. Any seeking after mere touches or experiences is really nothing but "soulishness", and can result in great spiritual deception. (Ibid, page 48)

People can be deceived by false spiritual experiences just as easily as false teaching and false prophecies. The demonic is just as much involved in either case, or more likely, familiar spirits. This is another reason that a Charismatic Reformation is needed.

It is easy for some people with a talent for putting words together to come up with great-sounding prophecies, even on the spur of the moment; as a result, the prophetic movement includes some prophets who give out great sounding, but false prophecies. And if you think about what the false prophets actually say, it really amounts to nothing of substance, just hot air. Just smooth sounding words to make people feel like they have received something, and make them want to buy their books and tapes. But there are no prophetic utterances with that type of content anywhere in the Bible.

(14) Nonsense Teaching and Scripture Twisting

Jesse Duplantis said:

> God has the power to take life, but he can't. He's got the power to do it, but he won't. He's bound, he can't. He says, "Death and life is in the power of" whose tongue? Yours. . . . <u>You choose when you live, you choose when you die</u>. Death and life is in the power of your tongue, not God's. (video on Youtube)

Who knew that Christians were choosing to die in sporting accidents, or die in car wrecks, or die of cancer? Lunacy.

There are probably thousands of videos on Youtube with horrible quotes from these WOF false prophets. A favorite of mine, that reveals their true spiritual state, is one that includes Creflo Dollar. He says in this quote what would happen if we were under the Old Covenant in his church. He would like to have people swipe a card to get into the main sanctuary, and it would detect if you are a tither or not. The tithers would be welcomed in, but guess what happens to the non-tithers:

> Security would go and apprehend them, and once we got them all together, we'd line them up in the front and pass out Uzis by the ushers and point our Uzis right at all those non-tithing members 'cause we want God to come to church, and at the count of three "Jesuses" <u>we'd shoot them all dead</u>. And then we'd take them out the side door there, have a big hole, bury them, and then go ahead and have church and have the anointing. (https:// KennethCopelandblog.com/2011/06/15/creflo-dollar-says-shoot-them-all-dead/)

Now that is scary. Nowhere in the Bible does it say to kill non-tithers. He also said that tithing correctly will keep you saved, in other words, it becomes a form of Eternal Security:

> If you tithe, and tithe correctly, it is impossible to go to hell. It will keep you in the presence of God. (*The Covenant Connector*,

World Changers Church International, 2001)

So in a manner of speaking, you can buy your way into heaven, just tithe and God will see to it that everything else is A-OK with your spirit.

There are Youtube videos that show Creflo Dollar standing in front of a church crowd, he shakes his Bible in the air and says:

> But a lot of other people say it's not about money, it's about peace, it's about joy, and it's about love. IT'S ABOUT MONEY!

WOW, this is so sick and disgusting, it is beyond words. But the crowds of people he speaks to, love it! You can see the clip in the video I created for this book.

Creflo Dollar went to Uganda in 2007 for a one-day crusade to break the curse of poverty off the country. But he would not go until the people raised the money to pay his $500,000 fee, plus another $100,000 for jet fuel for his private plane. They raised the money, but they are still poor!

Paul Crouch was well known for his twisted WOF teaching. He said on August 22, 1999:

> "Force God to perform a miracle by planting thousands of dollars and your last dollar ... Do you have a sick child? Don't go to Jesus in prayer, plant cold cash into TBN, and God will make your child well." (www.bereanpublishers.com/david-wilkerson-blasts-faith-preachers/)

Jesus said:

> Enter at the narrow gate, for wide is the gate and broad is the way that leads to destruction, and there are many who are going through it, because small is the gate and narrow is the way which leads to life, and there are few who find it. (Matthew 7:13-14) (MEV)

We all know what those verses mean, but the WOF teachers who are not following God, twist them to fit their false doctrines. Joseph Prince said:

> . . . he's not talking about heaven and hell . . . But once you have received Christ you are saved forever, and yet there are many Christians on this broad way. Amen. . . . It's not talking about the life to come it's talking about this life. Nowhere did Je-

sus say that few there are that find eternal life. Narrow is the way that leads to life, not eternal life. . . . <u>So these verses are not talking about the life to come, it's talking about our present life</u>.

Notice the first word in the verse, "enter," its main meaning is to go from one place into another place, as when you enter a room. And that is the picture which we are given in these verses, we are entering another place through a gate. So it cannot refer to entering this life; are we not already in this life?

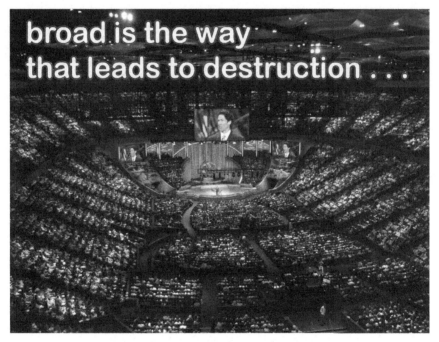

Joel Osteen's church in Houston.

(15) Brief Summary

One of the arguments used in an effort to prove the false ministers are actually true ministers, is that they can cast out demons, because Jesus said that Satan cannot cast out Satan. But Jesus also said that some false ministers will stand before him on the Day of Judgment and say that they cast out demons and healed the sick in His name. What this shows is that they are not intentionally followers of Satan, they actually think they are

Christians and think they are following the teachings of Christ, but they are deceived, because the desire for wealth is idolatry. (Except for the few who are indeed followers of Satan.) They have enough of the truth to be able to cast out demons the same as Catholic priests can cast out demons, but since they are guilty of idolatry (the prosperity gospel), they are practicing both Christianity and paganism. This is why they can cast out demons but will be cast into hell on the Day of Judgment.

About WOF doctrines, the *Christian Expositor* writer says:

> It is a system of thinking that has been generated by a group of men drawing from each other's teachings with an amalgamation of Christian theology, mysticism and Gnosticism bound together by one of the most fanciful methods of Scripture interpretation ever devised. www.thechristianexpositor.org/page7.html

Amen.

I originally wrote a whole book by the title of *The Prosperity Gospel Exposed: And Other False Doctrines*. I took it out of print in Jan. of 2017 because I was planning to publish a revised and updated edition. But while doing the research, it became apparent that the book needed to be refocused towards the false prophets who are teaching the false doctrines, which became this book. I have included only three chapters from the original book, though there is much more material, and I may yet publish a smaller edition of it.

Chapter 9:
The Prosperity Gospel Exposed

(1) Seeing Things Wrong

There is a misunderstanding among some people about what the doctrine called the *prosperity gospel* actually is and is not. We are not asked to choose between two opposites: either a belief that Christians should be poor, or that they should be rich. Neither is true. There are even theologians who have written on the subject who do not know what the doctrine is; they lump all Christians who believe that God is alive and working among his people with the label of *prosperity gospel*. This is false.

God is in fact answering prayers and healing people today, but many people who believe this do <u>not</u> believe the prosperity gospel. It is very wrong to claim that all Pentecostals and Charismatics believe the prosperity gospel, even though it has spread far and wide. <u>The *prosperity gospel* says that God will make you rich if you send an offering to the preacher on TV, or even give to your local church, and that God wants you to be rich.</u>

God has promised in the Bible that those who pay tithes will be greatly blessed. God said he will *"open for you the windows of heaven and pour out for you a blessing, that there will not be room enough to receive it"* (Mal. 3:10) (MEV). This is *not* the prosperity gospel, but the verse is sometimes wrongly used to claim that God will make you rich. If this verse supports the wealth gospel, then all you would have to do is pay tithes and you will become rich, simple as that. There would be no need for preachers on TV to teach on the subject of how to get rich, and ask you to buy their books and CDs to learn principles of Biblical prosperity. Nor would it be necessary to send them money in order to get any kind of financial blessing. If God has promised to make us rich, then it would be very easy for all Christians to become rich. But that is *not* what the Bible teaches.

Unlike what some people claim, I believe we should pay tithes because God has told me to pay tithes, and my prosperity is better when I do. And I no longer desire wealth, and have never even owned a new car. But when I pay tithes my needs are met; that is Biblical prosperity.

Out of one side of their mouths, the prosperity preachers say that the purpose of their ministry is to help people get out of debt and to help people prosper so they can give large sums of money to spread the gospel. But out of the other side of their mouths they teach that you can have whatever material goods you want, such as a luxury home or a *Rolls Royce*. So don't let any of the false prosperity preachers fool you into believing that they are not talking about living in luxury, I have read their books, so I know what they teach.

What they are teaching is that if you give to preachers, especially themselves, God will make you rich enough to own a *Rolls Royce*, like some of those preachers own, which they bought with donations from people hoping to get rich. John Avanzini said:

> Don't worry about missing out on the good life. As long as you fulfill God's purpose in your giving, God will loose abundance into your hands.

In addition, Avanzini teaches that in order for the Great Commission to be completed, that Christians must take over all the wealth of the world, because the cost is so great. But on the other hand, he teaches that God always supplies the needs for every minister he calls, so that none of them should ever lack for anything. So why are you asking for money? But the fact is, the Gospel has already been preached into most of the world, so it will not require all the wealth of Wall Street to complete the task. Christians already have enough, they are just spending it on themselves.

You can call them *Prosperity Pirates*, or *Prosperity Pimps*, as they are almost true yet false prophets. There are many preachers and teachers in this movement that are motivated by greed, but there are many local pastors who are teaching the prosperity gospel and WOF doctrines and are merely deceived because they believe the lies of the big name preachers. They have been deceived by the prosperity teachers like I was once deceived.

I read books by the big name prosperity preachers and was a firm believer in the prosperity gospel, but the more money I gave the poorer I became. I gave money in offerings for the purpose of getting rich and commanded angels to bring me money, but I am thankful to God that he did not prosper me so I could recognize the error of this teaching. Wisdom is the true wealth of the Kingdom:

> Wisdom is supreme; therefore get wisdom. Though it cost all you have, get understanding. (Proverbs 4:7) (NIV)

> Choose my instruction instead of silver, knowledge rather than choice gold, for wisdom is more precious than rubies, and nothing you desire can compare with her. (Prov. 8:10-11) (NIV)

Let me make it perfectly clear that the Bible does, in fact, teach that God wants to prosper us, but *biblical prosperity* is not the same as the prosperity gospel. God does not want us in poverty, but when we receive blessings, it is not for our own enrichment, but so we can help other Christians who are in need. There are many Christians in India, Africa, and China who have no shoes to wear, some have barely enough clothes to cover their bodies. God will give us more income than we need so that we can give towards meeting those needs. God does not give us money so we can buy a yacht or a big diamond ring, but that is what Christians in America are doing with the money God has given them.

Although God does make a few people rich, very few, because he wants to reward them in this life, or wants them to have a ministry of giving, it does not apply to the average Christian. Those few Christians who are genuinely blessed with wealth do not need to be taught how to acquire wealth. If you have the call-

ing to be rich, then you will not have to seek after wealth or follow a step-by-step plan to get rich, money will find you. But most
Christians are not called to be rich and will never be rich, no
matter how much money they send to TV preachers.

Oral Roberts was one of the biggest prosperity preachers in
history and popularized the phrase, *"I'm not your source, God is
your source."* In other words, *Don't ask me for help because I will not
help you.* I used to send him money and actually heard him say
on TV that he will not feed you and he will not pay your electric
bill, but if you send him money to help him stay on TV that God
will feed you and God will pay your electric bill.

He said people should send money to him <u>even if it was their
last dollar</u>! This is an abomination and is actually the opposite of
what the Bible teaches. Those who have money must give to
those who don't have money; and that includes wealthy preachers on TV. They should be giving to the poor, instead they are
taking money from them. It is not like they need the money to
preach the gospel; <u>teaching on TV that God wants you to be rich
is *not* the gospel</u>!

> The city's rulers govern for bribes, the priests interpret the Law
> for pay, <u>the prophets give their revelations for money</u>--and they
> all <u>claim that the LORD is with them</u>. "No harm will come to us,"
> they say. "The LORD is with us." (Micah 3:11) (GNB)

Rather than the above prophecy applying only to people who
lived when the prophet Micah spoke those words, could this
verse be a prophecy about the state of Charismatic Christianity
today? It certainly describes the prosperity pirates.

The prosperity gospel is the biggest hindrance to the spiritual
growth of Christians in the Charismatic Movement and a blight
to Christianity in general. The doctrine of greed is, perhaps, the
largest single reason that many people turn away from the Charismatic Movement, and even causes people to turn away from
Christianity! Yet, the fastest growing group of Christians today is
the Pentecostals and Charismatics. People love to hear that God
wants them to be rich.

The prosperity gospel is one of the most ruinous doctrines in

the Church today; it is not just harmful, destructive, and dangerous, it is the opposite of the true gospel and, therefore, an evil lie
from the pit of hell. The true gospel does not want us to be poor,
but it also does not want us to be rich because wealth can so easily separate us from God.

> Two things I ask of you; deny them not to me before I die: Re-
> move far from me falsehood and lying; give me <u>neither poverty</u>
> <u>nor riches</u>; feed me with the food that is <u>needful</u> for me, <u>lest I be</u>
> <u>full and deny you</u> and say, "Who is the LORD?" or lest I be poor
> and steal and profane the name of my God. (Proverbs 30:7-9)
> (ESV)

Christianity used to battle paganism, it now battles materialism, but it is a battle Christians in North America are currently
loosing. Materialism has overcome a large percentage of Christians in North America. Of all Christians, preachers in particular
like to drive Cadillacs and Lincolns and other luxury cars, as if a
luxury car is evidence of God's blessings, and somehow validates
their ministry. Rick Joyner said:

> We esteem highly those who overcome during times of persecu-
> tion, darkness and evil, as we should, but the greatest overcom-
> ers of all may be those who have overcome the lukewarmness
> generated by prosperity and comfort. (*The Harvest*, p. 82)

History tells us that Saint John Chrysostom (c. 349–407) lived
a fasted life. When he became Patriarch of Constantinople, he
donated his large salary to benefit the poor. Do you see anyone
doing that today? It happens, rarely. He founded several hospitals in Constantinople that cared for the poor.

Even churches that do not teach the prosperity gospel generally have members who are more prosperous than they were 100
years ago, and are caught up in the American life-style of con-
sumerism; more, bigger, newer. They want the big house, the
new car, the big screen TV, and the latest video game systems
and telephones.

The American Dream is not the Biblical model. Apparently
most Christians are not aware that the Bible teaches that wealth
can cause spiritual blindness.

Avanzini wrote a whole book, which was given away free by TBN, about Mark chapter 4, wherein he claimed that Mark 4 teaches the doctrine of great abundance, yet in the entire book he never once mentioned Mark 4:19 that says, "*the <u>deceitfulness of wealth</u> and the desires for other things come in and choke the word, making it unfruitful*" (NIV). Amazing! Jesus said earthly wealth can deceive you, choking out the truth of God's Word. And the prosperity preachers have been so blinded by their own greed, they pass right over that verse like it's not there. They have been deceived by their desire for wealth!

The above passage contains a very important truth that is being totally overlooked, not only by the prosperity preachers but also by most of Christianity in America today. The overall teachings in the Bible show us that it is not good to be in poverty, but also that it is not good to be rich. Solomon wrote Proverbs, and he understood the corrupting influence of wealth; therefore, he knew that people can have too much wealth. He knew that wealth deceives people into becoming materialistic; it deceives people into depending on it for security rather than God.

> He who trusts in his riches will fall, but the righteous will flourish as a branch. (Proverbs 11:28) (MEV)

> The righteous also will see and fear, and will laugh in contempt, 7 "See, this is the man who did not make God his refuge, but trusted in the abundance of riches, and grew strong in his own wickedness." (Psalm 52:6-7) (MEV)

Notice that in the above two passages, the "righteous" are not the rich. The prosperity preachers avoid passages such as these because they clearly contradict the get-rich gospel.

As further evidence for their teachings, the prosperity preachers point out that Abraham, Job, and Solomon were rich. But they fail to mention that Abraham did not live in luxury but lived in a tent; a tent that was not filled with expensive "stuff" like our homes in America today. He had lots of sheep and cattle but he had few material possessions (since he traveled from place to place), so he cannot be compared to the wealthy preachers today who have huge mansions and wear diamond watches.

Abraham also had many full-time employees; Genesis 14:14 says he had 318 trained fighting men, he also had many shepherds, plus all their wives and children. The total must have been several thousand which he fully supported. He did not pay them a low wage that cannot supply one person with housing and food. All his workers had all their needs met, of that I am sure. Also, it is likely that he did not live much better than his employees. Some rich Christians today are rich because they own businesses and pay their employees slave wages. Nowhere in the Bible does it say that Abraham thought he deserved to be wealthy, or tried to become wealthy.

Yes, Solomon was very wealthy, but he was a great king of a great nation, YOU are not! So just because he was wealthy, does not mean that you can expect to become wealthy. That is absolute nonsense. He also had hundreds of wives, do you expect the same? And, he did not ask for wealth, but wisdom.

The prosperity preachers like to talk about how wealthy the Israelites were when they left Egypt. They left with much of its wealth. What they fail to tell you is that God later asked them to give that wealth for the construction of the Tabernacle and the Ark of the Covenant. Even though they did not have to give it all, what good did the gold do them in the desert? They could not buy food or even clothing, so God had to provide them with manna and make their garments not wear out. It is clear that God did not give the Israelites the wealth of Egypt so they could live in luxury, but so they could give it to God, which did *not* include giving it directly to priests. The priests did not become wealthy.

The false prophets of materialism point out that Jacob reaped a hundredfold harvest during a famine. Yes, but they fail to mention that it only happened once, and that during another famine Jacob had to send his sons into Egypt to buy grain from pagans. Should we then expect pagans to be the source of supply during lean years? No, you cannot take something from the Old Testament that happened to one person one time and apply it to everyone today. The hundred-fold harvest was only an example of what is possible if God wills it, not what will happen every time if you have enough faith, or plant enough seed money. Did Jacob lack faith during the second famine? No, it was simply God's will for him to buy grain from Egypt so his family would move to Egypt where they would grow into a nation and be delivered by Moses.

The false teachers even twist the fact that Jacob had money to buy grain as an example of their prosperity message. In this famine there is a 99% likelihood that Jacob sold more sheep and cattle than he normally would have, because there was not enough water and grass for them all. This could have been the source of the money he used to buy grain, but even if he had enough money without selling any cattle or sheep, that is not evidence of wealth, but only of having enough. If he did not have the money to buy the grain they needed, then he would have starved to death. Having enough money to buy what you need to eat is NOT wealth! Will the stupidity ever end?!

The prosperity preachers point out that the whole nation of Israel was sometimes extremely prosperous, but they fail to mention that the Israelites were very prosperous even while they were worshiping the golden calves set up by Jeroboam. The southern kingdom of Judah was also prosperous while worshiping idols:

> Their land also is full of silver and gold, and there is no end to their treasures; their land is also full of horses, and there is no end to their chariots. 8 Their land also is full of idols; they worship the work of their own hands, that which their own fingers have made. (Isaiah 2:7-8) (MEV)

That passage could describe present-day America. The prosperity preachers fail to mention that throughout history there have been many nations that had great wealth. Many of the Egyptian Pharaohs had great wealth as did the city-states of Babylon, Athens, and Rome. Are we to believe that these pagans were blessed by God for being pagans and giving to the pagan temples!

Consider this, when Nebuchadnezzar invaded Israel he carried off all the gold that was in the temple. Here we have the case of God giving the wealth of Israel to a pagan king who used it to build a solid gold statue of himself. Why are the prosperity preachers not using this example as a teaching lesson? Maybe they are afraid God will send someone to carry off their gold because of their greed!

A final story illustrates how these false ministers are going farther and farther into deception with magic and superstition like the New Age movement. The following was reported online by a person who attended a church conference in Tinley Park, Illinois. John Avanzini was teaching at the conference and revealed a couple of new scams which he uses to prey upon the gullible.

He used several references in the Bible about stones that are said to speak, though it was metaphorical. But since he is stupid, he gave magical properties to the stones. He even passed out a smooth stone to everyone in the audience and instructed them to rub their stone whenever they faced financial issues.

Later he presented more new insight on how to get rid of credit card debt. It seems you must give a huge gift on your credit card to him, and "*something happens in the spirit world*" which is supposed to outsmart the credit lenders. To pay off your mortgage, just make a gift equal to your mortgage payment, and if you don't own a home, then $500 will work against future debt. The people flocked to the front to give their credit card numbers and cash offerings. Everyone left that night a lot poorer than when they arrived, but with their lucky rubbing stones. (Ingrid Schlueter, www.sliceoflaodicea.com/)

Giving to God is supposed to be one of the most important things that we can do as Christians; yet, when God was actually here in the flesh he never took one offering; he never once gave the people an opportunity to give directly to God in human form. Perhaps because, according to Jesus, if we want to give directly to him we should give to the poor (Matthew 25:31-46), NOT TO A RICH PREACHER ON TV.

If Jesus came today do you think he would live like the ministers listed above? No! He would set an example by not living in opulence. He would have a nice house, but not a mansion. You would never see Elijah living in a palace. He did not run away from Jezebel to his summer home, he slept under a tree. Are these prosperity preachers greater than Elijah? Jeremiah said:

> And Jehovah said to me, The prophets prophesy lies in My name; I did not send them, nor have I commanded them, nor did I speak to them. They prophesy to you a false vision and a <u>worthless divination</u>, and a thing of no value, and the deceit of their heart. (Jeremiah 14:14) (MKJV)

Kenneth Copeland said, *"God told me whatever your heart can believe you can have it in 2016."* You can have whatever you can believe for. I guess Paul did not have much faith, because he was homeless, hungry, and in rags at the time that he wrote 1 Cor:

> Even to this present hour we both hunger and thirst, and are poorly clothed and beaten and homeless. (1 Cor. 4:11) (MEV)

But that must have just been for 2016, LOL. Richard Roberts is Oral Robert's son. He first wife said:

> "We lived like characters in a novel or a made-for-TV movie about the beautiful people," Richard Roberts's first wife said. The fruits of Seed Faith included a Beverly Hills house, a Mercedes and a Jaguar, and vacations in Palm Beach and the South Seas. (*Grand Theft Jesus: The Hijacking of Religion*, by Robert S. McElvaine, page 68.)

(2) Dangerous Money

Jesus said:

> And I tell you, make friends for yourselves by means of <u>unrighteous wealth</u>, so that when it fails they may receive you into the eternal dwellings. (Luke 16:9) (ESV)

In this passage Jesus said that you should give your wealth to others while you are here on Earth, which will make them so grateful that they will be present to welcome you into heaven. So by giving to those in need you actually create friends for eternity. This is the proper use of earthly wealth, which Jesus literally calls "unrighteous." It says the same in the original Greek. How can people read that Jesus called wealth *unrighteous*, yet believe that God wants us wealthy? People who follow these blind guides will fall into the ditch with them.

The parable of the sower is found in Mark 4 and Luke 8:

"[The seed] are <u>choked by the cares and riches and pleasures</u> <u>of life</u>, ... (Luke 8:14) (MEV)

Here it clearly says that life's riches can choke out the truth of God's Word! If the <u>riches of this world can choke out the Word</u> <u>of God</u>, then Christians <u>should be very careful to not have a lot</u> <u>of those riches</u>. As it stands now, the gold-loving preachers do not believe the above statement, and preach that Christians should be millionaires. Satan is the one who wants Christians to become wealthy because he knows the harm it will do us.

Many rich people actually live cursed lives, such as J. Paul Getty who had one child die of a brain tumor, another committed suicide at age 48, another became a drug addict. His granddaughter Irene said, "*I hate money... I don't want to be a Getty*" (Interview on Dateline NBC, 1996). Irene was a drug addict with AIDS. Her brother suffered a drug overdose and became nearly a vegetable. Many rich people have lived the same kind of nightmare.

Today, there are more wealthy people in the United States than ever before. In 2015 there were 145,000 people worth 25 million or more, 1.2 million worth 5 - 24 million. The total number of millionaires in 2015 was 10.4 million, up 300,000 from 2014, and continuing to grow. And in 2016 America had a mere 536 billionaires, more than double the next country, China, with 251. (www.cnbc.com/2016/03/07/record-number-of-millionaires-living-in-the-us.html, and en.wikipedia.org)

Many of the super-rich do <u>not</u> plan to leave all their wealth to their children because they know the harm that it does, so they are giving away billions of dollars to hospitals, universities, and other charities. Oscar Shaffer, a rich hedge fund manager, is one of those who believe the rich should leave their wealth to charities. He said, "*I know a lot of people, sons and daughters of wealthy people, whose wealth has basically crippled them*" (*Untold Wealth: The Rise of the Super Rich*, CNBC, 2008).

Even people who win the lottery suffer greatly in so many ways that most of them wish they had not won. This happens so frequently that it is called "*the curse of the lottery.*" Several TV documentaries have been produced and articles written detailing the trouble that follows lottery winners.

> One Southeastern family won $4.2 million in the early '90s. They bought a huge house and succumbed to repeated family requests for help in paying off debts. The house, cars and relatives ate the whole pot. Eleven years later, the couple is divorcing, the house is sold and they have to split what is left of the lottery proceeds. The wife got a very small house. The husband has moved in with the kids. Even the life insurance they bought ended up getting cashed in. "It was not the pot of gold at the end of the rainbow," says their financial advisor. (*8 Lottery Winners Who Lost Their Millions*, by bankrate.com)

Typical results from winning the lottery are: divorce, lawsuits, family problems, drug addiction, bankruptcy, debt, and sometimes even death. Most winnings do not last more than a few years. You might think that only non-Christians are affected in this way, but you would be wrong. Winning the lottery destroys Christians as well. Jack Whittaker had a good life before winning the lottery, and even owned a construction company:

> In 2002, Jack Whittaker won the largest individual payout in U.S. lottery history. "I can take the money," Whittaker said at the time. "I can take this much money and do a lot of good with this much money right now."

> But it didn't work out like that. Whittaker's life was consumed by hardship, including the death of his beloved granddaughter Brandi, who was a victim of a drug overdose, and the breakup of his marriage. "If I knew what was going to transpire, honestly, I would have torn the ticket up," said Jewell Whittaker, Jack Whittaker's ex-wife. (*Curse of the Lottery Winners: Winning Millions Often Results in Hardship*, ABC News, 3-11, 07)

Even though this family was confirmed Christians, the money destroyed them. Another Christian was Billie Bob Harrell Jr. who won 37 million dollars in the Texas Lottery. He had so many problems he ended up committing suicide:

> "He was a good Christian man. But this money created a fantasy world for him. And unfortunately this was something that he lived out in real life. He gave into temptation and that's not an unusual thing to happen, when you have a large sum of money." (Darly LePage, certified financial planner. lotterypost.com)

The author of the above article also said, "*When you win a large sum of money, you would think that your problems go away. In reality, a new set of problems come in.*" Yet, people are gullible enough to believe that God wants them to be rich! <u>Stop listening to those lying servants of Satan! Those lying snakes; wolves in sheep's clothing</u>!

Tertullian (160-220) said, "*Nothing that is God's is obtainable by money.*" Yes, it is true that <u>some Christians can be wealthy</u>, but they need to be careful of the warnings in the Word of God, and they need to share their wealth with poor Christians in Asia and Africa, and even here in America.

(3) Sowing Seed

Don Basham, one of the founders of the Charismatic movement, relates his experience with giving and receiving:

> Some years ago I felt strongly urged by the Lord to give $150 to a fellow minister in need. I obeyed, even though at the time that $150 represented about 75 percent of my total financial resources. That simple act of doing what the Lord wanted was followed by months of unexpected prosperity.
>
> A few years later, in a time of relative abundance, I gave $1,000 to another ministry I felt was worthy of support. But this time there was no flood of blessing in return. At first I felt resentful that God hadn't been impressed by my generosity. But eventually, I acknowledged that the second gift had been my idea, not God's. God let me give the gift, but He hadn't told me to give it. (*The Way I See It*, p.106)

I can relate a similar story. One time God told me to give $25.00 to a particular evangelist, which was a lot of money to me, and within a month my income almost doubled, but even then it was still only about $300 per month. Does that mean every time I give $25, or an equal percentage of my present income, that I can expect my income to increase that much? Not a chance.

The key here is that Don Basham and I had obeyed God when God told us to give. Obedience is better than sacrifice. The increase in income was not a sowing and reaping principle, it was a reward for obeying God. I had given more than that before to the same minister with no noticeable return. If God tells you to give money to someone you can be confident that you will be rewarded one way or another, because you obeyed, not because you sowed a seed. If God does not tell you to give, you will still be rewarded, but not to the same extent, and it may only be with heavenly reward. If God does not tell you to give you cannot expect a monetary return because there is no sowing and reaping principle that works like the prosperity gospel says it does.

Here is a popular verse of the prosperity preachers:

> Be not deceived. God is not mocked. For whatever a man sows, that will he also reap. 8 For the one who sows to his own flesh will from the flesh reap corruption, but the one who sows to the Spirit will from the Spirit reap eternal life. (Gal. 6:7-8) (MEV)

Now, this appears to be a straightforward message of sowing and reaping that can be applied to cash, but let's take a closer look. Notice the underlined words, *"the one who sows to his own flesh will from the flesh reap corruption."* Your flesh is destined to die, so sowing to make the flesh happy and comfortable will not bring a good harvest, but only corruption. Sowing to the flesh includes spending your money on material comforts and luxuries. Therefore, your sowing should be spiritual, that is to bring a spiritual harvest. This view of the passage is proven by the context. Paul continues:

> 9 And let us not grow weary in doing good, for in due season we shall reap, if we do not give up. 10 Therefore, as we have opportunity, let us do good to all people, especially to those who are of the household of faith. (6:9-10)

Here Paul said the Galatians should sow spiritual seed by doing good works, such as providing food and clothing for poor people, or helping those who are sick, "especially" Christians. If Paul heard a preacher say that the above passage refers to sowing money and getting more money back, Paul would probably punch him in the face.

Avanzini's book about Mark chapter 4 is full of gross error. He said the parable is about sowing and reaping money. Jesus said:

> Then He said to them, "Do you not understand this parable? How then will you understand all the parables?" (4:13) (MEV)

Jesus said this parable should be the easiest of all the parables to understand, so if you do not understand this easy parable, how can you understand any of the other parables? So it is no surprise that Avanzini does not understand the parable in Mark 4, which is the easiest of all to understand! Here is the parable and Jesus' interpretation:

> 3 "Now listen! A farmer went out to scatter seed in a field. 4 While the farmer was scattering the seed, some of it fell along the road and was eaten by birds. 5 . . . other seeds fell where thornbushes grew up and choked out the plants. So they did not produce any grain. 8 But a few seeds did fall on good ground where the plants grew and produced thirty or sixty or even a hundred times as much as was scattered."... (Mark 4) (CEV)

Avanzini said the first part of the parable is about actual farming. It should be clear to anyone with good sense that this parable is not about farming. What the farmer is spreading is the message of the Kingdom of God. Mark 4 continues:

> 15 "The seeds that fell along the road are the people who hear the message. But Satan soon comes and snatches it away from them. . . . 18 The seeds that fell among the thornbushes are also people who hear the message. 19 But they start worrying about the needs of this life. They are fooled by the desire to get rich and to have all kinds of other things. So the message gets choked out, and they never produce anything. 20 The seeds that fell on good ground are the people who hear and welcome the message. They produce thirty or sixty or even a hundred times as much as was planted." (Mark 4) (ESV)

Avanzini said that Jesus gave two parables, but that is false. Jesus gave one parable, then he interpreted it, there are not two parables here. Avanzini said that in the second parable, actually the interpretation, the agricultural seed has become money: "*There you have it. When you give your money into the gospel, God automatically gives it seed-power.*"

Jesus never said the seed represented money, he said it represented the <u>Word of Almighty God!</u> If the seed is the Word, it's not money. Nothing could be more blasphemous than to say a reference to God's Word actually refers to money! This false teaching is an abomination!

The correct interpretation of the parable in Mark 4 is this: The ground represents the hearts of men and women. The seed represents the Word of God. So it's not money that produces the crop, but the Word of God which is sown into the hearts of people. Some people receive the seed, that is, hear the Word of God being preached, but they allow the cares of this life rob them of the truth. These people receive the Christian faith but barely grow and do not produce any fruit. Other people hear the truth but <u>because of their desire for wealth, the truth is choked off</u> and they never grow to become mature Christians. Some people are like the good ground that produces a great crop by growing spiritually to produce much fruit such as a Godly family, using their money to feed the hungry, etc.

Continuing in Mark 4, verses 21-25 refer to understanding the truth of God's Word:

> He said to them, "Is a candle brought to be put under a basket or under a bed and not to be set on a candlestick? 22 For there is nothing hidden except to be revealed; neither is anything kept secret except to be proclaimed. 23 If anyone has ears to hear, let him hear."

> 24 He said to them, "Take heed what you hear. The measure you give will be measured for you, and to you who hear will more be given. 25 <u>For to him who has will more be given. And from him who has not will be taken, even what he has.</u>" (Mark 4:21-25) (MEV)

These verses say that God intends for all truth to come to light, but not everyone will understand. It says whoever rightly divides the Word of God will be given even more understanding so he may understand more of God's Word than he now does. And if anyone does not rightly divide the Word, what little understanding he does have will be taken away.

As you would expect, Avanzini said the passage refers to understanding how to receive a great harvest of money. He claims that you must understand what the Bible teaches about wealth in order to receive a return from your seed money. Here are his words:

> Clearly our Lord is telling us that with this new insight, the more you understand about Him and His Word when you give, the greater your rate of return will be. . . . The more understanding you have, the greater your return will be, for he who has understanding will receive, and he who doesn't have understanding, even the wealth he has will be taken from him.

Avanzini said that if you give without the proper understanding of the prosperity message, that God will actually cause you to become poorer. In other words, if you do not believe in the prosperity message you will become poor, even if you give money to churches, missionaries, and preachers. If this were true then there should be no wealthy Christians except those who believe in the prosperity message. Wow, so it is evident that the prosperity preachers are just plain stupid. Do they even know to come indoors out of the rain?

Because people have given them many millions of dollars without getting a return, the false teachers have also developed the doctrine that the seed must remain in the ground for a long time before it will grow to produce a harvest. So, the reason you do not get anything back is because you have not waited long enough; even money-seed must be allowed to grow, which is pure nonsense.

How many years does it take for God to find someone a job? God is more than able to get someone a job today, if you have applied for jobs, then you could be hired immediately! No, it does not take a long time for God to act; this nonsense is just a cover so that they can continue to get your money even though you are not increasing in wealth. Avanzini actually makes an unintentional confession below:

> I can personally testify to the difficulty that goes with this waiting time, for my wife and I have been through it. Waiting caused us to look like fools to our family. It was as if we were standing still financially. Everyone seemed to be doing better than we were. We gave and gave, and then just gave some more. However, no matter how much we gave, we just didn't seem to be getting ahead, as the others in our family were. All we could see were the stalks. Oh, yes! God met our needs, but we <u>didn't seem to be accumulating anything</u>.

He reveals here that he wanted more than his needs met, he wanted to "accumulate" money and things. He shows his greed and materialism. He reveals his desire for financial gain and that he gave money with the wrong motives so he could use the money on material pleasures. He goes on to reveal that his trust is not in God, but in money:

> How wonderful it is when the farmer thrusts in the sickle and takes the harvest! . . . This glorious feeling is especially wonderful when it comes in the financial realm. You have unspeakable joy when the fear of insufficiency is gone from your life.

How can anyone who fears insufficiency have any trust in God? What a shame that he put so much trust in money, rather than God to supply what he needs. But the fact of the matter is, when you give money for the purpose of getting lots of money back, which is the whole doctrine of the prosperity preachers, then you are giving with wrong motives, so God will not prosper you. The Apostle James said:

> 2 . . . You covet but you cannot get what you want, so you quarrel and fight. You do not have because you do not ask God. 3 When you ask, you do not receive, <u>because you ask with wrong motives, that you may spend what you get on your pleasures.</u> (James 4:2-3) (NIV)

Nothing is said in this passage about not receiving from God because they did not give money as seed. God will give to those who ask, if they are in need, or desire to use the money to help the poor and the spread of the Gospel. What this passage says is that many people do not receive from God because they are asking out of greed; they want jewelry, expensive cars, expensive homes, etc. <u>The above passage alone proves the entire prosperity message is totally false</u>. In spite of what the above passage says, the money preachers say that asking is not enough, we must give money (to them) before we will get anything! Of course they would say that, that is the only way they can afford their millionaire-lifestyles.

The prosperity gospel says, *"God has blessed me with two coats, why has he not blessed you with a coat? You need to give some seed money to the preacher and God will give you a coat."* While the true gospel says, if you have two coats you should share with the person who has none:

> Produce fruit that is consistent with repentance! . . . He answered them, "The person who has two coats must share with the one who doesn't have any, and the person who has food must do the same." (Luke 3:8, 11) (ISV)

Of course many people have more than one coat, the important point we should get from those verses is the principle of sharing. Can you now see how *off* the prosperity gospel is? It is all about getting stuff from God, but the true gospel says sometimes our needs are met by other people giving to us, which means we should give to others and not expect God to do it directly. But, you may say, what about this other verse?

> "Give, and it will be given to you: Good measure, pressed down, shaken together, and running over will men give unto you. For with the measure you use, it will be measured unto you." (Luke 6:38) (MEV)

This is one of the favorite prosperity passages, because it seems to clearly show the prosperity message. But Jesus does not contradict himself, so is he here telling us that when we give money to a preacher that we will get back a whole heap of cash? No. In context, Jesus was teaching reciprocity, as the verses just before that one show:

"Judge not, and you shall not be judged. Condemn not, and you will not be condemned. Forgive, and you shall be forgiven." (Luke 6:37) (MEV)

Taking into consideration everything Jesus taught about money and giving, and the context of this verse, he was saying you reap what you sow. If you do good to others, good will happen to you. This is the basic philosophy that Jesus taught and the apostles taught. It does not refer to giving money to a preacher, but giving to others in general. It does not mean that if you sow money you get even more money, but it means if you give money, food, or clothing, to help people in need, when you are in need someone will help you. At the most, it could mean that you will not come into great need, but it does not mean that God will give you piles of money when you give to a preacher on TV.

People who help other people are greatly loved, and those who are helped will do just about anything for them. This is one reason people who help other people will receive back in heaps. If you give generously to others, you will be given to. And if you find yourself in need there will be no lack of people willing to run to your aid. It makes no direct reference to sowing and reaping literal cash.

People who give gifts to other people at Christmas or birthdays are more likely to receive gifts from others at Christmas or birthdays. Giving generously to others should be a way of life, and if it is, then you will be given to just as generously as you gave to others; "*with the measure you use it will be measured to you.*"

(4) Abundance of Possessions

. . . I came that they may have life, and that they may have it more abundantly. (John 10:10) (MEV)

This is another verse the prosperity preachers use to support their claims that Christ wants us to have abundant possessions. But they disregard what Jesus said in Luke:

Then He said to them, "Take heed and beware of covetousness. For a man's life does not consist in the abundance of his possessions." (Luke 12:15) (MEV)

Since Jesus does not contradict himself, there can be no question about it, abundant life is not abundant possessions. And we should be careful least we start thinking that it is. Many people have been deceived by riches, they have been overcome by greed so much that they believe abundant life equals abundant possessions, or an abundance of money in the bank.

What's more, in John 10 above, the Greek for "life" here is zoe (2222, Strong's number), which relates to the spiritual life. Why didn't Luke use bios (979), which refers to this physical world and refers to *"duration, means, and manner of life"* (CWD). Because <u>Jesus was not talking about material abundance but spiritual abundance</u>. Bios is translated "possessions" in 1 John 3:17, *"If anyone has material possessions and sees his brother in need . . ."* (NIV). So when the Bible referred to this physical world, it used "bios," which means Jesus was *not* referring to the material side of life when he said he came to give us abundant life; it means abundant *spiritual* life. The Apostle John said:

> I pray that all may go well with you and that you may be in good health, even as your soul is well. (MEV)

This verse does not say that we should become financially prosperous as our spirit grows in Christ, which is what the false teachers claim. But it does say that the person John was addressing (Gaius) was doing well spiritually, and John prayed that Gaius should also do well or prosper in all other areas of his life, just as his soul was prospering. But that does not mean wealth.

It should be clear by now that, that in the Bible, to prosper does not mean to become rich. Jesus did not contradict himself and neither did his apostles contradict him. Here again we must look at the teachings of Jesus and the apostles as a whole. To prosper means to have everything you need in all areas of your life. It does not refer to having lots of unnecessary luxuries. It means having enough clothes to wear for all occasions, but it does not mean having several closets full of expensive clothes.

The writer of Hebrews made it clear that we should not even desire more than what God chooses to give us: *"Keep your lives free from the love of money and be content with what you have*" (Hebrews 13:5) (NIV). Do the prosperity preachers tell you to be content with what you have? No! In an issue of *Charisma Magazine*, a Christian singer said:

> "Although God has blessed us, I need something that catapults me into the stratosphere financially. I don't need to be just pretty well off. I need to be wealthy, extremely wealthy, and I don't even mind saying it." (July 2000)

God help us. Do you see what is happening with the prosperity gospel? It is causing many people to become consumed by greed. The preachers of the get-rich gospel are causing many people to become dissatisfied with what God has provided. Creflo Dollar has the people in his congregation to shout to God, "*I WANT MY STUFF, I WANT MY STUFF!*"

The get-rich doctrines cause people to give to God out of greed, to command angels to bring them money, to demand that God give them the money he owes them, and it is all the fault of the prosperity pirates. People who are not content with what God provides are in danger of God's judgment.

The false prophets of greed don't teach you about the judgment of God that came upon the Hebrews because they were not satisfied with what God chose to give them. God provided manna for the people to eat, but the people soon tired of it because they actually ate better while they were in Egypt. The people mumbled and complained and asked for meat, so God sent them tons of quail. But before they could even eat it, while it was still in their mouths, people started dying from a plague (Numbers 11:33). Many people died of the plague, because they were not satisfied with what God provided.

Though we are under the grace of the Gospel, people can still bring judgment upon themselves by becoming unhappy with God because of their humble circumstances and wanting more.

(5) Comments

After I published the *Prosperity Gospel Exposed* in 2011, along with videos to promote it, there have been many comments posted to the videos and the website. Here is part of a typical comment:

> The devil sold the "church" the lie that poverty is the way to go. The bible say's Jesus became poor, so that we might become rich. When we criticize without offering a solution -what good is that?? . . . You think God is poor??? Why does His family have to be poor??? . . . (G. Emerson, Mesa, Arizona)

The get-rich preachers are lying to people, telling them that those who do not believe in the prosperity gospel believe that we should be poor. In case you are a follower of the WOF, there is no Protestant church that teaches such nonsense. Just drive by the parking lots of any church in town and you will see all the nice cars, so most other Christians are NOT POOR. And they do not teach poverty, but they know that God does not promise to make us rich! Biblical prosperity is NOT becoming wealthy; it is having your needs met and even having enough to share with those who are poor.

It is also a lie that Jesus died on the cross so you can become rich; that is an abomination. The dangers of wealth have already been shown in this chapter. Jesus died for our sins, so we can have eternal life, that is what Paul was referring to when he said, *"though he was rich, for your sake he became poor, so that you by his poverty might become rich"* (2 Cor. 8:9) (ESV).

It is also a lie that Jesus was materially rich in heaven and died on the cross so that we can become rich in material goods here on earth. It means rich in the same way that Jesus was rich in heaven. In heaven, gold is not worth much because it is used for pavement. You think Jesus was materially rich in heaven? Did he have a room piled with gold coins and gold goblets? What does a spirit need material things for? Nothing, that's what. Spirits do not sleep so they do not need a bed, they do not need a closet full of clothing, they do not need to travel in a car, they do not need to buy food, etc. If they want a change of garment they just think about it and it happens. Earthly riches are worthless in heaven.

Neither my first book nor this one merely criticizes without offering a solution; truth is the solution, believe the truth.

Chapter 10:
Satan's Ministers

(1) In League With Satan

If all the above is not enough to shock you to your core, there is another type of false minister who is even worse than all of the above. This group of ministers are not merely deceived, they know they are in league with the devil. You may have heard of movie stars and rock stars who made deals with the devil to become rich and famous; well, preachers have done it also! Paul said that Satan appears as an angel of light, therefore it is not a surprise that Satan literally has followers who are big name preachers:

> For such are false apostles and deceitful workers, disguising themselves as apostles of Christ. 14 And no wonder! For even Satan disguises himself as an angel of light. 15 Therefore it is no great thing if <u>his ministers also disguise themselves as ministers of righteousness</u>, whose end will be according to their works. (2 Cor. 11:13-15) (MEV).

These are the genuine wolves in sheep's clothing. I mentioned how most of the books and websites that expose the WOF and prosperity gospel are actually against all forms of Pentecostalism, and against all forms of the move of the Holy Spirit; this is why they are ignored by Pentecostals and Charismatics. And this is why I first scoffed when I saw websites and videos that claimed there are big name preachers who were literally in league with the devil.

I scoffed when I saw pictures of these preachers who clearly had their hands and fingers forming the sign of Satan. I thought to myself how the preachers were just gesturing with their hands and happened to move their fingers into the same configuration that is used by Satanists. But I recently saw a video that blew my mind, it was an absolute shocker. It seems that Satan requires his ministers to acknowledge him by signs <u>and words.</u>

On a video you can clearly hear Jessie Duplantis teaching, and then in a slightly lower volume and a little faster than normal, he said, *"I'm with Satan."* At another time Duplantis says, ". . . you become a son that serves, [slight pause] Satan."* Really, you can tell that it is his voice and not dubbed in by editing the video. In this book you just have to take my word for it, but when you hear it for yourself it is very powerful. Therefore, I copied the video and cut it down to the important parts. You can watch it on my website www.usbibleprophecy.com or on Youtube by the title: *Satan's False Prophets Exposed.*

The video also has Kenneth Copeland speaking to Satan. After taking, or perhaps while taking an offering, he pretends to speak in tongues on and off to disguise what he actually says. At one point he says, *"Tie my money, Satan."* I take this to mean that he is making sure that the money given is credited to Satan, and not God.

The Bible says that the Holy Spirit will bring things to our memory (John 14:26). I used to watch Benny Hinn on TV and one time a woman was laid out by the power of his counterfeit anointing and I thought I heard him say, *"Satan take her."* I remember thinking to myself that he did not say what it sounded like he said, and I am sure that everyone else who heard it thought the same thing, but <u>now I see that he really said it.</u>

In another part of the video, Hinn interviews a woman who believes she has been healed. He is holding the microphone in his right hand and stands to the left of the woman. Hinn's assistant is standing on the other side of the woman and he raises his hand with fingers outstretched and then does the sign of Satan and holds it there. Hinn considers it too noticeable, so he moves the microphone from his right hand to his left and then brushes the other man's fingers to remove the sign of Satan. Here are the still pictures:

Open hand

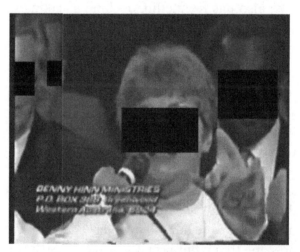

Sign of Satan

Officially, the sign of Satan means that the two fingers sticking up represent the horns of a goat, and the two fingers bent down and the thumb represent the Father, Son, and Holy Spirit are in subjection to Satan. Often the thumb is seen sticking up, but it is really supposed to be bent as well.

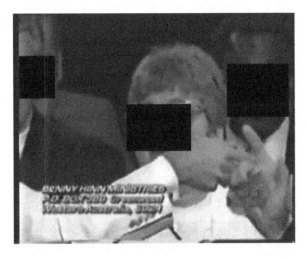

Hinn moves microphone to his left hand and brushes fingers.

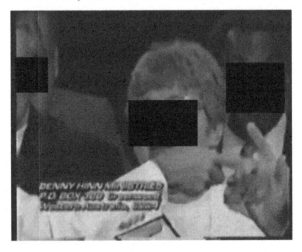

No more sign of Satan.

It is in slow motion in the video. Shocking? Yes, but when I learned the above information I said to myself, "*Finally, proof that they belong to Satan.*" You may want to say, why would they have a pact with Satan? Have they no fear of hell? Why would <u>anyone</u> make a deal with the devil? But they do it all the time, and many more even worship Satan.

You may say that they spend their time teaching on the Bible, but if you think about what they teach, it is off-the-wall lunacy.

They teach lies and confusion. You may say that they help people become Christians. Yes, it is possible for people to get saved and filled with the Holy Spirit under the ministry of an almost true yet false prophet. But if someone is converted expecting God to make them rich, then they are not converted to Jesus and the Father, they become worshipers of the golden calf. It is therefore a false conversion.

This is what Satan wants. Satan is ok with you being a Christian if you are a deceived Christian, because the hardest people to convert to the truth are the people who think they have it already. It is very hard for deceived people to see and know the truth. <u>Satan's lies are the most deadly when they are mixed in with truth</u>. So what they teach is designed to keep you from the truth and keep you deceived and keep you defeated.

The deals could have gone down something like this: Satan sends one of his emissaries to a preacher and offers a deal. The preacher can keep preaching and preach whatever he wants, but he must acknowledge Satan with the sign and with words in some of their messages. Then Satan will cause them to become rich and famous preachers. But what they do not realize is that once they make the deal, they no longer hear from God, if they ever did, but Satan now speaks to them in the place of God.

These false prophets are not only teaching useless garbage, but they are actually speaking to Satan in their messages and the people still give them tons of money! They must be laughing all the way to the bank. Kenneth Copeland said on a video that in the entire history of his ministry he had taken in over 1 billion dollars. WOW, all given in an effort to get money back from God, but there was no return on money bound up by Satan!

I must give credit to the fellows who dug up the footage and created the original 1-hour video: The video says, "*God's reddened ark*" at the start and at the end gives credit to Bill Koulaxizellis for the Toronto footage. The first posting of the video which I found was dated July of 2013, by John Oganyan. He died in 2015 at age 35. Did Satan, or one of his followers, kill Oranyan?

I am not afraid of Satan's attacks; Satan has been trying to kill me for almost 25 years. In late 1993 I decided to do something that Satan did not like, and immediately I heard a demon audibly threaten me. It said, in a high-pitched squeaky voice, "*You do that and I'll kill you!*" Shortly after that, a group of educated people, mostly "Christian*s,*" began meeting together to plot how they could destroy me by any means possible. I was accused of every crime in the book, even framed for crimes, and other people not connected to that group have also tried to destroy me; it's a miracle I am still here. I reached the end of my rope several times, but God saved me. Since they cannot kill me or send me to prison, they spread slander everywhere I go. Some of them have died from various causes, yet they continue. They believe they are doing God a favor, but they are really doing the devil's work. It is surprising how easily demons can influence people by putting thoughts into their minds.

More investigation needs to be done to find more of these statements that prove these preachers are Satanists, but there are many thousands of hours of video footage to watch, so it would take thousands of people watching them for weeks to find more proof. If you have any of those video tapes or DVDs please watch them and send me a copy of the footage or at least send the name of the tape or DVD: okmedia@gmail.com.

There are other preachers that should also be examined to see if they present the same evidence of being in league with Satan, which are Joyce Myers, Rodney Howard Brown, Joel Osteen and any rich and famous preacher, not just WOF preachers. I am sure that NOT all TV preachers are in league with Satan, but they could still be Satan's puppets.

Brown can be seen on my video giving the sign of Satan. He is also good buddies with K. Copeland. Brown is seen on the video speaking at a Copeland convention. Likewise, Joyce Myers is seen giving the sign. She is also seen wearing a blouse with upside down crosses printed on it. The upside down cross has a long history in Catholicism because it is the way Peter died, but Satanists use it as a symbol of disrespect and mockery of the sacrifice of Christ on the cross. No Protestant preacher in his/her right mind would wear a garment with upside down crosses on it.

(2) Dumber than Rocks

Jesus referred to the Holy Spirit as the "*Spirit of Truth:*"

> But when the Spirit of truth comes, He will guide you into all truth. . . (John 16:13) (MEV)

This verse tells us why these big name WOF preachers teach so much lunacy, they do NOT have the Spirit of Truth. One leader spoke out about the growing heresy in the Charismatic Movement in 2010 in an issue of *Charisma Magazine*'s online prophetic bulletin, *Prophetic Insight*. Loren Sandford said:

> I find myself beyond appalled and deeply concerned about a trend I have seen developing in the body of Christ for several years now. I believe this trend is propelling us toward a crisis in the charismatic Christian world that may well derail and destroy revival before it can take firm root.
>
> It seems that in the quest to become more and more supernatural many have increasingly wandered away from the plumb line of solid Christian doctrine and responsible, accurate interpretation of the Scriptures. The resultant weirdness flowing from key leaders in various places is leading many followers into what can only be called heresy. (Sept. 27, 2010)

Perhaps the reason false doctrines are growing is because God is removing the good sense that people once had; they refuse to believe the truth, but instead desire wealth and other strange spiritual experiences and seek after them as if they were a lost child. The majority of the false doctrines within the Charismatic Movement are coming from the Word of Faith group. Here are some of their shockingly stupid teachings. Jesse Duplantis said:

> I've never had the Lord say, "Jessie, I think that car is a little too nice." I've had vehicles and the Lord said, "Would you please go park that at your house. Don't put that in front of my house. I don't want people to think that I'm a poor God." (Duplantis, *When Will we Yield To The Anointing of Wealth II*, April 10, 2005)

Hank Hanagraf reports on some other lunatic teaching and lies of Jesse Duplantis:

After clarifying that he is not just a millionaire but a multimillion-aire, Jesse says to Hagee, "The Lord, I give him the glory, is my comforter. If he is my comforter, Dr. Hagee, I live in comfort. That's not only spiritually—that's physically too. Because when you've got some stuff it brings you comfort." Jesse goes on to pontificate that those who would say otherwise "know nothing about the Bible." (Jesse Duplantis, Praise The Lord, Trinity Broadcasting Network, July 11, 2003) (www.equip.org/audio/word-of-faith-revisionism/)

"When you've got some stuff it brings you comfort." WOW, clear-ly he has his focus on material goods instead of the things of the spirit. The Holy Spirit is the Comforter, not material goods! Du-plantis thinks that after God created all the animals that they were just like mannequins, stiff and lifeless until Adam gave them life! This is one of the most amazing displays of stupidity I have ever heard:

God made a horse and didn't have the foggiest idea what a horse was. . . . Did you know that they were not alive when He brought them [to Adam]? . . . "and whatsoever Adam called eve-ry"-- what? "living." They weren't alive. . . . He named 500,000 species and life came into them, and he gave you creative abil-ity and He says, "Produce life." . . . They were just like Adam, mannequins formed. God didn't know what they were. . . . He said, "Adam, do what I do. That's why I give you domin-ion." (www.youtube.com/watch?v=DDYyym5tD20)

God traveled to earth in a space ship called light. (K. Copeland, *What Happened From the Cross to the Throne*, Tape)

Justin Peters says about Benny Hinn:

Hinn maintains that unless signs and wonders accompany the preaching of the gospel, then the gospel in and of itself has no power. This statement alone is more than sufficient to prove that he really has no understanding of the true transformational pow-er of the Gospel of Christ as recorded in the written Word of God (Luke 16: 27-31; Romans 1:16). (www.gty.org/library/ blog/ B140207/has-benny-hinn-repented)

Benny Hinn is well-known for having taught that each person of the Trinity is also a trinity, with a body, soul and spirit, mak-ing 9 in the Godhead, LOL. He has also taught that female humans originally gave birth out of their sides! (*Christianity in Crisis for the 21ˢᵗ Century*, page 11, Hank Hanegraaff)

Creflo Dollar can be seen on video on Youtube teaching that Jesus was not God because the Bible says God does not sleep or slumber, yet it says Jesus was asleep in the boat! Another LOL moment. Why is this dumb? God is spirit, so he does not need to sleep, but while Jesus was here on Earth he had a human body that required him to eat and sleep just like any other human body, but that does not mean that he was just a mere human, no, he was both God and man. This was established in the *Chalcedonean Creed* and believed by all branches of Christianity, except WOF, Jehovah's Witness, and other cults.

(3) Benny Hinn: Big Time Liar and Counterfeit

On a guest post on the *Grace To You* website of John MacArthur, Justin Peters relates information that is well known about Benny Hinn, showing that he is a lair:

> Claims he and a Catholic priest channeled the power of God to heal practically every patient at a hospital in Sault Sainte Marie, Ontario, Canada. (Hinn, Welcome Holy Spirit (Nashville, TN: Thomas Nelson Publishers, 1997), pgs. 232-235.)

> Claimed to have video of Jesus walking around in one of his meetings. When asked to show the video, his staff said it had been "misplaced." (I attempted to get an audience with Hinn but was refused. I was successful only in speaking with one of his staff at Hinn's ministry headquarters in Grapevine, Texas.)

> On Dec. 31, 1989, Hinn went into a trance and said God was giving him (in real time) prophecies about major events that would occur before the end of the next decade. Hinn predicted the total collapse of the American economy within a decade. He declared that during the 1990s the East Coast would be ravaged by earthquakes; a female would be elected as president; Fidel Castro would die in office; a "short man dictator" would arise; the rapture of the church would occur; and the homosexual community of America would be destroyed by fire "in '94 or '95, no later than that." (Hinn, audio clip recorded Dec. 31, 1989, at Orlando Christian Center. Audio on file.)

> Claimed that an image of Jesus appeared on the wall of his

church and "stayed for eight weeks." Hinn says, "Even the people who studied the Shroud of Turin came to see this image. . . . the mouth [of Jesus] would move, the Lord's mouth would move ... but His mouth would only move as I was preaching." (Hinn, TIYD program with Oral Roberts as guest. Video on file.)

Claimed (repeatedly) that he once saw a man raised from the dead on the platform on which he was standing. When later questioned by a reporter about the incident he said, "I did not see it. In that one case we did hear about it." (Benny Hinn interview with unknown reporter. Video on file.)

Claimed to have a department that verifies all his healings. ("I have spoken with a former employee of Hinn who says not only that the healings are not verified but that such a department does not even exist.") (www.gty.org/library/blog/B140207/has-benny-hinn-repented)

Healing is genuine, but it rarely happened in the extremely large healing crusades you have seen on TV by Benny Hinn. Hinn makes many claims, but few if any have ever been verified. Several news organizations have tried to verify the healings reported by the world's most famous "healer" but they are unable to do so. Kathryn Kuhlman published several books filled with documented healings that were investigated by journalists and confirmed by doctors, but Hinn has never published such a book. He claims to have documented cases but never provides this evidence to the news media, even after repeated requests.

What about the people on stage who say they have been healed? Many times Hinn has declared people healed of cancer or AIDS on the platform but when they are followed by journalists or film crews to their doctors, they discover they were not healed. They truly believe they have been healed because the symptoms have gone away, but when they go home the symptoms return. This is the reason that the healings cannot be verified. This happens because our minds make us think that we have been healed; I will explain.

Let me tell you what happened to me many years ago. I was visiting a friend and he had forgotten to turn the heat on and it became very cold during the night. I was sleeping on the couch with a blanket, but it was not enough to keep me warm. But I did not know that the heat was not on, I thought I heard the heat come on frequently during the night, but as it turned out it was not the heater but the refrigerator coming on in the kitchen not far away from the couch. I was shivering in the cold and then I would hear what I thought was the heater come on, and because I expected to get warmer, I actually got warm. I stopped shivering and went back to sleep. But some time later I would wake up cold and shivering and I would wait until the "heater" came on again, then I would get warm again and go back to sleep. This went on all night. But I never actually got warm, it was my mind which made me think I was getting warm because I was expecting to get warm.

This is exactly what is happening to the people who believe they have been healed in Hinn's crusades. Their symptoms go away because they are expecting their symptoms to go away, but they are not really healed.

Another reason the symptoms go away for some people is because of the presence of God. Even though Hinn is a false minister, the many thousands of people in the auditorium are praying and worshiping God, so they can feel God's presence. God said in his Word that where two or three are gathered in his name he will be in the midst of them. And the more people there are in one place worshiping God, the more of his presence there is. It is in this atmosphere that people believe they are being healed, so the symptoms go away, but they have not been healed.

This is called the placebo effect. When drug companies test their drugs they give some people the real drug but others get a sugar pill without knowing it. Some people will believe they are getting better when they are only taking the sugar pill. This is such an established fact of the human brain, that no drug can be approved unless it is tested this way. Some people taking the sugar pill will even have drug side effects, but it is all in their minds.

There are, of course, a very small number of people who get healed, probably because of their own faith and God's sovereign will, in spite of the false prophet who is leading the service, but the vast majority of those who go onto the platform and declare that they have been healed, later find that they have not been healed.

This is why only inward healings that cannot be seen from the outside are ever even claimed to have occurred. No one who is totally paralyzed is ever proclaimed healed. No one who was badly burned is ever shown with new skin; the list goes on. Only people with arthritis who can now move their arms or can now walk easily, or who have asthma but can now breathe without difficulty, etc. But the symptoms return in a few hours.

God still heals today, but not through Hinn. I originally believed that his anointing is made sterile because of his greed. But I now believe it is merely counterfeit. His counterfeit anointing can knock people down but cannot heal them. When he takes offerings he tells people that if they need a really big miracle, they should plant a really big seed, inferring that you can buy a miracle. People who give this way will not be healed.

He claims that he never touches a penny of the ministry's money, but he gets a large salary, and the ministry pays for his expensive house overlooking the Pacific Ocean, including the property taxes. It has over 7,000 square feet with seven bedrooms and eight bathrooms worth $12 million dollars. The house is located in a private cove with security guards. So is he getting any money from the ministry? YES!

And according to documents smuggled out of the ministry offices by employees who want people to know the truth, he stayed in the Presidential suite at the Savoia Hotel in Milan, Italy, that cost over 10,000 American dollars for one night. It was recorded as a ministry expense. He always stays in the Presidential or Royal suites at high prices. The ministry even pays for a phalanx of body guards and a police escort! How full of self-importance and pride can you get?

No wonder people are not being healed the way they could be healed if he were a true man of God. God does not honor greedy ministers who are full of pride. Therefore, Hinn is nothing but a charlatan. I once classified him as one of the almost true yet false prophets who lead people into idolatry because he is also a wealth-gospel preacher who spends a lot of time pulling for money in all his crusades, but now I know he is literally one of Satan's false ministers.

I attended probably three of his crusades. And I know for a fact that in at least one of them, perhaps all, he spent a full hour, a literal 60 minutes, asking for money. This was a full hour of twisting peoples' arms for money before the offering buckets were even passed!

Last but not least, Hinn's true spiritual condition is revealed when he stated on TBN, about his critics: "*Sometimes I wish God would give me a Holy Ghost machine gun. I'd blow your head off!*" In other words, wanted to send power to kill his critics. That's called murder. (www.azquotes.com/quote/ 688275)

(4) A Letter to the Assembly of God

Here is part of a letter that was sent by an Assembly of God pastor to Thomas Trask, the General Superintendent, about Benny Hinn, dated July 16, 1995. This letter resulted in Hinn resigning his ordination through the AOG:

Friday, July 14, I attended a Benny Hinn Crusade service in East Rutherford, NJ. . . . Since he was now a colleague in this great Fellowship, I decided to go and ask the Lord to minister to me through this man who now enjoys the endorsement of our movement and our leadership.

Out of that four hour-long service, many questions were raised in mind so I am writing to you- my Pastor- heavy in heart; confused; and in need of answers.

To give context to my further remarks know that I am 40 years of age and have served the Lord in the Assemblies of God- sometimes wisely and sometimes not so wisely- for 20 years. . . .

The service began with a self-congratulatory 5 minute video about the grand goals of Benny Hinn to reach the world and an appeal for "partners" who would be granted certain special privileges in future crusades for their support. That is standard stuff for evangelists and traveling ministries.

The next segment of the service was praise/worship and it was wonderful. . . .

Following the praise, Benny used time "warming up" his audience with light humor and extended remarks . . .

Then, after another song or two, it started to get heavy. A grand lead-up to the offering started. For about 30 minutes Hinn treated us to an exhaustive listing of his achievements for Christ around the world with the clear implication that he was God's man of the hour. Then, with <u>manipulation that was beyond any standard of integrity</u>, we were instructed to faithfulness in our giving TO HIM. A minimum of $100 was set and $1000 was suggested. To further cap it off, Benny reminded us that if we failed to give to the Lord in obedience, "<u>God would surely collect from us within the next year</u>," possibly through financial disaster or business problems. . . . His warning was to spare us those kinds of problems. Is this lapse of ethics any less serious in God's eyes than the recent lapses of Jim Bakker which were held to be so contemptible?

Following the offering, Benny presented a message on the "Blood of Christ." Given his new prominence as an example for Spirit-filled, fire-fresh, A/G pastors (i.e.; his inclusion in the recent Signs and Wonders Conference) I would have hoped for better than we got! It was a rambling, not well researched, presentation of God's Holy Word. His <u>interpretations and conclusions sometimes were drawn from thin air, a tendency that has created heresy problems for him in the past</u>. . . .

The concluding 35-50 minutes were, in my humble opinion, the most grotesque display I have ever seen put on in the Lord's Name. There are no words to adequately describe . . .

"TOUCCHHH!" he screamed over and over into the microphone while flinging his arms at groups and individuals. Sometimes he ordered ministry teams members to stand a person up so he could have a second and even third go at them with his TOUC-CHHH! I was unable to ascertain what was supposed to be happening or accomplished in Jesus' precious Name. <u>There was no appeal for conversion, re-dedication, or even healing.</u> It seemed {to me, at least} to be little more than a frenzy of blessing seeking. . . .

If I write as one over-wrought, please forgive me. As I moved closer to see what was happening, I became intensely nauseated. I trembled, but not from the power of God. What shook my body was a combination of powerful emotions that included both terror and fury at the blatant manipulation of people that was going on . . .

Is this the new direction of our great and wonderful Fellowship? Is Benny Hinn the new exemplar of things desired in our ministries?

. . . Far too much of what passes for seeking the fresh Fire of the Spirit today is really just a seeking after another spiritual high. The self-centered attitudes of this age are in the church and we say, "Bless me, Lord, and make me happy" while forgetting the call to sacrifice. Thank you for your response.

Yours humbly in His service, JDS

(5) Kenneth Copeland

As shocking as the previous quotes from Copeland are, the next one will blow your socks off. He teaches that Jesus died spiritually and was taken to hell by Satan, then Jesus was born again in hell and took the keys of death and hell away from Satan. But worse than that, he believes <u>he could have died for the sins of the world himself</u>:

"The Spirit of God spoke to me and He said, "Son, realize this. Now follow me in this and don't let your tradition trip you up." He said, "Think this way: a twice-born man whipped Satan in his own domain." And I threw my Bible down . . . like that. I said, "What?" He said, "<u>A born-again man defeated Satan</u>, the firstborn of many brethren defeated him." He said, "<u>You are the very image, the very copy of that one.</u>" I said, "Goodness, gracious sakes alive!" And I began to see what had gone on in there, and I said, "<u>Well now you don't mean, you couldn't dare mean, that I could have done the same thing</u>?" He said, He said, "Oh yeah. If you'd known . . . had the knowledge of the Word of God that He did, <u>you could have done the same thing because you're a reborn man too.</u>" (*Substitution and Identification*, 1989, tape #00-0202, side 2) (*Christianity in Crisis*, Hank Hanegraaff, page 187)

This is wrong on so many levels. Even though this book is not intended to be a theological apologetics book against the Word of Faith movement; there are already books out there on that, I must point out the glaring heap of stupidity and nonsense above. First, notice that Copeland is claiming that Jesus was just an ordinary man when he died on the cross and went to hell. If you are WOF, let me explain that Jesus was not just a man, because he was born of a virgin of the Holy Spirit, making him the *"only begotten Son of God."* But even more than that, he was the Word of God, and it was the Word of God that created the universe, as it says in the Gospel of John 1:1-3.

In the quote above, Copeland claims that God told him that if he was alive 2000 years ago that he could have died for the sins of the world, because he is also *"a reborn man."* Or perhaps he was saying he could have defeated Satan in hell because he is a reborn man. Really?

Now, this first assumes that Copeland is actually born again, and if he really is born again, how did he become born again? Because of the death and resurrection of Jesus. But if Copeland were alive 2,000 years ago, he would not have been a reborn man prior to the death and resurrection of Jesus. Before the death of Christ, Copeland would have been an unregenerated man.

Is he claiming that he could have died on the cross and gone to hell and been reborn? No, God supposedly said he could have conquered Satan because he already is a reborn man. But if he is a reborn man, how could he have died on the cross and gone into hell? Was he going to be reborn a second time? What a bunch of convoluted mush. TOTAL LUNACY.

If you do not understand how messed up Kenneth Copeland is, then you do not understand basic Christian doctrine, that says Jesus was the Son of God, and born of a virgin, and sinless, that is why his blood paid for the sins of the world. Whereas Copeland would not have been any of those things had he been alive 2,000 years ago. He would NOT have been the Son of God, he would NOT have been born of a virgin, he would NOT have been sinless, therefore, he could NOT have died on the cross for our sins or defeated Satan. The Bible says that Jesus was sinless:

> You know that He was revealed to take away our sins, and in Him there is no sin. (1 John 3:5) (MEV)

> "He committed no sin, nor was deceit found in His mouth." (1 Peter 2:22) (MEV)

Does Copeland think he would have been sinless? Jesus also had the power to forgive sins (Mat. 9:5); does KC think he could forgive sins? Here are more of his embarrassingly messed up statements:

> "How did Jesus then on the cross say, 'My God.' Because God was not His Father any more. He took upon Himself the nature of Satan. And I'm telling you Jesus is in the middle of that pit. He's suffering all that there is to suffer, there is no suffering left . . . apart from Him. His emaciated, little wormy spirit is down in the bottom of that thing and the devil thinks He's got Him destroyed. . . ." (Believer's Voice of Victory (television program), TBN, 21 April 1991.)

> "That Word of the living God went down into that pit of destruction and charged the spirit of Jesus with resurrection power! Suddenly His twisted, death-wracked spirit began to fill out and come back to life.... Jesus was born again — the firstborn from the dead the Word calls Him — and He whipped the devil in his own backyard." (*The Price of It All*, page 4-6.)

Being firstborn from the dead refers to his resurrection to immortality, not his spirit being reborn!

> **Pray to yourself**, because I'm in yourself and you're in Myself. We are one Spirit, saith the Lord. (*Believer's Voice of Victory*, Feb. 1987, p.9)

> I say this with all respect so that it don't upset you too bad, but I'll say it anyway. When I read in the Bible where he [Jesus] says, 'I Am,' I just smile and say, 'Yes, I Am, too!' (*Believer's Voice of Victory* broadcast on TBN, recorded 7/9/87)

> God is the biggest failure in the Bible. . . . the reason you've never thought that is because He never said He was one. (Praise-a-thon, broadcast on TBN, recorded 1988)

WOW, Copeland prays to himself! Has he asked his followers to pray to him yet? Satan wants to exalt himself and bring God down in any way he can, so he instructs his followers to tell lies about God, like calling God a failure!

> God is a being that stands somewhere around 6'2, 6'3? (*Following the Faith of Abraham*, tape # 01-3001)

> God is someone "very much like you and me.... A being that

stands somewhere around 6'2," 6'3," that weighs somewhere in the neighborhood of a couple of hundred pounds . . . (Spirit, Soul and Body I, tape, side 1.)

God weighs approximately 200 lbs. (Spirit, Soul, and Body; Tape #1)

Heaven has a north and a south and an east and a west. Consequently, it must be a planet. (*Spirit, Soul, and a Body* 1, 1985, audio tape #01-0601, side 1)

Do you want a hundredfold return on your money? Give and let God multiply it back to you. Invest heavily in God; the returns are staggering. Every man who invests in the Gospel has a right to expect the staggering return of one hundredfold. (*Laws of Prosperity*, Page 67)

Jesus existed only as an image in the heart of God, until such time as the prophets of the Old Testament could positively confess Jesus into existence through their constant prophecies. (*The Power of the Tongue*, pp. 8-10)

Every Christian is a god. (*Force of Love*; Tape #2-0028) (*Believer's Voice of Victory*, broadcast July 9, 1987)

(The above quotes found at: www.victorstephens.com/ victorstephenswebsite_115.htm, & www.biblebc.com/Studies/_derived/ sourcecontrol_why_i_am_ not_a_charismatic.htm, & www.equip.org/ article/whats-wrong-with-the-word-faith-movement-part-two/, & https:// treeoflifeblog.com/tag/little-gods/ and others.)

Copeland even brags about being a billionaire, but if you listen close to his bragging he briefly mentions that his ministry took in a total of a billion dollars from its beginning. So he is not a billionaire, nor is his ministry worth a billion, that is false representation. You must be worth a billion dollars in total assets to be a billionaire, not have taken in a billion total. That is just more Copeland falsehood.

He is a total loon that is NOT hearing from God. <u>He is clearly hearing from a spirit, but it is not the Holy Spirit</u>. Like Jesus said, when you follow a blind leader, both will fall into the ditch.

So it should come as no surprise that KC has met with the Pope, and had "*Bishop Tony Palmer, a bishop of the Anglican Episcopal Church in the United Kingdom,*" speak at a "*Copeland pastor's conference calling for unity between Catholics and Protestants*" (6/30/14, www.worthynews.com/16631-pope-francis-met-televanglelists-kenneth-copeland-and-james-robison-video).

In spite of all his aberrant teaching, Copeland has a following of probably millions of Charismatic believers! He is clearly operating by demonic influence, rather than the Holy Spirit. If you still do not understand that WOF teaching is twisted beyond crazy, I recommend you learn the basics of the Christian faith.

God is tolerating these false prophets, for now, but their followers are in great danger of missing the Rapture. I can assure you that Laodiceans will not make the Rapture, and most WOF believers will not because they are greedy for money.

What makes Copeland even more dangerous, is that he has created what amounts to a denomination. There are churches that are either officially or unofficially affiliated with his ministry. One local WOF church even includes Copeland's logo at the bottom of its website.

I believe it is significant that Satan's false prophets have chosen to join the WOF movement, it is tailor made for them.

Chapter 11:
Strange Fire and God's Judgment

In this chapter we will discuss the meaning of "strange fire," and how it applies to the WOF movement today. Not only is the prosperity gospel idolatry, and strange things are happening that I believe are being done by "familiar spirits." But some "miracles" are not miracles at all, but just old-fashioned fakery.

In Leviticus 10 we have the story of Nadab and Abihu who offered strange fire to God and were struck dead. They prepared incense and put fire upon it:

> And Nadab and Abihu, the sons of Aaron, each took his censer and put fire in them; and they put incense on it and brought strange fire before Jehovah, which He had not commanded them. (Lev 10:1) (LIT)

The Hebrew for "strange" is zur (zoor), Strong's number (2114). It means:

> A primitive root; to turn aside (especially for lodging); hence to be a foreigner, strange, profane; specifically (active participle) to commit adultery . . .

Normally a priest would put incense upon the altar and the fire of God would come down and consume it, as with the animal sacrifice. But Nadab and Abihu took ordinary fire and burned the incense; thereby it was not the fire from God but a counterfeit fire, a false miracle. In response, God sent fire down and consumed Nadab and Abihu. Nadab and Abihu did something that God had not approved; therefore, it was foreign or profane to God. It was the same as if you took something from a pagan god and offered it to God. When people offer to God their financial offerings for the purpose of gaining wealth, it is strange fire because greed is idolatry.

But we need to discover the reason why Nadab and Abihu offered their strange fire. I believe we can find the answer in the preceding verses in Leviticus chapter 9:

> And Moses and Aaron went into the tent of meeting, and when they came out they blessed the people, and the glory of the LORD appeared to all the people. And fire came out from before Jehovah and consumed the burnt offering and the fat on the altar. And <u>all the people saw, and cried aloud, and fell on their faces</u>. (9:23-24)

This is what happened: Moses and Aaron did something, God sent fire from heaven, then the people cried aloud and fell on their faces. Nadab and Abihu saw how the people reacted, and they wanted the people to look at them with the same awe and reverence as they did Aaron and Moses, so they prepared incense, then put the fire on it themselves. This means <u>they faked a miracle</u>. God does not like it when people fake miracles and claim that God did it.

Jesus said the only unforgiveable sin is blasphemy of the Holy Spirit, which is when someone says a true miracle from God was done by the power of Satan, or demons. The opposite is when you claim a fake miracle is done by God, or when a miracle done by familiar spirits is a genuine miracle from God; so <u>this is also serious sin</u>.

Many ministers today want signs and wonders to happen in their ministries: *"Look at me, look what I can do, be awed, be amazed."* So they often fake it by planting gems, or angel feathers, or gold dust. They desire the same thing that Nadab and Abihu desired. Sometimes this desire results in false doctrines that are unusual, or special, doctrines that most other churches are not teaching. Adam Clarke commentary states:

> Here we find Aaron's sons neglecting the Divine ordinance, and offering incense with strange, that is, common fire, <u>fire not of a celestial origin</u>; and therefore the fire of God consumed them. . . . The most awful judgments are threatened against those who

either <u>add to, or take away from, the declarations of God</u>. (ACC)

J. Lee Grady of Charisma Magazine writes:

> . . . people in some streams of the prophetic movement are claiming to have visitations from Aimee Semple McPherson, William Branham, John Wimber or various Bible characters. And we are expected to say, "Ooooooo, that's so deep"-and then go looking for our own mystical, beyond-the-grave epiphany. (*Strange Fire in the House of the Lord*, located at www.charisma mag.com)

Grady sees it exactly right, ministers want others to look at them with awe, as though they are special, so they are claiming miracles or teachings from God that do not come from God, but are faked. But are ministers falling dead like Nadab and Abihu? Yes.

William Branham (1909 – 1965) is credited with being the first faith healer to travel the county with a tent, holding healing revivals. He started as a Baptist about 1941, and held meetings in the world's biggest stadiums and meeting halls. He is credited with many healings and in operating with the Word of Knowledge by knowing things about people in his meetings. But his downfall was his exaggerated claims of numerous visions and angelic visitations, and that an angel was at all his meetings, and that he was led by this angel. He claimed he had a special birth and was specially chosen of God to bring in the return of Christ. He claimed he met with the seven angels who were to open the seven seals in Revelation which had begun to open. Fake claims of visions or visits from angels can be classified as false miracles. He said denominations were under the power of the antichrist.

> In 1963 Branham revealed that he had come in the "spirit of Elijah" to warn people to flee their "dead churches and denominations and pledge their loyalty to the prophet of the last days." (*Counterfeit Revival*, Hank Hanegraaff, page 151)

I am not saying that all his claimed miracles were false, many were doubtless genuine, but he made many false claims, or was led by an angel, which is not Biblical. Jesus did not say he would send us angels to lead us and bring us miracles, but that he would send the Holy Spirit. Branham was killed when a drunk driver hit him head-on in 1965, at the age of 56. His followers expected him to rise from the dead.

Jack Coe was a faith healer who followed on the heels of William Branham. He began as an Assembly of God preacher after World War 2. He was accused of misusing money and had an *"extravagant lifestyle and home."* He was kicked out of the Assembly of God, but it is not clear whether it was because he was misleading the public by claiming that people who go to doctors would eventually take the mark of the beast, or that he was making exaggerated claims of healings that could not be verified; both were true. He warned that people who opposed him were in danger of being struck dead by God. He was suddenly struck with bulbar polio and died a few weeks later at Dallas Parkland Hospital in 1956 at age 38. (Ibid, page 153)

Next to die was A. A. Allen. I saw a video of A.A. Allen in which he allegedly had oil oozing from his hands, and claimed a man was healed of a short leg. As Allen pulled on one leg, it supposedly grew right before your eyes; but that is an old trick that hucksters have used for decades to con people. I know two people that both say that a preacher said they had a short leg and that it grew out. Nonsense. If someone has a short leg, they will know it long before they become an adult because it will cause great back pain and will mess up your spine. Long before you become an adult you will be walking with a shoe with a thicker sole. So when you see a short leg healing done on someone, know that it is a 99% likelihood that it is fakery.

There seems to be a growing number of lying ministers who claim to grow out a short leg. It is an old con, and when you see it just know what it is, a lie, a faked miracle. There are not millions of people with one leg shorter than the other and not know it, it is a lie. It is very easy to make the legs look as though one is shorter than the other, and very easy to make them look like they are now the same length.

Every time I see that on TV, especially Sid Roth's show, I say, *"There's another lying conman (or conwoman)."* They apparently have no fear of God. Be warned, fakers!

Allen was also kicked out of the Assemblies of God in 1955 after he was arrested for driving drunk. But he continued preaching, and became the most well-known faith-healer in the nation. He spread the prosperity gospel and gave out anointed cloths for donations of $100 or $1000. At one time he was on 58 radio stations daily, and 43 TV stations, and his monthly *Miracle Magazine*, had a circulation of 350,000. Allen was known to wear flashy suits and say, *"Jeee-uh-zuss!"* (*Time*, March 7, 1969). He is the preacher that Hollywood remembers most, and became their model for faith healers in movies for many years.

Time Magazine said, *"In the current issue,* [of Miracle Magazine] *a teenager named Yodonna Holley from Globe, Ariz., testifies that 'I received fillings in my teeth' during a camp meeting"* (*Faith Healers: Getting Back Double from God*, March 7, 1969). Allen had over 2,000 acres in Arizona called Miracle Valley where he held camp meetings with a church that seated 4,000. On this property he lived in a *"twelve-sided house of wood and cut stone, with a swimming pool under a simulated stained-glass canopy"* (Ibid); that is until his sudden and untimely death.

He was found dead in 1970 at age 59 in a hotel room. After his death the coroner said he died of liver failure due to acute alcoholism. His close associate who took over his ministry, wrote in 1999 that Allen and --

> . . . other evangelists had wheelchairs available for people who had bad backs and couldn't stand in a healing line for hours. But when the evangelist got to them and pulled them up out of the wheelchair, some in the audience thought they were walking for the first time or that they had come to the revival in that wheelchair. (*Only Believe: an eyewitness account of the great healing revivals of the 20th century*, by Don Stewart, Revival Press, 1999, page 115)

The inference here is that Allen and the other evangelists made the most of it when they came to the people in the wheel chairs, but who could actually walk, *get out of the wheel chair in Jesus name!* This means he was faking miracles. I know that he had many genuine healings in his meetings, but that was not good enough, and he felt that God needed some help!

Then in 1973 another prosperity preacher and faith healer, Gordon Lindsay, died suddenly during a Sunday church service at age 66. In more recent years several ministers have died at a relatively young age, including Billy Joe Daugherty of Tulsa, OK at age 57, in 2009. I will not begin to speculate here as to what the divine cause was for his death, I have not researched his teaching or his church; all I know is that he was a Word of Faith preacher. In 2007 his church moved into their new sanctuary that cost 32 million dollars.

More recently, Jill Austin died as reported by CBN news on Jan. 15, 2009 at age 60. It is ironic that she had a false prophetic ministry, yet, died genuinely prophetically:

> Austin entered emergency surgery last Tuesday after doctors found that her <u>intestines were twisted and cutting off her blood supply</u>. Parts of her stomach, intestines and colon were removed because of infection. (www.cbn.com/cbnnews/us/2009/january/well-known-prophetic-minister-dies-/)

The Holy Spirit was supposed to have been her *"best friend,"* so why did she die like that? She apparently started out as a true prophet of God, but joined the false revival and taught on angelic visitations, portals, and all the other twisted teachings of the counterfeit revival. So it is no surprise that her insides were all twisted up. We should take this as a warning from God. Judgment begins at the house of God.

Another big name person in the Prophetic Movement, John Paul Jackson (1950-2015), died at age 64. He was known to lift himself up by claiming that an angel visited his mother and told her she was going to have a special child and to name him John Paul. He also believed the prosperity gospel.

Then Kim Clement died at age 60 (1956-2016). He was also part of the Prophetic Movement, and in the prosperity gospel.

What about those who have not died? I am not going to claim that God kills every preacher that makes false claims, or how long he will allow it to continue before taking action. But people need to take warning.

Chapter 12:
Prophetic Voices Crying in the Wilderness

This chapter contains articles and messages written by other ministers who are greatly concerned about the prosperity message and general materialism and backsliding of Christians today (reprinted here by permission, or only short quotes from books).

The first article compares the lifestyle of a well-known TV preacher with Francis Asbury, who was a circuit rider; that is, a preacher who traveled a particular route each year on horseback.

(1) The Circuit Rider vs. The Televangelist

by Pastor Michael Edds

In my continued research on the "old wells of revival" I have discovered some incredibly contrasting bits of information. One of the top televangelists in the nation was recently invited to preach in Baltimore, Maryland. His terms for coming were #1. That he must be picked up by a limousine at the airport, #2. that he must have $1,000 spending money, #3. That he must be guaranteed at least $10,000 in offerings. This same televangelist/ pastor lives in a multimillion-dollar mansion, eats in the finest restaurants and wears the most expensive tailor-made suits. His writings and speaking engagements have garnered millions of dollars. He brags that he is a role model of the prosperity message of our day. He pastors a mega church, appears on national and international television, has authored many books and draws tens of thousands to hear him. To his credit, he is a powerful, commanding speaker. However, please contrast this to the following life and ministry of the great circuit rider, Francis Asbury in the late 1700s and early 1800s.

While still in his 20's, Bishop Francis Asbury left his home and family forever in England to come to a wilderness called America. He came to be a traveling preacher/evangelist in a nation with little infrastructure such as roads, decent housing, few hotels and restaurants, poor sanitation and dangerous drinking water, few medical professionals and limited law enforcement. The nation had recently plunged into a violent war of independence against Asbury's native land of England. The American frontier was also ablaze with war between the colonist and Native Americans tribes.

Asbury was not greeted upon his arrival by a limo. He had to purchase a horse on which he traveled 8,000 miles a year for over 40 years. His financial reward was $60 a year, much of which he gave away or sent back to England to help his parents. He wore hand-me-downs not tailor made suits. He had no retirement, no insurance, no dental plan, and no 401K. He set no fee for his ministry.

What he did receive, he often gave away. He traveled on "roads" on which his horse sank many times knee-deep in mud. If a road did not exist, he would lead his horse over the steep, rocky inclines of the Appalachians to reach a pioneer community. Many times, his feet and legs were bloodied and bruised by the horrific journey. When he came to a river where there was no bridge or ferry, he would swim his horse across. Numerous times he was nearly drowned by an angry, swollen stream. His "hotel" on many occasions was on a dirt floor in an overcrowded, rat- infested frontier cabin. Often times he slept in the woods, on a mountain ledge or in a damp cave.

Many days he would travel over 60 miles with nothing to eat. The paths and roads he traveled were full of dangers from murderers, thieves, wolves, bears, poisonous snakes and roaming bands of Native Americans with whom the frontiersmen were at war. If he met someone who needed a cloak, food or money, he would take what he had and give it to the person in need. Asbury sought out the forgotten, hidden places of early America. He traveled from New England, to the Midwest, and to the Deep South spreading the Gospel of Christ. When he would meet a person who was ill, he would minister to their physical needs with the last medication he had. He demanded nothing of others in order to come into a community. The demands he made were on himself. Frequently, his body would be racked with pain, illness, fever, hunger and weakness. His physical being would cry out for rest and nourishment. However, his spirit ruled his body. When truly unable to travel, he would mount his horse and ride for 8 hours or more through blinding snow storms, torrential rain or in oppressive heat. He too had been invited to Baltimore. In 1816 he was traveling by buggy through Virginia headed to the annual conference in Baltimore. However, he was dying.

His last sermon was preached in Richmond. He had to be carried into the meeting room. He commented, "I am too weak to walk but not to preach." They sat him on a small table and he ministered the Word for the last time. He made it as far as Spotsylvania twenty miles north of Richmond. He body was rapidly failing. He stopped at a friend's house on Saturday. Shortly before he left this world he was asked, "Do you feel Jesus precious?" Summoning his last remaining strength, the great circuit rider raised both hands in victory. Minutes later he laid his head on a friend's hand and gently slipped away to be with the Lord. He owned no mansion, no land, and no bank account. His net worth was what he wore on his body. He was buried in a borrowed grave plot.

When Asbury came to America, there were few Methodist believers and fewer preachers. At the end of his ministry, there were over 200,000 Methodist believers and almost 8,000 ministers. He impacted lives of thousands upon thousands. He changed the very course of American history. Among his converts were poor farmers, merchants, Governors of several states, frontiersmen, slaves, Native Americans, State Supreme Court Justices, attorneys, physicians, house wives, children, youth and people from all walks of life. He gave all he had. He sought nothing for himself. His passion was to bring salvation and the Light of the Gospel to those in darkness of sin. He loved a nation and made it his own even though he was not her native son.

Quite a contrast between the Circuit Rider and the Televangelist! One was selfless, the other selfish. One was people-centered, the other ego-centered. One was a Kingdom builder, the other an empire builder. One drew souls into the Kingdom of God, the other drew the masses into an arena. One demanded of himself, the other demanded of others. One gave freely, the other commanded a price. One was a servant, the other a celebrity. Hebrews 11:32-38 speaks about the real heroes of the faith: They were, "tortured, not accepting deliverance, that they might obtain a better resurrection. Still others had trial of mocking and beatings, and of chains and imprisonment. They were stoned, they were sawn in two, were tempted, were slain with the sword. They wandered about in sheepskins and goatskins, being destitute, afflicted, tormented... they wandered in deserts, and mountains, in dens and caves of the earth.... of whom the world was not worthy."

How long are we going to tolerate the "superstar syndrome" in the church? How long are we going to feed the ego and pocketbooks of these self-seeking charlatans, regardless of how articulate they are? How long will we continue to pack their arenas and buy their CDs, DVDs and books? How long will we pick them up in limos, and line their wallets with thousands and thousands of dollars to spend on self? How long will we tolerate apostasy???

My God, how far we have fallen!! God is calling on us as His people to repent and turn from our wicked ways. He is calling us to seek HIS face. I am praying that God will overthrow this current, perverted religious system and will fulfill Jeremiah 3:15 and give us shepherds after His own heart.

(2) What has become of the American church? What is this sickness spreading in the body of Christ?

by J. Lee Grady

Some bigheaded preachers demand rock star treatment. If the apostle Paul were around today he might throw rocks at them.

Just when I thought we charismatics had finally taken enough abuse from the egomaniac ministers in our midst, I've learned that some of our leaders are taking things to a new extreme. We've moved beyond the red carpets, limousines and entourages of the 1990s. A new strain of the celebrity virus is spreading in large segments of the church.

One friend of mine in Texas recently inquired to see if a prominent preacher could speak at her conference. The minister's assistant faxed back a list of requirements that had to be met in order to book a speaking engagement. The demands included:

* a five-figure honorarium
* a $10,000 gasoline deposit for the private plane
* a manicurist and hairstylist for the speaker
* a suite in a five-star hotel
* a luxury car from the airport to the hotel (2004 model or newer) [This was written in 2007.]
* room-temperature Perrier [imported bottled water]

This really makes me wonder how the apostle Paul, Timothy or Priscilla managed ministering to so many people in Ephesus, Corinth and Thessalonica. How did they survive without a manicurist if they broke a nail while laying hands on the sick?

I was relieved to know that this celebrity preacher's requirements in 2007 did not include a set of armed bodyguards- because I just might want to jump uninvited into her Rolls-Royce and say a few words.

It gets worse, if you can believe it. At a charismatic conference in an East Coast city recently, a pastor stood on a stage in front of a large crowd and smugly announced that the guest speaker was "more than an apostle." Then the host asked everyone to bow down to the person, claiming that this posture was necessary to release God's power.

"This is the only way you can receive this kind of anointing!" the host declared, bowing in front of the speaker. Immediately, about 80 percent of the audience fell prostrate on the floor. The few who were uncomfortable with the weird spiritual control in the room either walked out or stood in silent protest.

So today, I guess it's not enough to feed a celebrity preacher's ego by treating them like a rock star. We also are required to worship him.

And apparently in some places you even have to pay big bucks to speak with him. In a city in the South, a well-known preacher is known to ask for money in order to secure a five- or 10-minute counseling session. The minister uses Proverbs 18:16, "A man's gift makes room for him and brings him before great men" (NASB), to support this bizarre practice. Some people are known to give more than $1,000 for a short meeting.

People on fixed incomes need not apply. (That would include

lepers, blind beggars, Samaritan women or any other social out-casts who were welcomed and healed by Jesus without pay-ment.)

What has become of the American church? What is this sick-ness spreading in the body of Christ? I don't know whom to blame more for it: The narcissistic minister who craves the atten-tion, or the spiritually naive crowds who place these arrogant people on their shaky pedestals. All I know is that God is grieved by all of this shameful carnality.

How far we have fallen from authentic New Testament faith. Paul, who carried the anointing of an apostle but often described himself as a bond slave, told the Thessalonians, "Having so fond an affection for you, we were well-pleased to impart to you not only the gospel of God but also our own lives" (1 Thess. 2:8).

New Testament Christianity is humble, selfless and authentic. And those who carry the truth don't preach for selfish gain or to meet an emotional need for attention. May God help us root out the false apostles and false teachers who are making the Ameri-can church sick with their man-centered, money-focused here-sies.

(Reprinted with permission from *Fire In My Bones*, Charisma & Christian Life, July, 2007. Copyright Strang Communications Co., USA. All rights reserved. www.charis-mamag.com.)

*   *   *   *   *   *   *   *

The minister being referred to in the above article is a very popular female TV and prosperity preacher. J. Lee Grady says he may want to jump into *"her Rolls-Royce,"* which tells us the ego-maniac minister is in fact a very wealthy woman with a private jet and a *Rolls Royce*. But to answer his question, the sickness that is spreading is called the Word of Faith.

(3) Modern Day Money Changers

by David Ravenhill

I'm convinced that the carnal, cunning, conniving, crooked crooks that Jesus drove out of the Temple are still among us today. These modern day moneychangers are forever devising new and deceptive doctrines to defraud God's people out of His/their money. These masters of deceit have now set up their changing tables throughout the Christian television industry.

I'm absolutely certain that if Jesus returned today He would walk into the vast majority of these television studios and overthrow the cameras, lights, monitors, and soundboards. He would unplug the microphones and scatter the makeup colors around as He went about destroying the stages and backdrops.

Several years ago now, a nationally know prophetic voice was told by the Lord, "I'm sick and tired of the prosperity message". If that was true then, how much more today. As far back as 1986, the top seven media evangelists took in over 750 million dollars. Now with the increased manipulation of 'seed faith teaching' that amount has no doubt been dwarfed by comparison.

Only a few days ago I was appalled as I watched and listened as Pastor Steve _____ [last name not in the original] zealously twisted and distorted the Scriptures to his own advantage. This 'brother' dared to distort the most sacred truth of all Scripture. He used The Day Of Atonement, that day when Jesus Christ the Lamb of God shed His blood for the sins of the world, to teach that how we give financially determines how God will respond to us throughout the coming year. My blood boiled as I listened. This 'brother' had finally crossed the line and was now on the verge of blaspheming the atoning work of our blessed Lord and Savior Jesus Christ, not to mention lining his own pockets with the proceeds. He might as well have been selling indulgences by inferring that God's favor toward us was based on our giving rather than God's unmerited grace and forgiveness through the gift of His Son. What made matters worse was that this same 'charlatan' was the guest of one of the nation's best known charismatic personalities. Within a day or so he was teaching the same message on a local Christian telethon. Neither the evangelist nor the network sought to correct his aberrant teaching - after all, the show must go on and that takes money, so how you raise it doesn't seem to matter anymore.

Why does almost every single Christian program have to end with some type of 'seed faith teaching'? If these men and women of faith really believed what they taught, they would practice what they preach and teach; after all what's good for the goose is good for the gander. Imagine how shocked you would be if your favorite televangelist and covenant partner were to send you a check in their next mailing for the amount of $1,000.00 with a personal note telling you he/she just wanted to sow into your life. Perhaps then I could believe that these men/women really believe and practice what they teach. Not only that, but they would never have to appeal for money again as God's return to them would result in a hundredfold increase. At least that's what they would have us to believe.

On a recent ministry trip to the Northwest, I was told by a pastor friend that his church had received a call from a well-known and anointed teacher in the Body of Christ. The caller was asking them for a contribution towards the purchase of a jet for their ministry. What a far cry from what the Apostle Paul taught when he prefaced his teaching on 'sowing and reaping' with these words; "For this is not for the ease of others and for your affliction, but by way of equality." (II Cor. 8:13-14)

Many pastors measure their success in terms of numbers -the larger the church the more successful their ministry. Itinerant ministries, not being able to brag about size, seem to fall for the notion that having one's own jet is how success is determined. (Once it was the Rolex watch). By the way, if you love and appreciate this fine teacher, pray that he won't get the desires of his heart - it will only lead to the leanness of his soul.

This is one man's attempt to appeal to the Body of Christ. Stop pandering to these moneychangers. These men and women live like kings while spending your money to buy mansions and jets for themselves. They dine in the finest restaurants, wear the latest designer fashions and then have the audacity to tell you that you can live the same way as long as you give to their ministry.

I opened my Bible the other day to Zechariah's wonderful prophecy concerning the first coming of Jesus, our great and glorious King. Listen to his words; "Behold your King is coming to you; He is just and endowed with salvation, humble, and mounted on a donkey, even on a colt the foal of a donkey" (Zechariah 9:9). What a far cry from the televangelist who comes high and mighty and traveling on his own jet!

If you are as sick and tired as I am about this waste of God's money, then for heaven's sake STOP SUPPORTING THESE PEOPLE. Give your money to your local church. There are tens of thousands of needy missionaries who barely have enough support to keep themselves alive. They are laboring long and hard under some of the most difficult and trying conditions. They would rejoice at the thought of an extra $10-30 dollars a month support. These are the real heroes of whom the world is not worthy. Help put these MONEY LOVING TELEVANGELISTS OUT OF BUSINESS and save another MISSIONARY FROM EXTINCTION. Together we can make it happen.

(4) Caught in the Web of Deception

by Bob Farley

Many Christian leaders and church members alike have fallen into sin through deception. Sexual sins and the break up of marriages are at an all time high! Addiction to pornography has become a national epidemic among Christian men. Deception is causing divorce, immorality, dishonesty and greed to run rampant in the church! The divorce rate among Christians is now running 8% higher than the divorce rate among the people of the world.

Dr. Billy Graham has said that, according to his research, at least 90% of all Christians in America are living defeated spiritual lives. (p. 5)

The world's influence on Christians in this generation has been much greater than the influence of the standards taught in the Word of God. This has caused the moral character of the average Christian in America to change. Christians are more tolerant and indifferent to many of the sins described in the Bible that are now commonplace in our culture. While we say we are standing against the tide, in reality we are simply a few decades behind the world's acceptance of 'new' moral standards. What was permissible by worldly standards in American society twenty or thirty years ago is now largely acceptable to Christians. Finding a Christian who has a fear of sinning is very rare these days.... (page 6-7)

[The author's brother, Dr. Charles Fraley, had a vision--]

The first vision I had was that of a large head of a "beast" --very fat looking-- hovering over America. It was swallowing up Christians in our country almost at will. The Spirit of the Lord showed me the meaning of this vision. This "beast" represented the <u>power of materialism and pleasure</u> in our country. It was swallowing up Christians by spiritually deceiving and then overcoming them through the influence of the materialistic and pleasure-seeking lifestyles that had developed in our society. Those Christians who were spiritually being overcome were not aware of what was happening. ... (page 13)

It is unfortunate, but it has been proven again and again that it takes an extended crisis before most people will listen and begin to seriously seek the Lord. The events of September 11 proved that to be true. The churches were full the next few Sundays following this tragedy. But how quickly we returned to the ways of the world. (page 18) (For copies of this booklet write to; Christian Life Outreach, 6438 E. Jenan Drive, Scottsdale, AZ 85254, or visit www.christianlife outreach.org.)

(5) The Fight Against Mammon (money)

This section contains extracts from the writings of Eberhard Arnold (1883-1935). He was active in the student revival in Germany before World War I, but just saving souls and leaving them to suffer deprivations did not seem right to him, so he studied the Scriptures and the Early Church Fathers and realized that he had to help the entire person, not just his soul. So he started a Christian commune. His observations are as relevant today as then.

*   *   *   *   *   *   *   *

I found myself in a very difficult situation, and I was deeply unhappy. I began to recognize the needs of people in a deeper way: the need of their bodies and souls, their material and social need, their humiliation, exploitation, and enslavement. I recognized the tremendous power of mammon, discord, hate, and violence, and saw the hard boot of the oppressor upon the neck of the oppressed. If a person has not experienced these things, he might think such words an exaggeration - but these are the facts.

Then, from 1913 to 1917, I sought painfully for a deep understanding of the truth. I recognized more and more that personal dedication to people's souls was not all that Jesus asked - that it did not fully express the being of God. I felt that I was not fulfilling God's will by approaching people with a purely personal Christianity and concerning myself with individuals so that they, like myself, might come to this personal Christianity. During those four years I went through a hard struggle. I searched not only in the old writings, in Jesus' Sermon on the Mount and other scriptures, but I also wanted to get to know the life of the working classes - the oppressed humanity of the present social order - and to share in their life. I wanted to find a way that corresponded to the way of Jesus, of Francis of Assisi, and also the way of the prophets....

Then hunger came to Berlin.... it soon became clear that Jesus' way is a practical one: he has shown us a way of life that is more than a way of concern for the soul. It is a way that simply says, "If you have two coats, give one to him who has none; give food to the hungry, and do not turn away your neighbor when he needs to borrow from you. When you are asked for an hour's work, give two. You must strive for His justice. If you want to found a family, see that all others who want to found a family are able to do so, too. If you wish for education, work, and satisfying activity, make these possible for other people as well. If you say it is your duty to care for your health, then accept this duty for the health of others also. Treat people in the same way that you would be treated by them. This is the law and the prophets. Enter through this narrow gate, for it is the way that leads to the kingdom of God."...

In this connection it became clear to us that the first Christian community in Jerusalem was more than a historical happening: it was here that the Sermon on the Mount came to life. We saw that it was more necessary than ever to renounce the last vestiges of privileges and rights and to let ourselves be won for this way of total love: the love that will pour itself out over the land from the breath of the Holy Spirit, the love that was born out of the first church community.

So we felt that we could not endure the life we were living any longer. We had to witness to the fact that Jesus concerned himself not only with people's souls but with their bodies as well. He made the blind see, the lame walk, and the deaf hear. And he prophesied a kingdom, a rule of God which was to change completely the conditions and the order of the world and make them new. To acknowledge this and live according to it - this, I believe, is God's command for the hour....

Our mission on behalf of the kingdom is to be the salt of the earth: to stem its injustice, prevent its decay, and hinder its death. The world must perish in order to be born again. But as long as salt remains salt, it restrains the fulfillment of evil in the world and acts as the power that will one day renew the earth....

The salt of the earth is where God is, where the justice of the future kingdom is lived out and the powers of the coming order promote organic life and growth. In other words, salt is present where the victorious energy of God's love is at work. God himself is the creative spirit who overcomes corruption, the living spirit who wakens the dead. He is the God of miracles who can bring forth new birth out of corruption and degeneration, replacing nausea and disgust with joy and well-being.

Finally, there is freedom from everything outward and unessential, a freedom that is ready to sacrifice all possessions and any amount of time, for it is love, love to enemies as well as to friends and brothers and sisters. It is freedom from earthly treasure, freedom from the cares and worries of possessions, a childlike joy in light and color, in God himself and all that he is and gives....

Not a single area of life should remain unaffected by this salt and this light. There is no responsibility in public life, including economics and politics, from which the city on the hill may remain aloof. Nowhere should the poison of decay be allowed to set in without being counteracted by salt. No wickedness must be allowed to lurk in the dark....

It serves the whole of life without letting itself be enslaved. It fights against all suffering and injustice without succumbing to the suffering and becoming unjust itself.... It is a lost cause to try to follow Christ in only one sphere of life....

So they are both poor and rich at the same time. They are people of faith who have nothing in themselves and yet possess everything in God. In spite of failing again and again, they try to reveal God's invisible nature through their deeds. Just as they themselves receive mercy, so they pour mercy on all in need. They are on the side of poverty and suffering, on the side of all who suffer injury, and they are ready to be persecuted with them for the sake of justice. They know that they cannot go through life without struggle and that their opponents' slander will fall on them like a hailstorm; yet they rejoice in this struggle and remain the peacemakers who overcome opposition everywhere and conquer enmity through love...

The entire Sermon on the Mount shows us the characteristics of this new justice - a gift of the future, a promise of God....

Gather no riches for yourselves! Know only the one treasure, the treasure in heaven. Your longing can have only one object. Your heart is either set on things, or else it is directed toward something entirely different. A divided heart leads to darkness and judgment. You can never serve God and money at the same time. What the heart longs for is decisive. Consequently, your worry about material things and your existence stems from the same godless spirit of mammon as accumulating wealth. Life that is given by God liberates from both worry and possession. Just as the birds and flowers in creation are cared for, so in the new creation there is abundance of food and clothing for those who trust in God and acknowledge his kingdom as the first and last....

Not all who call themselves Christians are connected to the same center, nor are they motivated by the same thing. The religion of many who confess to the name of Jesus Christ has nothing to do with God or the coming kingdom....

Is not the great world organization that names itself after Christ serving a god other than the God whom Jesus confessed? Has not the institutional church sided with wealth and protected it; sanctified mammon, christened warships, and blessed soldiers going to war? Has not this church in essence denied him whom it confesses? Is not the Christian state the most ungodly institution that ever existed? And are not the state and the organized church, which protect privilege and wealth, diametrically opposed to what is to come: God's new order?

Nobody can serve two masters. Nobody can serve God and mammon. The message of Christ had to do with the "trans- valuation of all values" - the coming kingdom of God. His first witnesses testified to a radically new order, an order concealed from those blinded by the god of this world. This god - the god of greed and murderous possessiveness - stands opposed to the kingdom of justice, unity, and love.

Mammon is the rule of money over people. It means dependence on income and finances instead of on God. We recognize that mammon is the enemy of God, but we cannot apply the lever that lifts it off its hinges: we ourselves are so dominated by it that we lack the strength to rebel.

The deepest human relationships are based not on mammon, but the spirit. No one of us can live in isolation; we are all interdependent. All of us are interrelated in groups, families, classes, and trade unions; in nations, states, churches, and all kinds of associations. And through our humanity we are interrelated in an even deeper way: through the love of God that flows from spirit to spirit and heart to heart, leading to organic, constructive fellowship.

But there is a devilish means that seeks to rob us of heart and spirit and God. This means is money. Money reduces human relationships to materialistic associations. It destroys the highest human goals. At first it may be just a means of barter, but later it becomes a commodity in itself. It becomes power. In the end, it destroys all true fellowship.

Money and love are mutually exclusive. Where mammon rules, the possessive will is stronger than the will to community. The struggle to survive becomes stronger than the spirit of mutual help. Where mammon rules, matter is stronger than spirit, and self-assertion stronger than solidarity. Mammon never motivates people to work in a creative way for a life of fellowship. Instead, it engenders the enslavement of the soul to circumstance. It is the spirit of lying, impurity, and murder, the spirit of weakness and death.

Jesus, the prince of life, declared war on this spirit, and we must declare war on it too. When our inmost eye has been opened to his light, it can no longer respond to what mammon demands. When our hearts are set on the future - when we expect God's kingdom - we can no longer accumulate property. We will turn our backs on everything present and live instead for freedom, unity, and peace.

Jesus entered the temple with a whip not to strike people, but to show his contempt for money: his father's house belonged to God, not to mammon. In the Gospel of Matthew, he exhorted the otherwise blameless rich [ruler] to confirm his love by selling everything: "Give all you have to the poor, and come follow me." . . .

This attack on the order of mammon resulted in his death. Yet life had the final victory. The men and women who had gathered around him in life waited for something new after his death. They waited for the Spirit. They knew that the spirit of love, order, and freedom was the spirit of God's kingdom. And this Spirit came upon them, bringing about a church: a fellowship of work and goods in which everything belonged to all, in which all were active to the full extent of their powers and gifts....

It is self-deception to think we can overcome mammon by violence, for violence is of the same evil spirit as mammon. We cannot drive out poison by means of poison. The new can be born only of the new; only out of life comes life; only of love can love be born. Only out of the will to community can community arise.

And community is alive wherever small bands of people meet, ready to work for the one great goal, to belong to the one true future. Already now we can live in the power of this future; already now we can shape our lives in accordance with God and his kingdom. The kingdom of love, which is free of mammon, is drawing near. Change your thinking radically so that you will be ready for the coming order!

*   *   *   *   *   *   *   *

Eberhard Arnold formed the Bruderhof Community commune, but because of persecution they fled to England. With the approach of World War II, the English became suspicious of Germans, so they moved to Portugal and eventually to the United States. Today they also have branches in England, Germany, and Australia, with about 2,500 members.

(6) Clouds Without Water

For *some strange reason*, rather than God sending rich Americans to Eastern Europe to plant churches, God has sent poor Africans. Henry Madava pastors *Victory Christian Church* with 6,500 members in Kiev, Ukraine. He has also planted 85 other churches in Ukraine and 23 in other parts of the world. Seven people have been raised from the dead and many others healed. Here is what he says about American TV preachers:

*   *   *   *   *

When the big guys who are on TV in the United States come here, my congregation is shocked because what they see on TV does not correspond to what they see in person.... Many leaders in America have received the anointing but they have become clouds without water. Most of them seem to lose the anointing. I wish the American church could keep the water in the cloud. (Quoted in, Lessons from *Ukraine: America: Please Don't Lose the Anointing*, by J. Lee Grady. Charisma Online)

(7) Crisis in The American Church

Another Nigerian pastor who also pastors a large church in Kiev, Ukraine, is Pastor Sunday Adelaja. Pastor Sunday is concerned about American Christianity:

*   *   *   *   *

There are several points that I see are responsible for the crisis in the American Church today. I got a better understanding of this after I started visiting North America four years ago. The first and foremost of these reasons is a lack of desperation for God.... Another problem I saw in the American Church is what I call the lack of fresh revelation from above.... There will be a fresh anointing on a fresh revelation, which unfortunately, we don't see in today's American church leaders.

The third problem I see in the American Church is materialism. .... This abuse is seen in Godly men and women eventually falling into the trap of the love of money.... Another problem connected with money is that the American Church doesn't seem to fully comprehend the purpose of the wealth God has entrusted into its hands. Though America is still the biggest and most generous giver in the world, we all know that what is given to missions is meager in comparison with what is spent on the minor issues of life....

Another problem I see in the church is ... I am certain this is a major doctrinal lie that Satan has planted in the church, worldwide, to kill her and take as many people as possible to hell. I'm referring to the doctrine of "once saved, always saved." The teaching that believers can never lose their salvation is the biggest, anti-New Testament doctrine in the world today.

The next area I see that has contributed to a weak church in America is the lack of emphasis on holiness in the churches. This, of course, could be a direct effect of the point above, "if you're going to heaven anyway, why live holy?" (www.godem bassy.org/en/news/newsfr.php) (Parts of this interview were published in the January 2005 edition of Charisma Mag.)

(8) A Dream About Fishermen in Shallow Water

by Michael D. Fortner

This section is my own: I dreamed that some fishermen were on small boats, and in competition with each other. They were trying to catch fish in shallow water, but all the fish were out in the deep ocean. But their nets were not long enough to catch fish in deep water. The water was also murky when it should have been clear.

One group sent divers down to see why they were not catching any fish. The divers saw other divers carrying large amphorae (clay pots) from the deep water into the shallow water and pouring out their contents onto the bottom of the shallow areas, and the fish were following, thus allowing them to be caught. When the fishermen saw that, they knew how their competitors were catching fish and they started doing the same.

The ocean bottom of the deep water represents where nutrients are, so this contains spiritual and doctrinal truth that people need. But because the church is so shallow and lacking in this area, the people are not getting the truth they need, so these churches are declining in membership. Those churches which are catching fish are taking some truth from the deep and mixing it with shallow teaching; in other words, they are compromising truth.

The deep ocean bottom is rich in nutrients and is being dumped into shallow water, and the fish flock to it in large numbers, thinking they are getting something good but they do not realize that the nutrients have become diluted in the shallow water, so it does not contain as much truth. This is the large-mega churches in America today.

If they were teaching the truth, they would have very long but narrow nets, because long nets that reach down to the bottom of deep water must be narrow in order to pull them in; otherwise they would be too heavy. The nets that are used in shallow water do not need to be long in depth, so they can be very wide and therefore can pull in many more fish because they can cover more of the bottom area. But they would not be able to catch any fish in the shallow water were it not for taking truth from the deep and dumping it in the shallow water. They are able to catch large amounts of fish only by compromising truth.

We all know who the fishermen are that use this method; they are all the mega-churches in the U.S.A., because they all teach people what they want to hear rather than hard truths that would cause some people to turn away, as Jesus himself taught hard truths.

Finding truth is like hunting a wild animal, it must be hunted and killed and butchered and cooked. It is hard work to find and eat this truth. But people prefer fast food that is very tasty and contains lots of filler and additives such as fat and sugar; so you are not getting as many nutrients and the fat can clog your arteries and kill you. So even when truth is made available, most people will pass it up in favor of the tasty mix of truth and lies. It has always been this way.

There are many things in the list of lies that tell people what they want to hear; here are the top 13, not necessarily in order of poison level:

1. You cannot loose your salvation, even if you deny Christ.
2. God wants you to be wealthy.
3. You can have anything you want, just confess it.
4. No Christian can ever have a demon in them.
5. It's OK to live in luxury as long as you pay tithes, while your Christian brothers and sisters are cold and hungry.
6. God wants you to be happy and successful in all areas of life; (unless you live in Africa or Asia, where God must want you to live in poverty, be beaten, imprisoned, and killed).

7. Nothing bad is going to happen until the Rapture occurs (Christians will not go through the Great Tribulation).

8. Every Christian will go in the Rapture, even Christians who lie, and commit adultery.

9. It is OK to gamble in casinos as long as you can afford to lose the money, and you are not addicted to it.

10. It's OK to engage in perverted sexual acts, as long as you are married.

11. We already have all the truth, so you don't have to concern yourself with seeking it, just believe what we tell you to believe.

12. Capitalism is ordained of God, therefore it is OK to pay people minimum wage, even though they cannot supply all their needs on that income.

13. God prospers those who are his children, and the opposite is also true, that poverty is always from Satan and a sign of God's disapproval, or your lack of faith.

(9) Woe! To The Money-Loving Christians

By Michael D. Fortner

Have you ever wondered why the Christians in America are prosperous while the Christians in Asia and Africa are poor? Is it because the Christians in America have more faith or are able to plant more seed money? No, it is because we live in America. The nonChristians are also prosperous! It is not merely faith or righteousness, it is our economy that is responsible for the prosperity in America. God has blessed America, generally, but the Christians are not using the money God has given them to help their poor brothers and sisters, therefore, God is going to take away their money.

The Bible says that greed is idolatry, which means the Christians in America are guilty of idolatry and the preachers are guilty of leading the people into idolatry. Even those preachers who do not teach the gospel of wealth teach that it is OK to be rich. It is not just the Charismatics who are guilty of materialism and idolatry. The parking lots of many churches are like Cadillac showrooms.

Therefore God is going to bring economic disaster upon America. God is going to take away the retirement accounts and vacation homes, the sports cars and diamond rings. God is going to teach the money-loving Christians in America a lesson that money cannot buy. God is going to give the money-loving Christians in America spiritual gold which comes only by being refined in fire.

Christians in America are eating up sermons about *"money cometh"* and *"who wants to be a millionaire."* There are millions of homeless Christians throughout the world who are NOT being helped by the prosperous Christians in America, therefore God is going to take the money away from the rich Christians who still don't have enough. Money is not going to "cometh," money is going to *goeth*. God's judgment has already begun, as Christians have lost millions with the collapse of Enron, Worldcom, IndyMac Bank, and other companies. Then in 2007 the global economic collapse began, but we did not realize it had started until well into 2008 when trillions of dollars were lost when the stock market dropped, and when several investment firms were exposed as frauds. Trillions were lost just as I had been warning about online for seven years, 2000-2007. Few people who read the warning believed it.

God commands that we share our wealth with those who don't have enough, but American Christians are using the money on themselves. Africa is not the Promised Land of Canaan; the Sahara Desert does not flow with milk and honey, therefore God expects us to help the poor Christians who live there.

(10) Reproach of the Solemn Assembly

By David Wilkerson
(The following was taken from one of his sermons.)

It has been prophesied that in this day of reproach, shame and disgrace, God is going to raise up a holy remnant who are going grieve and weep over this defilement. . . God will have a remnant that will not sit idly by while all of these things invade the Church. God says, "I will have a people that are not going to be satisfied to go their merry way and just ignore what is happening as Charlatans and money-mad false prophets are coming into the House of God and destroying everything in sight." . . .

Wake up elders. Wake up pastors. Wake up shepherds. Take a look at the Church. Get the burden. Carry it. Why should we take on the burden of the reproach of the Solemn Assembly? Joel said, "because there is a rotten seed being planted." A gospel is being preached that is withering everything that is in sight. Everything that is green and Godly and pure is being withered. The seed is rotten, there is a famine of hearing the pure Word of the Lord, there is no pasture. The flocks are desolate and hungry. The rivers are drying up. A strange fire is devouring the pastors. Ezekiel says that Shepherds are trampling down the good pasture and eating the best for themselves. What are the shameful disgraceful things that are happening in the Church of Jesus Christ today?

First of all it is the rotten seed that is being preached by covetous Shepherds. This is known as the Prosperity Gospel. This is one of the greatest reproaches that the Church of Jesus Christ ever perpetrated since Christ. This perverted gospel is poisoning multitudes - even in China, Africa and all over the world. It is an American gospel invented and spread by rich American evangelists and pastors. Rich! It alarms me that so many people can hear the tapes and see videos that are coming out of these prosperity conferences and not weep over them. This poison has spread all over the world. . . .

Some of you will not receive it. If you have been feeding your soul on Copeland or Hagin's tapes, you are not going to like what you hear. Folks, I am a shepherd, I've been called by God. I made this church a promise. As long as we are in this pulpit, if we saw wolves in sheep's clothing coming to rob the flock, we would stand up and cry out against it. It is up to you to do something about it. . . .

Here is what grieves me most. This was preached. "The Holy Spirit can't be poured out upon you until first you are in the money flow. Until you are prospering, the Holy Ghost can not do His work."

Think of it! How does this affect you? What does it do to your spirit when you see poor people who are living from pay check to pay check and suddenly he says, "run for the money" and people are running wildly everywhere and they say as they run, they are claiming the riches.

Then I see people withering like snakes out of their seats onto the floor. I see the evangelist going up and hissing like a snake and people falling everywhere. Folks, what is going on?

The Reproach of the Solemn Assembly! The prophet called them "greedy dogs, ungodly watchmen". Folks, if you had the heart of God and the burden of the Lord you would be crying out with Isaiah, "they are blind watchmen, ignorant, dumb dogs, sleeping, loving to slumber, yea, greedy dogs which can never have enough.

(11) 1968 Prophecy by 90-year-old Woman in Norway

This prophecy was given by a 90 yr. old woman in Norway in 1968 about events leading up to the second coming of Christ. An Evangelist by the name of Emanuel Minos wrote down what the lady said, but because it was so extreme, he put it away. In about 2015 he reviewed the prophecy and was amazed that much of what she predicted has taken place. The prophecy, with E. Minos:

The woman from Valdres was a very alert, reliable, awake and credible Christian, with a good reputation among all who knew her. This is what she saw:

"I saw the time just before the coming of Jesus and the outbreak of the Third World War. I saw the events with my natural eyes. I saw the world like a kind of a globe and saw Europe, land by land. I saw Scandinavia. I saw Norway. I saw certain things that would take place just before the return of Jesus, and just before the last calamity happens, a calamity the likes of which we have never before experienced.

She mentioned four waves:

1. "First before Jesus comes and before the Third World War breaks out there will be a 'détente' like we have never had before. There will be peace between the super powers in the east and the west, and there will be a long peace. (Remember, that this was in 1968 when the cold war was at its highest. E. Minos) In this period of peace there will be disarmament in many countries, also in Norway and we are not prepared when it (the war)

comes. The Third World War will begin in a way no one would have anticipated – and from an unexpected place.

2. "A lukewarmness without parallel will take hold of the Christians, a falling away from true, living Christianity. Christians will not be open for penetrating preaching. They will not, like in earlier times, want to hear of sin and grace, law and gospel, repentance and restoration. There will come a substitute instead: prosperity (happiness) Christianity.

The above paragraph clearly describes the prosperity gospel and other lukewarm doctrines being preached in America today.

"The important thing will be to have success, to be something; to have material things, things that God never promised us in this way. Churches and prayer houses will be emptier and emptier. Instead of the preaching we have been used to for generations - like, to take your cross up and follow Jesus, – entertainment, art and culture will invade the churches where there should have been gatherings for repentance and revival. This will increase markedly just before the return of Jesus.

3. "There will be a moral disintegration that old Norway has never experienced the likes of. People will live together like married without being married. Much uncleanness before marriage, and much infidelity in marriage will become the natural (the common), and it will be justified from every angle. It will even enter Christian circles and we pet it – <u>even sin against nature</u>. Just before Jesus return there will be TV programs like we have never experienced. (TV had just arrived in Norway in 1968. E. Minos)

The *"sin against nature"* refers to homosexuality, which has also come true.

"TV will be filled with such horrible violence that it teaches people to murder and destroy each other, and it will be unsafe in our streets. People will copy what they see. There will not be only one 'station' on TV, it will be filled with 'stations.' (She did not know the word 'channel' which we use today. Therefore she called them stations. E. Minos.) TV will be just like the radio where we have many 'stations,' and it will be filled with violence. People will use it for entertainment. We will see terrible scenes of murder and destruction one [after] the other, and this will spread in society. Sex scenes will also be shown on the screen, the most intimate things that takes place in a marriage." (I protested and said, we have a paragraph that forbids this kind of thing. E. Minos.) Then the old woman said: "It will happen, and you will see it. All we have had before will be broken down, and the most indecent things will pass before our eyes."

4. "People from poor countries will stream to Europe. (In 1968 there was no such thing as immigration. E. Minos.) They will also come to Scandinavia – and Norway. There will be so many of them that people will begin to dislike them and become hard with them. They will be treated like the Jews before the Second World War. Then the full measure of our sins will have been reached." (I protested at the issue of immigration. I did not understand it at the time. E. Minos.)

The tears streamed from the old woman's eyes down her cheeks. "I will not see it, but you will. Then suddenly, Jesus will come and the Third World War breaks out. It will be a short war." (She saw it in the vision.)

"All that I have seen of war before is only child's play compared to this one, and it will be ended with a nuclear atom bomb. The air will be so polluted that one cannot draw one's breath. It will cover several continents, America, Japan, Australia and the wealthy nations. The water will be ruined (contaminated?). We can no longer till the soil. The result will be that only a remnant will remain. The remnant in the wealthy countries will try to flee to the poor countries, but they will be as hard on us as we were on them.

"I am so glad that I will not see it, but when the time draws near, you must take courage and tell this. I have received it from God, and nothing of it goes against what the Bible tells.

"The one who has his sin forgiven and has Jesus as Savior and Lord, is safe."

There is also a video on Youtube that gives another translation of the same prophecy: search for: *A Prophecy from 90yr old lady in 1968.*

(12) A Chinese Leader Speaks Out

Because America sends a lot of money, Bibles, and literature to China, a Chinese Church leader went to America expecting to find super-spiritual Christians on fire for God, but that is not what he found:

Before I traveled to the West I had absolutely no idea that so many churches were spiritually asleep. I presumed the Western church was strong and vibrant because it had brought the gospel to my country with such incredible faith and tenacity.

Many missionaries had shown a powerful example to us by laying down their lives for the sake of Jesus. On some occasions I've struggled while speaking in Western churches. There seems to be something missing that leaves me feeling terrible inside. Many meetings are cold and lack the fire and presence of God that we have in China.

In the West many Christians have an abundance of material possessions, yet they live in a backslidden state. They have silver and gold, but they don't rise up and walk in Jesus' name. In China, we have no possessions to hold us down, so there's nothing preventing us from moving out for the Lord. The Chinese church is like Peter at the Beautiful Gate. When he saw the crippled beggar he said, "Silver or gold I do not have, but what I have I give you. In the name of Jesus Christ of Nazareth, walk!" In a similar way, I pray that God might use the Chinese church to help the Western church rise up and walk in the power of the Holy Spirit. . . .

Multitudes of church members are satisfied with giving their minimum to God, not their maximum. I've watched men and women during offering time in church. They open their fat wallets and search for the smallest amount they can give. This type of attitude will never do! Jesus gave his whole life for us, and we give as little of our lives, time, and money as we can give back to God. What a disgrace! Repent! This may sound strange, but I even miss the offerings we used to give in China.

On numerous occasions, the leader of a meeting would announce, "We have a new worker who is leaving tomorrow to serve the Lord." Immediately every single person would completely empty their pockets of everything they had. With that money, the worker would buy a train or bus ticket and leave the next day. Often this money was not just everything we had in our pockets at that time, but everything we owned in the whole world. Just because you have a church building doesn't necessarily mean Jesus is with you. He is not welcome in many churches today. In Revelation 3:20 Jesus said, "Here I am! I stand at the door and knock. If anyone hears my voice and opens the door, I will come in and dine with him, and he with me." Often this verse is used as an invitation for salvation, but actually the context Jesus was speaking in was very different.

He was standing outside the door of the church of Laodicea, knocking to get in! (Brother Yun, *The Heavenly Man*, pages 295-298)

Did you notice anything? He said he expected the American Church to be alive, but he found it dead. Jesus said the same thing: " *'I know your works. You have the reputation of being alive, but you are dead"* (Rev. 3:1) (ESV). The reason the Western Church has backslidden is because it has been deceived by false doctrine and prosperity. This refers to a large percentage of American Christianity, not just the WOF and prosperity gospel churches.

Another Chinese Church leader, Samuel Lamb, suffered imprisonment for twenty years! He stated:

"Our churches in China are undergoing persecution; your churches in the West are undergoing delusion." (*Voice of The Martyrs*, May 2000, page 1)

The Western Church believes it has been given wealth as a reward from God, but the wealth should be shared with Christians in Asia and Africa who do not have enough to meet their personal needs, and help them preach the Gospel.

Chapter 13:
Conclusion

I believe the evidence is overwhelming, that the WOF is full of false prophets and false doctrines; that the Toronto inspired revivals are a mixture of Holy Spirit and false spirits, and that the Prophetic Movement could be worse than both of them, with their counterfeit trips to heaven and appearances of a false Jesus.

The quoted message from Jesus given to Steven Dobbs, says there will be many *"counterfeit visions from the enemy, counterfeit experiences of heaven, fake appearances of Jesus."* I believe that people have gone to heaven, like Apostle Paul, but I do not believe that many people have frequent *authentic* trips to heaven.

One fellow named Bob Jones apparently had the power to take someone's hand and immediately they would go on a trip to heaven together. If this was genuine, I would have expected him to have been a super-saint, but the evidence says otherwise.

John MacArthur reported in his book, *Strange Fire*, that Bob Jones admitted giving hundreds of false prophecies, yet he was a huge figure among the Kansas City Prophets at Mike Bickle's church, and Rick Joyner's church. And he remained highly praised even after some horrible stuff was revealed:

> It had come to light that Jones was using false "prophecies" as a means of gaining trust from women whom he then abused sexually. "The sins for which [he was] removed from ministry include[d] using his gifts to manipulate people for his personal desires, sexual misconduct, rebelling against pastoral authority, slandering leaders and the promotion of bitterness within the

body of Christ." He nevertheless returned to the charismatic limelight after a short hiatus, and as of this writing, he is still speaking in charismatic churches, presenting himself as an anointed prophet of God, and making prophecies that are demonstrably false and often patently ridiculous.' Thousands of gullible charismatics still hang on his every word—as if all the scandal and false prophesying never happened. The fact that Jones's online biography compares his ministry to that of the prophet Daniel only heightens the blasphemous nature of the whole fiasco. (page 111)

It is my understanding, that he did occasionally have an accurate prophecy. Therefore, there can be no doubt that Bob Jones was one of the almost true, yet false prophets.

We should not reject all spiritual experiences, and should not reject all signs and wonders just because so much of it is false; we just need to use discernment to know what is true and what is false. Discernment is greatly lacking throughout the Charismatic / Pentecostal movement today.

It is truly shocking that churches which are not WOF, or not in the false revival, will invite a WOF or false revival preacher to speak at their church or conference. This is giving credibility and even sanction to their false doctrines and evil spirits. We must STOP THIS NOW. We must speak out against those false ministers and false revivals and call them what they are. It is not love that allows people to remain in that deception without calling it what it is. We must not associate with them in any official capacity . Paul said that we should not even eat with people who claim to be Christians, yet are greedy:

But now I am writing to you to stop associating with any so-called brother if he is sexually immoral, greedy, an idolater, a slanderer, a drunk, or a robber. With such a person you must even stop eating. (1 Cor. 5:11) (ISV)

Sometimes you must cut off an infected arm or leg or the poison in it will enter the rest of the body and kill the whole body. There must be a separation between the Charismatics who support the falsehood discussed in this book, and those who do not support it, otherwise all Pentecostal and Charismatic churches are in danger of being infiltrated. Derek Prince said:

> [A] false church will emerge from the true church, leading some
> believers astray as part of Satan's agenda for the end of the
> age. . . . Christians must <u>discern the true church from the false</u>
> <u>church in order to separate themselves from the false church</u>
> and the wrath she will incur . . . (*Protection*, 2008, p. 99, 108)

The false church has emerged, and we must call it what it is
and separate from it. If the WOF doctrines do not get into your
church, the false spirits of the "river" will get in. If not those,
then the prosperity gospel or the gold dust will get in. And one
will lead to another. We cannot blindly believe that it will not
infiltrate your church, it has infiltrated my previous church, and
thousands more. If you are attending one of these churches, get
out now; find a church that teaches sound doctrine.

And I expect the falsehood and deception to get even worse. I
would not be surprised to see a picture of a prosperity preacher
begin to weep until you send in an offering. So we must have no
fellowship with the almost true yet false prophets and the almost
true yet false revivals. The revivals think they have the river of
God, but there is a sewer flowing into the river.

Critics of this view will point out that people have been
healed. People have also been healed through the prayers of a
Roman Catholic priest, or after praying to Mary or one of the
Saints. The critics will say that God does not bring division, but
Jesus said, "*I did not come to bring peace, but a sword*" (Matthew
10:34).

The Charismatic Movement was not originally dominated by
the wealth gospel, but thanks primarily to TBN and other Christian networks, the wealth gospel has infected much of the Charismatic Movement and even Pentecostal churches like a plague.
Because the desire for wealth is idolatry, these churches have
been taken off track by idolatry. Therefore, all of those churches
will continue to go farther and farther away from sound doctrine
unless those in the movement repent and reform.

If a plane that took off from JFK airport in New York flying
to LAX in Los Angeles were just one degree off course, it would

end up 40 miles over the Pacific Ocean, south of the LA area. [*] If two planes are flying side by side, and one of them is on course and one is only 1 degree off course, they will at first appear to be going the exact same direction, but the more time passes the wider the space between them will get until they can no longer see each other. All churches that refuse to renounce the prosperity gospel or WOF doctrines will continue moving away from the truth. [*] (www.irrefutablesuccess.com/2010/04/one-degree-off-course/)

In 2000 I heard Carlton Pearson, a prosperity preacher in Tulsa, say on TV, "*Who wants to be a Millionaire? 'Operation No Lack'--Send for the tape series.*" Not long afterwards he began to teach the doctrine of Universalism, that all people will eventually be saved. He even says that it was God who told him this lie. As a result, most of his congregation left, and his large church closed its doors and went into foreclosure. But he is still preaching, just to a smaller crowd in a different location.

God will not be mocked. All the get-rich preachers will eventually become failed preachers, or killed by God, like others have been. All ministers who refuse to stop preaching the gospel of wealth or WOF, in spite of numerous calls of correction from many people, will likely be led down the path of counterfeit miracles, demon spirits, and other doctrines of demons that will ultimately lead to death or hell, or both. Some ministers actually have spirits of sorcery and divination at work in their ministries and don't know it. People who allow themselves to have hands laid on them by these ministers may at first believe they have been healed, but could end up worse off, as we have seen in this book.

The wealthy preachers in America are clouds without water. They have no power and frequently push people down when they pray for them, which is itself strange fire because they are faking results of the anointing.

Charismatics need to openly renounce and repent of teaching and believing the false gospel of wealth, and start sharing what they have with those in need. There are Christians in many nations of the world that have no shoes to wear, or no clean water to drink. Just buying them a few chickens will improve their stand-ard of living. Perhaps they need tools they can use to earn a living.

We need to open our eyes and see the truth of what the Bible teaches about *"unrighteous mammon."* To prosper is not to have wealth, that is NOT biblical prosperity, that is Loadicean pros-perity. Biblical prosperity is having enough, and even more than enough so you can share it with others, not way more than you need so you can live in luxury.

All of Christianity in America needs revival, but the WOF and Toronto Blessing churches need reform. If they were to re-pent of the prosperity gospel and evil spirits that are allowed to operate, and start helping our poor brothers and sisters here and around the world, it could change the world, and the way the world views Christianity, and help to win many to Christ.

In the famous words of Peter, *repent and turn to God that your sins may be wiped away* (Acts 3:19).

But we have renounced disgraceful, underhanded ways. We refuse to practice cunning or to tamper with God's word, but by the open statement of the truth we would commend ourselves to everyone's conscience in the sight of God. (2 Co 4:2)(ESV)

See the last page for other books written by the author.

Bibliography

Adelaja, Sunday. *Church Shift*. Lake Mary, FL: Charisma House, 2008.

Arnold, Eberhard. *The Early Christians in Their Own Words*. Rifton, NY: Plough Publishing House, 1998.

Bae, Kenneth. *Not Forgotten: The True Story of my Imprisonment in North Korea*. Nashville: Thomas Nelson, 2016.

Basham, Don. *The Way I See It*. Grand Rapids, MI: Fleming H Revell, 1986.

Barna, George. *The Second Coming of the Church*. Nashville: Thomas Nelson, 2001.

Fee, Gordon. *The Disease of the Health and Wealth Gospels*. Regent College Publishing, 2006.

Floyer, Sir John. Fortner, Michael D. *The Sibylline Oracles: Revised and Updated*. Lawton, OK: Trumpet Press, 2011.

Gushee, Dr. David P. "What Would Jesus Say About Wealth?" www.ncccusa.org/ poverty/sermon-gushee.html.

Hayes, Richard B. *The Moral Vision of The New Testament*. Harper: San Francisco, 1996. (Quoted in, *Embezzlement: The Corporate Sin of Contemporary Christianity?*, by Ray Mayhew, ebook.)

Hill, Steve. *Spiritual Avalanche*. Lake Mary, FL: Charisma House, 2013.

Kinnaman, David, and Gabe Lyons. *UnChristian*. Grand Rapids: Baker Books, 2007.

McNemar, Richard. *The Kentucky Revival*. Lawton, OK: Trumpet Press, 2011. Originally published in 1808.

MacArthur, John. *Charismatic Chaos*. Grand Rapids: Zondervan, 1992.

Schaff, Philip. *The Apostolic Fathers with Justin Martyr and Irenaeus*. Grand Rapids, MI: Wm. B. Eerdmans Publishing Company, reprint 2001.

Sider, Ronald J. *Rich Christians In an Age of Hunger: A Biblical Study*. Downers Grove, IL: Inter-Varsity Press, 1977.

Sloan, Allan. "Can Need Trump Greed?" *Newsweek* 28 April 1997

Staniforth, Maxwell. *Early Christian Writings: The Apostolic Fathers*. New York: Barnes & Noble Books, 1968.

Srygley, Fletcher Douglas. *Seventy years in Dixie: recollections, sermons and sayings of T. W. Caskey and others*. Nashville, TN: Gospel Advocate Publishing, 1893.

Strom, Andrew. *Why I Left the Prophetic Movement*. Revival School, 2007.

Strom, Andrew. *Kundalini Warning: Are False Spirits Invading the Church?* Revival School, 2015.

Sullins, D. *Recollections of an Old Man: Seventy Years in Dixie, 1827-1897*. Cleveland, TN, 1910.

Yohannan, K.P. *Revolution in World Missions*. Carrollton, TX: AFA Books, 2004.

For a *fresh* look at Bible prophecy, see the book series: *Bible Prophecy Revealed*, by Michael D. Fortner.

Book 1: Includes new important insights on Daniel's 70th week, the four beasts of Daniel 7, the ten toes, and how the EU will break partly break apart. Shows America several times, and shows that the whole world of the Bible is not the entire planet but merely the Middle East / Mediterranean world, so the beast will not rule the entire planet.

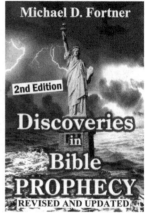

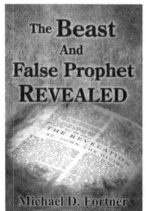

Book 2: Provides the history of the beast and how and why it is based in Islam, and how it is even now trying to rise again.

Book 3: Proves that America is Babylon the Great harlot and will be destroyed in a nuclear holocaust at the end of the Great Tribulation.

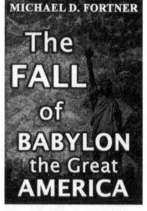

Book 4: Shows that the darkness connected with the return of Christ is caused by nuclear war and asteroid impacts. Includes many other prophecies from the *Book of Enoch, Sibylline Oracles, Pseudepigrapha, Apocrypha,* and even modern prophets which agree with and shed more light on the biblical prophecies, both Catholic and Protestant prophecies.

Made in the USA
Las Vegas, NV
17 December 2022

63022124R00128